In memoriam Roger Prior who should really have written this book

Contents

Acknowledgements:
Source and secondary material

University of Cambridge Digital Library Forman and Napier Casebooks
https://cudl.lib.cam.ac.uk/
Folger Library Shakespeare Documented https://shakespearedocumented.
folger.edu/exhibition
British Library First Edition of Shakesperare Sonnets 1609 https://
www.bl.uk/collection-items/first-edition-of-shakespeares-sonnets-1609
The Bodleian First Folio https://firstfolio.bodleian.ox.ac.uk/
University of North Texas Digital Library https://digital.library.unt.edu/
ark:/67531/metadc86/m1/22/
Archive The Passionate Pilgrime https://archive.org/details/passionatepil-
gri00shakrich/page/n81/mode/2up
Gutenberg Every Man in his Humour http://gutenberg.reading-
roo.ms/5/3/3/5333/5333-h/5333-h.htm
University of Aberystwith Shakespeare's Bust http://www.sidthomas.net/
pdf/paperpdfs/144.pdf
John Shakespearehttps://www.jstor.org/stable/3844266?read-
now=1&seq=13#page_scan_tab_contents

I am deeply indebted to the following who over the years have taken trouble
to answer my queries and correct my misconceptions: Dr Yasmin Arshad,
University College London, Andrew Ashbee, Lucy Bamford, Sir Jonathan Bate,
Harold Bloom, Derby Museums, Charlotte Bolland, National Portrait Gallery,
John Boneham, British Library, Andrée Brooks, David Bryant, Susan Cerasano,
English Colgate University, Howard Coutts, Bowes Musem, Professor Kather-
ine Duncan-Jones, Charles Duff, Maureen Duff, John Eddowes, Cynthia
Harrod-Eagles, Professor Deborah Howard, John Hudson, Richard Jarvis,
Peter Levi, Morgan Lloyd-Malcolm, William Lyons, Peter Matthews, Bruce
O'Neil, Joshua Nash, Berkeley Castle, Netty Nicholson, Andrew Parrott, Sir
Roger Norrington, A.L.Rowse, Jane Rylands, Philip Rylands Peggy Guggen-
heim Museum, Jenny Senior, James Shapiro, Crispian Steele-Perkins, Ian
Steere, Sir Roy Strong, Sir Anthony Wagner, Thomas Woodcock, Garter King
of Arms, Georgianna Ziegler, Folger Library.

I found myself continually returning to pioneering work on the Bassano
family by David Lasocki and Roger Prior both in print and correspondence.
Peter Jensen's encyclopedic knowledge of Shakespeare and the Sonnets was
pivotal in forming my final conclusions, some of which were at odds with his
good advice.

Bibliography

Peter Ackroyd: Shakespeare the Biography
G..P. V.Akrigg: Shakespeare and the Earl of Southampton
Dr Yasmin Arshad: 'The Enigma of a Portrait: Lady Anne Clifford and Daniel's Cleopatra', The British Art Journal. Vol. XI, No. 3 (Spring 2011), 30-37
Andrew Ashbee: Records of English Court Music
Shaul Bassi and Alberto Toso Fei: Shakespeare in Venice
Jonathan Bate: Shakespeare and Ovid
Jonathan Bate: Soul of the Age
Jonathan Bate and Dora Thornton: Staging the World Shakespeare
Jonathan Bate: The Genius of Shakespeare
Harold Bloom: Shakespeare The Invention of the Human
Bill Bryson: Shakespeare
William Byrd: Songs of Sundrie Natures edited David Mateer
Riccardo Calimani: The Ghetto of Venice
Oscar James Campbell: The Rader's Encylopedia of Shakespeare
Mary Chan: Music in the Theatre of Ben Jonson
Tanyia Cooper: Searching for Shakespeare
Michael Dobson and Stanley Wells: The Oxford Companion to Shakespeare
Katherine Duncan-Jones: Shakespeare an Ungentle Life
Richard Dutton: Mastering the Revels
John Goss: Shylock
Germaine Greer: Shakespeare's Wife
Charles Hamilton: In Search of Shakespeare
Philip Henslowe: The Diary of Philip Henslowe
Anthony Holden: William Shakespeare
Anthony Hoskins in the Society of Genealogists journal
Leslie Hotson: Shakespeare by Hilliard
John Hudson: Shakespeare's Dark Lady
Peter Jensen: The Secrets of the Sonnets
Peter Jensen: The Secrets of the Sonnets Book 2
Peter Jensen: Shakespeare's name Code
Frank Kermode: Shakespeare's Language
Frank Kermode: The Age of Shakespeare
Aemilia Lanyer: Salve Deus Rex Judæorum, edited by Susanne Woods
David Lasocki with Roger Prior: The Bassanos, Venetian Musicians and Instrument Makers in England 1531-1665
Peter Levi: The Life and Tims of William Shakespeare
Morgan Lloyd Malcolm: Emilia
Peter D. Matthews: Shakespeare Exhumed The Bassano Chronicles
Peter D. Matthews: Genesis of the Shakespearean Works
Edward Muir: Civic Ritual in Renaissance Venice
Charles Nicholl: The Lodger, Shakespeare on Silver Street
John Nichols: The Progresses and Public Processions of Queen Elizabeth I:
John Julius Norwich: A History of Venice
Tina Packer: Women of Will

G.A.Philipps: Crown Musical Patronage from Elizabeth 1to Charles 1 Music & Letters Vol.58, No.1

Roger Prior: Shakespeare's Visit to Italy. University of Maltam Journal of Anglo-Italian Studies 2008 Vol. 9

Roger Prior: Was King Edward lll a Compliment to Lord Hunsdon? Connotations Vol.3 No.3

Roger Prior: More (Moor? Moro?) Light on the Dark Lady Financial Times, October 10 1987

Cecil Roth: Doña Gracia of the House of Nasi

A.L.Rowse: Sex and Society in Shakespeare's Age

A.L.Rowse: Shakespeare's Self-portrait

A.L.Rowse: Shakespeare's Sonnets

A.L.Rowse: Shakespeare the Elizabethan

A.L.Rowse: The Poems of Shakespeare's Dark lady

A.L.Rowse: William Shakespeare

William Shakespeare: Shakespeare's Sonnets edited Katharine Duncan Jones

James Shapiro: 1599 A Year in the Life of William Shakepeare

James Shapiro: 1606 William Shakespeare and the Year of Lear

James Shapiro: Contested Will

James Shapiro: Shakespeare and the Jews

Emma Smith: Shakespeare's First Folio

Ian Steere: Shakespeare a Hidden Life Sung in a Hidden Song

John Stowe: Survey of London

Lytton Stracjey: Elizabeth and Essex

Horace Walpole: Anecdotes of Painting in England

Alison Weir: Elizabeth the Queen

René Weis: Shakespere Revealed

Bryan H. Wildenthal: Early Shakespeare Authorship Doubts

Ian Wilson: Shakespeare the Evidence

Michael Wilson: Nicholas Lanier Master of the King's Musick

Michael Wood; In Search of Shakespeare

1 Peter Bassano and Francesco da Mosto on the Ponte di Alpini, Bassano del Grappa from BBC TV's Shakespeare in Italy

Anyone with an interest in Shakespeare may have wondered why he used Italy as a setting for so many of his plays, what, or who - apart from some obvious Italian authors - inspired him do so, and whether he ever visited the country?

The reason for my writing this book is my belief that it was the daughter of a Venetian, Emilia Bassano, the musician and poet and my first cousin, twelve times removed, who aroused Shakespeare's interest in Italy. It was primarily Emilia who initiated his interest, but it was three of her Bassano cousins - the brothers Arthur, Andrea and Jeronimo - who befriended Shakespeare and took him on a three month trip to the North of Italy in the autumn of 1593.

Emilia Bassano was first identified as the Dark Musical Lady of the Shakespeare Sonnets in 1970 by A. L. Rowse, the Elizabethan historian and Fellow of All Souls, Oxford. He discovered her, not in a work of Shakespeare, but in the diaries of Simon Forman, the Elizabeth astrologer and medical practitioner, which were owned by the Bodleian Library in Oxford. As Shakespeare's lover Emilia exerted an enormously strong and long lasting influence on the playwright. Emilia was a musician and poet and the young mistress of Henry Carey, Lord Hunsdon, best known to us as the patron of Shakespeare's company of actors, The Lord Chamberlain's Men.

John Hudson's impressively researched and powerfully argued *Shakespeare's Dark Lady* proposes that Emilia wrote the complete Shakespeare canon. In *Shakespeare Exhumed* and the follow up book *Genesis of the Shakespearean Works* Dr Peter D. Matthews argues that Emilia and her immediate family were the creators of the works of Shakespeare. How I wish they were correct, but I don't believe they are, mainly because Emilia's known writing doesn't compare to the outstanding poetry and moving rhetoric of the Shakespeare plays. At her least inspired, some of the verses are reminiscent of William McGonagall *In glittering raiment shining much more bright, Than silver Starres in the most frostie night* for example. (*Salve Devs* to the Ladie *Arabella* 6-7)

If Simon Forman's comment about her *she can hardly keep secret* was true, Emilia would never have possessed the self-control to keep quiet about the success of Shakespeare as a playwright and poet, if in fact she had been "Shakespeare". By the time her prose book *Salve Devs Rex Judæorum* was published in 1611 Shakespeare had written nearly forty plays and his authorship of them widely acknowledged. In *Salve Devs* Emilia's dedication to Princess Elizabeth refers to her first named publication as *the first fruits of a woman's wit*

My view of Emilia's contribution to Shakespeare's writing is that she inspired him by her outstanding personality, her looks, her musicality, knowledge of Italian and the Veneto and formidable use of language, and in that sense my ideas are much closer to that of Morgan Lloyd Malcolm's Shakespeare's Globe Theatre commission, *Emilia.* This fiercely feminist play, written close on the heels of the *Me Too* movement, with an all female cast, suggests that Shakespeare not only fell deeply in love with Emilia, but was equally in love with her spoken rhetoric and *woman's wit* to the point where he wrote some of his female text *verbatim.*

Many of the female characters in Shakespeare's plays are based on Emilia Bassano, the obvious ones bearing her Christian name (including a male version of it) these are Aemilius in *Titus Andronicus*, Emilia in *The Comedie of Errors*, Æmilia in *Othello*, Emilia in *The Winter's Tale*, Emilia in the Fletcher/Shakespeare collaboration *The Two Noble Kinsmen.*

Emilia's character, her broad and detailed classical education, fierce intelligence, quick wit, scalding tongue and mercurial temperament can be detected in Rosaline in *Loues Labour's lost*, in Hermia in *A Midsommer nights Dreame*, in Beatrice in *Much adoe about Nothing.* in Rosalind in *As you Like It*, in Cressida in *Troilus and Cressida*, in Cleopatra in *Antony and Cleopatra* and in

Katerina in *The Taming of the Shrew*. In *The Shrew*, the name of Katerina's long suffering father, Baptista, who pays for lute lessons for his daughter, is also the name of Emilia's father. Emilia's father played the lute, gave lute lessons and imported the instruments.

Apart from the names I have already mentioned, there are a number of Emilia's relatives whose names have been adopted by Shakespeare; her cousins Ludovico (*Othello*) and Isabella (*Measure for Measure*) and her half-sister Angelus (*A Comedy of Errors*) - these three could of course just be a coincidence.

What is unlikely to be a coincidence are the names of two characters who appear in *The Taming of a Shrew* - an early version of *The Taming of The Shrew* performed at the Rose Theatre in 1593; the list of characters includes an Emelia and an Alfonso, the name of Emilia's husband, they were married on 18th October 1592. *The Taming of a Shrew* contains an impassioned declaration of love to Emelia, naming her twice.

Many of Shakespeare's works - poems as well as plays - strongly hint at the biographical nature of his relationship with Emilia and Henry Wriothesley, 3rd Lord Southampton. This triangular relationship runs intermittently from one of his first plays, the *Two Gentlemen of Verona* to his last, *The Two Noble Kinsman*.

Emilia, with her Venetian ancestry - a state noted for its acceptance of sexual freedom - was also the inspiration for Venus in *Venvs and Adonis*. The start of her amorous association with the elderly Lord Hunsdon, Patron of Shakespeare's company, the *Lord Chamberlain's Men*, is alluded to in the *Rape of Lucrece*.

The venue of Shakespeare's first encounter with Emilia and her view of subsequent events is disclosed in a *Louer's Complaint*, published as an appendix to the Sonnets. The first *Dark Lady* sonnets weren't composed until after the birth of Emilia's son, Henry, which I date to May 1593.

I have devoted a number of chapters to biographies of the three main protagonists. Shakespeare's life has been the subject of thousands of books, Southampton and Emilia much less so. Comparative knowledge of their lives is necessary to understand how three people from completely different backgrounds could be thrown together in such an emotional maelstrom.

Robert Greene's pamphlet *Groats-worth of Witte, bought with a million of Repentance* is well-known to those with an interest because of its early first carping reference to Shakespeare's presence in London by 1592. Three protagonists in Greene's *Groatsworth* possess Italian names, the brothers, Roberto and Lucanio who get involved in some Machiavellian intrigue with Lamilia, a courtesan who possesses a beautiful and enticing face, who sings and plays the lute.

In 1592 at the age of 23, Emilia, then unmarried, became pregnant. By this time she had an association with Lord Hunsdon - forty three years her senior - for some four or five years. An assumption, gleaned from the 1597 diaries of

Simon Forman where he writes *she was pa[ra]mour to my old L. huns-Dean that was L. Chamberline* was that Lord Chamberlain Hunsdon was the father.

I will question this assumption - my theory, more than hinted at in a line in the very first Dark Lady sonnet (127) - and suggest that Emilia's son, Henry, wasn't Hunsdon's but was Shakespeare's. If I am correct, although the physical love affair between William and Emilia was relatively short-lived - probably three years, or less - Shakespeare's putative paternity goes a long way to explain why the playwright was so obsessed with her throughout his creative life and why their affair continued throughout her pregnancy, her shot-gun marriage to Alphonso Lanier and the birth of her child.

For more than thirty years I earned my living playing the trombone, an instrument that has been 'in the family' for at least four centuries, however I didn't learn about that fact until 1990. It was then that I discovered that I am descended from Antonio Bassano, the eldest of a family of six Venetian Jewish brothers - all six of them professional musicians, mainly wind players and instrument makers - brought to England by King Henry VIII in 1539 to improve musical life at the English Court.

Shakespeare puts asunder the names of my ancestor, as two separate and important characters - Antonio and Bassan[i]o - in *The Merchant of Venice*. In his 1576 will, Baptista refers to his wife as Margaret Bassanio and Elizabeth I's livery accounts for 1568 the family name is spelt Bassanio. There can be no doubt that Shakespeare had the family in mind when he used the name.

In the final scene of *The Merchant,* Shakespeare forces the magnificently proud Shylock to convert to Christianity, something that the Bassanos had already appear to have done some eighty years before the play was written. Might it be that Elizabethan audiences recognised in the names Antonio and Bassanio two *conversos* or *marranos*, characters of Jewish origin, who had accepted, or more probably - like Shylock - been forced to accept conversion to Christianity?

When the Bassano brothers finally settled in England they left their father, Jeronimo, behind them in Venice. Jeronimo was a sackbut player in the *Pifferi,* the Doge's wind consort, the sackbut is easily recognisable an early form of the modern trombone. Some, perhaps all, of Jeronimo's sons also played the sackbut.

With no knowledge of this ancient family profession, when I discovered it, I was astonished that I should find myself earning my living in precisely the same way that Jeronimo Bassano had done five centuries before. An occasionally recurring *leit motif* of this book will be the concept of genetically inherited talent, temperament and physical features.

One of my very first professional engagements was on-stage of the Old Vic, when the theatre was home to Sir Laurence Olivier's National Theatre Company. In 1965, before I joined the company, a critic for The Times, wrote about what was to become a very long running *Much adoe about Nothing.:-*

> *A nattily uniformed town band parades the streets blaring forth crudely harmonised marches: the troops swagger back from the war in dress swords and plumed pill-box hats and are mobbed by a welcoming crowd of frock-coated civilians. And as for civic statuary, Zeffirelli has provided it in the shape of self-assembling monuments - ethereal girls who drift on and freeze into Ondines at the base of a fountain, and an unearthly warrior who clambers on to a pedestal and takes up martial stance as a local hero covered in bird droppings. (The Times 17.2.65)*

Two years later, in the autumn of 1967, I joined the blaring *Messina Town Band*, in residence at the Old Vic, as its single trombone player. I found myself, nattily uniformed on-stage surrounded by some of the most influential actors of their generation, in what felt like an extended family of performers. It is likely that my Bassano ancestors, particularly the second generation would have played in the Elizabethan theatre, I'm sure they too, felt an identical camaraderie with their fellow entertainers.

By 1967 the cast included Derek Jacobi as Claudio, Frank Finlay as Dogberry, Ronal Pickup as Don John, Albert Finney as Don Pedro, Caroline John as Hero, Gerald James as Leonato but most significantly, Maggie Smith and Robert Stephens as the bickering, sonnet-writing lovers, Beatrice and Benedick. All of the cast had been encouraged by Zeffirelli to speak with Italian accents.

During the long periods when the six strong Messina Town Band was relieved from its on-stage duty, whilst my fellow musicians relaxed in the canteen, I stood at the off-prompt side of the stage watching the action, spellbound, and listening to, as well as learning, the dialogue - by osmosis - between Beatrice and Benedick. This without any knowledge that it was Emilia's recycled words - alternating affection with vitriol - that had been put into Beatrice's mouth.

Zeffirelli was a hugely inspiring director of actors and opera singers too, as anyone who has seen his *Tosca* with Callas, Bergonzi and Gobbi can testify. When Hero has been denounced at the altar and Beatrice pleads with Benedick to kill Claudio, he is eventually persuaded after his initial refusal, by a solemn question to Beatrice with his dagger held by the blade, cruciform *Think you in your soul the Count Claudio hath wrong'd Hero?* to which she replies *Yea, as sure as I have a thought, or a soul.* It was at moments like this that I was held me captive, so began my love of the theatre. I was delighted to learn that the BBC has recently rescued from oblivion its studio recording of the Old Vic production.

I later learned that Zeffirelli had commissioned Robert Graves to modernise some of Shakespeare's text, to the great disapproval of most of the cast and all

Shakespearean purists in the audience, but coming at this with no previous knowledge of the words, the text even in this adulterated form, with its superb rhetorical delivery, made a great impression on me.

The exchanges that I witnessed between the actors in question - Robert Stephens and Maggie Smith - was given an added frisson by the on-stage/off-stage relationship that had developed between the two actors during the run of the production. Maggie Smith, gorgeously attractive, was single, but Robert Stephens, who had experienced an unhappy working-class upbringing in Bristol, was trapped in a turbulent marriage to his second wife, the actress, Tarn Bassett. Robert Stephens had fallen desperately in love with Maggie Smith - within the confines of the theatre, a secret difficult to maintain - and had made her pregnant, which hastened his second divorce. Maggie Smith was to become Robert's third wife, they were to have two children together, Chris Larkin and Toby Stephens, both were to achieve great success as film actors.

At a distance of four decades since I witnessed the event of a London based actor from the provinces, unhappily married, beginning a passionate affair, resulting in pregnancy, I detect a strong sense of the historical parallel between Shakespeare and Emilia from nearly four centuries earlier.

I wasn't the first musician, in a state of ignorance of his work, to have been strongly drawn to Shakespeare. In the course of performances of *Hamlet* and *Romeo and Juliet*, in Paris, the Stratfordian began a new role as the life-long inspiration for Hector Berlioz, the composer. For Berlioz, the man, he provided another occupation, that of a 'stage-door Johnny' who persisted in pursuing Harriet Smithson, the Irish actress, who he'd seen play Ophelia and Juliet, until she finally agreed to marriage.

Hamlet was to inspire a three movement work, *Tristia*, very rarely performed these days. The movements were *Méditation religieuse*, *La mort d'Ophélie* and *Marche funèbre pour le dernière scène d'Hamlet*, and with its salvo of muskets, is an ordnance precursor to Tchaikovsky's *1812 Overture*. Amongst other Shakespeare inspired works, *Le roi Lear*, *Roméo et Juliette*, *The Tempest* and *Béatrice et Bénédict* flowed from Berlioz's pen. We can of course add to this list, compositions, orchestral and vocal by Britten, Finzi, Mendelssohn, Prokofiev, Sibelius, Shostakovich, Tchaikovsky, Vaughan-Williams, Verdi, Walton and many others.

Many of the plays contain songs and the task of setting them to music fell to at least two of Shakespeare's contemporaries; Thomas Morley, who was a neighbour of Shakespeare's in the parish of St Helen's Bishopsgate and Robert Johnson, who was probably related to Margaret Johnson, Emilia's mother. There is something particularly attractive to musicians about the way Shakespeare chooses his words, structures his ideas that ensures a musical and convincing flow of the text.

Within the last fifty years great progress has been made in the performance of Baroque and Classical music by scholars researching historic instrumental practice, this has been greatly assisted by the use of urtext scores, that is, only using the notes written by the composers, not the editions made by well-meaning musicians which were sometimes whimsical and often potentially misleading.

Throughout this book I have tried to use the earliest sources, albeit with some curious spelling and punctuation, because they provide us with the words as they were written at the time. When I started to look at the source material, it came as something of a surprise to me, that many modern editions of Shake-speare have radically different words, and therefore meanings, to the earliest sources.

Whatever Emilia Bassano's connections with Shakespeare might have been, she remains a remarkable woman in her own right, particularly for the age in which she lived. In 1611, two years after the Shakespeare Sonnets were published, at the age of 42 and under her married name of Lanyer, she published a collection of poems and prose which she entitled *Salve Devs Rex Judærum* (*Hail God, King of the Jews*), a title she reveals occurred in a dream, some years before.

Some commentators believe that this collection contains the first ever example of a country house poem, *The Description of Cooke-ham,* a precursor to Ben Jonson's *To Penhurst* by five years. As well as this important innovation, Emilia has been shown as a very early example of a woman writing from a woman's point of view, and so her work has been championed by the gender studies departments of many English speaking universities, particularly in America.

It was my privilege to briefly renew my acquaintance with Robert Stephens in the Spring of 1991. My old friend, the composer, Eddie Gregson, had been commissioned by Adrian Noble, the newly appointed director of the Royal Shakespeare Company, to write the music for the series of Plantagenet plays at Stratford. Eddie, knowing of my interest, telephoned and offered me two complimentary tickets.

At the time, my wife, Kathy was heavily pregnant with our first child. It came as a pleasant surprise when I read the cast-list in the programme to discover that Robert Stephens was playing Falstaff, a role that Harold Bloom champions as Shakespeare's greatest character.

Following Robert Stephen's departure from the National Theatre in early 1970s, the breakup of his marriage to Maggie Smith in 1973, and the estrangement of his two young sons, he suffered a long career slump, exacerbated by bouts of depression, coupled with a burgeoning reputation for heavy drinking.

This chance to revitalise his performing career was presented by Noble who remained a great enthusiast for Robert's work, and felt that he deserved a new start, and courageously offered him the role of Falstaff in *Henry IV*. Since pay for the actors in the national companies was poor and hedonistic living expenses for Robert were high, he didn't immediately accept the offer but was finally persuaded.

Although he had aged dramatically since we worked together, over two decades earlier, none of the old larger-than-life stage personality had diminished. A much younger cast, who in the early 1990s had been brought up in acting-schools much more geared towards producing performers for film and television than the Olivier, Gielgud, Schofield, Wolfit school of rhetoric in which Robert retained his position, were left in the shade by this Falstaff portrayal.

The generally complementary press reviews for this production, encouraged Adrian Noble in 1993 to offer Robert the final thespian accolade, the role of *King Lear*. Critics praised Robert's performance which balanced the spectacular effects by stressing the vulnerability and poignant humanity of Lear.

At the likely instigation of HRH the Prince of Wales, Robert Stephens was knighted in 1993, but two years later, at the age of 64, he was dead.

When Kathy and I went back-stage at the RSC Theatre in Stratford to see Robert, we reminisced about the Zeffirelli production of *Much ado*. Before we left his dressing-room, he sang us the song, set to music by Nino Rota that he remembered from lines Shakespeare gives to Balthasar, but Zeffirelli gave to Benedick.

Sigh no more, ladies, sigh nor more;
*   Men were deceivers ever;*
One foot in sea and one on shore,
*   To one thing constant never;*
*   Then sigh not so,*
*   But let them go,*
*   And be you blithe and bonny;*
Converting all your sounds of woe
*   Into. Hey nonny, nonny.*

Sing no more ditties, sing no mo,
*   Or dumps so dull and heavy;*
The fraud of men was ever so,
*   Since summer first was leavy.*
*   Then sigh not so,*
*   But let them go,*
*   And be you blithe and bonny,*

It is a nice irony that it is in the songs from within the plays, that Shakespeare, the author, often reveals himself as Shakespeare, the man.

Emilia left this world in April 1645 exactly three hundred years before my arrival in it. I come to writing this unanticipated book, not as an author or literary scholar, but as a musician drawn towards Shakespeare by quirks of fate

1. Emilia Bassano The Dark Musical Lady

Take, oh take those lips away,
that so sweetly were forsworne,
And those eyes: the breake of day
lights that doe mislead the Morne;
But my kisses bring againe, bring againe,
Seales of loue, but seal'd in vaine, seal'd in vaine

Measure For Measure (1.1.1718-23)

This book will highlight the lives and characters of the three main protagonists alluded to in the Shakespeare Sonnets - the poet, the young man and the Dark Lady. Proposing the identity of the Dark Musical Lady from the Shakespeare Sonnets has occupied the ingenuity of playwrights, academics, and novelists for years; George Bernard Shaw, Jonathan Bate, Hildegard Hemmerschmidt-Hummel, Duncan Salkeld and Simon Andrew Stirling have all provided different candidates; Mary Fitton, a Lady in Waiting to Elizabeth I, John Florio's wife Aline, Lord Southampton's wife, Elizabeth, Lucy Negro, a notorious London prostitute, and Jane Davenant, the Oxford Inn keeper's wife, and mother to Sir William Davenant, who as well as being Shakespeare's Godson, when in his cups, claimed to be the poet's illegitimate son too.

In 1973, in the pages of *The Times*, A. L. Rowse named Emilia Bassano as his candidate. This was long after Shaw's suggestion but before Bate's, Hammerschmidt-Hummel's, Salkeld's and Stirling's. In Rowse's opinion, which he regarded as infallible, by a stroke of good fortune, he discovered the true identity of the *Dark Lady* when he wasn't looking for her in the casebooks of Simon Forman held at Oxford's Bodleian Library. Forman was a physician, (we might say a quack doctor) a caster of horoscopes - like Elizabeth I's favourite, Dr Dee - but also a regular play-goer, diarist and efficient casebook recorder.

The fact that Forman had been hauled up in front of the medical regulators and fined, more than once, for practicing medicine when unqualified didn't seem to deter a well-heeled clientele from consulting him. Rowse, a renowned and immensely popular historian and Fellow of All Souls College, Oxford, whose speciality was the Elizabethan period, which, in his case, encompassed a profound love of the works of Shakespeare and the music of the period, was researching Forman's notebooks for information on the stage performances of the Shakespeare plays.

A number of Forman's clients were associated with Shakespeare's circle and his known interests, including two of Hunsdon's daughters, Lady Hoby and Lady Scrope, Henry Writhiosley and Elizabeth Vernon, Earl and Countess of Southampton. Southampton was Shakespeare's dedicatee of *Venvs and Adonis* and *Lucrece*. Another client was Frances Howard, who'd set her cap at Southampton when he was still single. Cressacre More, grandson of Sir Thomas More. Two of Shakespeare's publishers, Richard Field and William Jaggard, the impresario Philip Henslowe and Marie Mountjoy, who was later to become the playwright's landlady at his Silver Street lodgings.

In 1612 Shakepeare's residence at Silver Street was to involve him as a witness in litigation, along with a fellow tenant, Humphrey Fludd, an English trumpet player in the former employ of the french King Henry IV. Shakespeare and Fludd were obliged to give evidence in a Mountjoy family dispute at the Court of Requests in Westminster. Fludd, like the lutenist John Dowland, was a spy on behalf of the English, returning from Dieppe in the summer of 1599 to disclose intelligence about the Spanish fleet. I imagine that as a French speaker Fludd was a welcome guest in the Mountjoy household.

Forman attended several Shakespeare plays and made notes on performance of four of them; *Macbeth, Cymbeline, Richard II* and *The Winter's Tale*. Forman's reputation as a philanderer will have reached the ears of Shakespeare's company when the actor Augustine Philips arrived home earlier than expected surprising his wife and Forman in *flagrente delicto.*

At the time of Emilia's first consultation with Forman in 1597 he was living in the Parish of St Giles, Cripplegate. In the previous year, Camilla Bassano, a cousin of Emilia had consulted Forman twice, so very likely, she had recommended him. It was known that Forman had attended performances at *The Globe* and had made notes about his visits to the theatre. Rowse didn't anticipate reading confidential information and a character description in the notes about a woman that made him metaphorically yell *eureka.*

The account of the lady fitted the timing, location, temperament, conduct, education of the Dark Lady as described by Shakespeare in the Sonnets; probably dark because of her Italian ancestry, married but with a child conceived out of wedlock, promiscuous, musical, haughty, inconstant and temperamental. Forman recorded her name as Emilia Lanier neé Bassano wife of the court musician Alphonso Lanier and noted her connection to Court and her domestic and financial situation.

On 17 May Forman wrote:-

she was pa[ra]mour to my old L. of huns-Dean that was L. Chamberline and was maintained in great pride and yt seames that being with child she was for collour maried to a minstrell [Alphonso Lanier]

On 3 June he wrote:-

[she] *hath bin married 4 years / The old Lord Chamberlain kept her longue. She was maintained in great pomp....she hath 40£ a year & welthy to him that maried her in monie & Jewels*

On 2 September he wrote:-

She hath been much favored of her mati [majesty] *and of mani noblemen & hath had gret giftes and bin moch made of and a nobleman that is ded hath Loved her well & kept her longe but her husband hath delte hardly with her and spent and consumed her goods and she is nowe very needy, in debt and it seems for lucres sake will be a good fellowe for necessity doth co[m]pell*

The nobleman that is dead, is Hunsdon. It is unlikely that the £40 a year settled on Emilia by him on her marriage continued after his death, which is why she is hard up. Rowse interpreted the last phrase as meaning Emilia was prepared to sell herself; sex for money. Not so dissimilar to Berowne's description of Rosaline *and by heauen, one that will doe the deede* (*Loues Labour's lost* 4.1.936)

When he published his discovery Rowse had entered an academic arena which the English Shakespeare Establishment regarded as its exclusive and well guarded territory. Almost without exception, the professors of English Literature questioned the veracity of his nomination. In two respects he had left himself open to serious criticism. He had misread the word *brave* for *brown* and *Millia* for *William* in Forman's ambivalent hand writing, two significant building blocks indicating that Emilia was dark skinned and married to a man named Will proved to be incorrect.

Responding to the claim in a letter to *The Times*, Sir Anthony Wagner, *Garter King at Arms*, a friend of the historian, suggested that Rowse had insufficient evidence to guarantee the truth of his discovery so confidently. Wagner had more than a passing interest, since he had recently registered the later Bas-

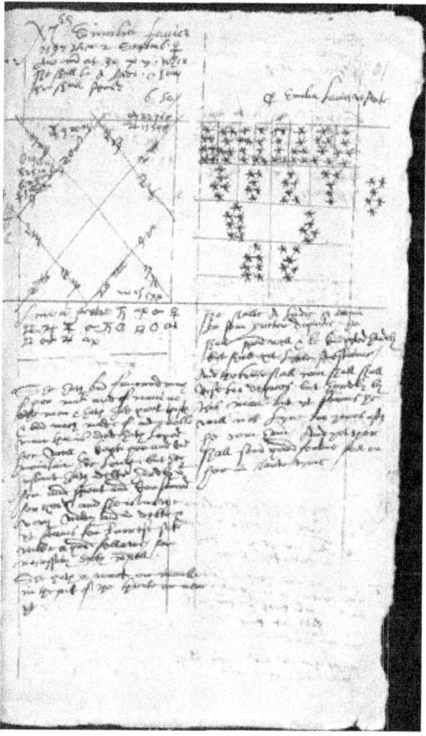

2 Forman Case Book Entry 2 September 1597

sano family pedigree with that of the Tudor and Stuart period of the family at the College of Arms. By the time I met him, Sir Anthony had succumbed to blindness, after complications from surgery, and so I read to him Roger Prior's article *More Light on The Dark Lady* from the *Financial Times*. Sir Anthony responded with "it looks as though Rowse was right, after all". Never for one moment did Rowse doubt that he was anything other completely correct in his identification, *it is she* he wrote to me.

Rowse had an unusual, probably unique, background for a Fellow of All Souls. He had been born into the humble home of an uneducated Cornish china clay worker and his wife who was in domestic service to the St Aubyn family on St Michael's Mount. Rowse told me there were no carpets, no books and no pictures in his childhood family cottage. Miraculously, he won a scholarship to Christ Church, Oxford when he was seventeen. Coincidentally, Christ Church own two silver mounted cornetti made by the Bassano family for the visit of James 1 to Oxford in 1605.

Rowse was successful in his determination to lose his regional accent to the point where it was completely undetectable. He was appointed a professor at his *alma mater* and during his lifetime published more than a hundred books reflecting his wide range of interests, but extensively on Tudor history.

Often his discoveries, as in the case of Emilia as the Dark Lady, were partly intuitive, but later proven to be correct by unknown documentary evidence. I hope that I am being instrumental in providing some of that evidence. As a homosexual Rowse remained single throughout his life. He regarded children as a dreadful nuisance to completing work and hated babies.

Roger Prior, lecturer in English at the Queen's University of Belfast, was a supporter of Rowse's nomination of Emilia from the beginning. He subsequently published research and contributed to books providing evidence that Emilia was the *Dark Lady*.

It is interesting that those involved as professional actors or directors in the theatre - Mark Rylance, Tony Haygarth, Margaret Wolfit, Tina Packer and John Hudson for example - seem much more willing to accept Rowse's nomination than the academic Shakespeare establishment. The prolific crime novelist, Agatha Christie wrote a letter to *The Times* in support of Rowse in which she attributed the character of Cleopatra to Shakespeare's experience of Emilia.

Considering that Rowse didn't discover Emilia Bassano in any work of Shakespeare, it has to be more than a coincidence that in the two Venetian plays - *The Merchant of Venice* and *Othello* - there is an Emilia in one and a Bassan(i)o in the other, and in another early play, *Titus Andronicus* there is an Æmlius and a Bassanius.

One would have hoped Shakespeare's choice of those names alone would have encouraged academics to explore Rowse's idea. Instead, many embarked upon a campaign to prove him wrong, and proclaimed his *Dark Lady* identification a distraction from Emilia's poetry.

Is there, though any evidence that Shakespeare met Emilia? Not so far, the *scrap of contemporary gossip* linking their names that Peter Levy claims would prove Rowse's identification. However, there are plenty of literary coincidences that link the two together. Here's one, the lines from the dedication to Lady Anne Clifford - known for her appearances in masques in stately homes - in Emilia's *Salve Devs* indicate that Emilia and Shakespeare were acquainted with one another's works

For well you knowe, this world is but a Stage. Where all doe play their parts, and must be gone

Jaques ingeniously develops Emilia's aphorism

All the world's a stage, And all the men and women, meerely Players; They haue their Exits and their En trances, And one man in his time playes many parts, His Acts being seuen ages (As you Like it 2.7:1078).

The Latin version *Totus mundus agit histrionem* was thought to be used as the Globe Theatre's motto when it was constructed in 1599.

Robert Greene accused Shakespeare of using other writers' ideas - the concept of plagiarism, as we know it, didn't exist then - did William seek her permission before adopting Emilia's turn of phrase, I doubt it?

As You Like It was thought to have been written in 1599, but not published until 1623 in the First Folio, twelve years after the publication of *Salve Devs*. Since there is no record of a public performance until the Restoration, Emilia can only have remembered the lines if she was at one of the two putative private performances at Wilton House or Richmond Palace - very unlikely - and so a personal exchange seems the only reasonable explanation.

The earlier *Dark Lady* sonnets are relatively complimentary, written before Shakespeare discovered her betrayal with his young friend and had his eyes opened to many sexual favours granted elsewhere *the baye where all men ride* (137.6). If he'd wanted to, there is no reason why the poet shouldn't have shared these earlier sonnets with his *Dark Lady.*

Here are Shakespeare's own words on his mistress's appearance, she is immediately identified as *black,* by which Elizabethans meant black haired and her eyes are *raven black.*

Sonnet 127:-

In the old-age blacke was not counted faire,
Or if it weare it bore not beauties name:

But now is blacke beauties successiue heire,
And Beautie slandered with a bastard shame.
For since each hand hath put on Natures power,
Fairing the foule with Arts faulse borrow'd face,
Sweet beauty hath no name no holy boure,
But is profan'd, if not liues in disgrace.
Therefore my Misteress eyes are Rauen blacke,
Her eyes so suted, and they mourners seeme,
At such who not borne fair no beauty lack,
Slandring Creation with a false esteeme,
Yet so they mourne becoming of their woe,
That euery toung saies beauty should looke so

The *bastard shame* accorded with Emilia's unfortunate position in the days of life before birth control. As you can see Shakespeare puns on heir/hair.

Emilia probably gave birth in May 1593, some six months after her marriage, by special licence, to Alphonso Lanier. Shakespeare and Anne Hathaway were also married by special licence, a legal facility which dispensed with statutory weekly public announcement of the Banns over three weeks, speeding up the conventional process, in the hope that pregnancy wasn't too obvious during the wedding ceremony.

There were many paintings owned and commissioned by the Bassano family. Nowell Bassano's 1651 will lists

a Picture of Sir Philip Sidney, four of my kindred, four pictures of my father, my wife's and my own, a picture of a good fellow painted on brass (rest of my pictures are in France)

John Bassano's 1671 mentions

Pictures of my great grandfather & my Uncle Andrea & my grandfather and grandmother

So I had always thought there would be a portrait of Emilia somewhere awaiting discovery. If anyone deserved a right to discover it in modern times, that right should surely go to an actor, playwright and poet. The late Tony Haygarth was just such. At the time of his discovery, Haygarth had been an actor for forty years, performing for all the major national companies, and had been productive as a poet and playwright too.

You will probably recognise his face from various television films: *Hornblower*, *The Mayor of Casterbridge*, *The Bill*, etc. and his distinctive Liverpudlian voice as that of Mr Tweedy in *Chicken Run*. He, like many actors was convinced by Rowse's Dark Lady identification and was moved to begin writing *Dark Meaning Mouse*, a three character play exploring the relationship between Emilia, Shakespeare and Forman. Whilst working on the play he investigated a Hilliard miniature known as *Mistress Holland* dated 1593 held in the Victoria & Albert Museum.

Here are some pertinent points makes about it

it is a portrait of an elegant young woman of pale complexion with black hair and dark eyes. She is wearing a white bodice decorated with stags, insects and trees. There is also a fleur-de-lis to the right of the picture. As was the custom in Elizabethan times, the image is painted onto velum on the back of a prepared playing card, in this case the five of spades. In the C18 the painting was thought to be Mistress Holland. In C19 it became known as Elizabeth, Lady Russell.

At first, Haygarth thought it was Emilia's Sister Angela who had married Joseph Holland, the antiqarian, but he realised that Angela died in the 1580s. He then wondered if the two sisters have been confused with the C18 and the C19 and the identification of Lady Russell just an incorrect one. Known portraits of Lady Russell, show her to have been fair-haired, unlike the sitter in this miniature. It is though more than coincidence that both Angela Holland and Lady Russell were important figures in Emilia's life. In fact had Lady Russell been alive when Emilia published *Salve Devs* she would have been included in the list of lady dedicatees.

3. Nicholas Hilliard: Emilia Bassano

Haygarth concluded that it was a portrait of Emilia. He explains

Under the magnifying glass I inspected the decorations on the white bodice described in the brochure as bees, trees and deer. I was staggered to see that the silkworm moths of the arms were identical to the "bees" on the lady's bodice, the four front legs, the turned-out antennae and the double wings. The trees could certainly be mulberries. What of the deer, the deer were in fact stags, with one of their forelegs raised - in heraldry this is known as the stag trippant. The lord whom Alphonso served at the siege of Rouen, in Cadiz, on the Islands Voyage to the Azores, and in Ireland was Robert Devereux Earl of Essex whose badge was the Stag Trippant. The fleur-de-lis in the right directs us to Emilia's husband whose family originally came from Rouen, where the symbol appears three times in "chief" in the arms of that city.

Some commentators rejected Haygarth's identification because they say that in 1593 Emilia would only have been twenty four, not twenty six, and that in 1593, she would have been heavily pregnant and the sitter clearly isn't. The sitter is in court dress and Emilia had ostensibly left the court immediately after her marriage. In response to this Haygarth explained

The painting informs us that the sitter is in her twenty-sixth year, as in "aetatis suae xxvi annis" which means she is "in the 26th year of her age" - and has therefore past her twenty-fifth birthday, but not yet her twenty-sixth. Next, I calculated Emilia's age at the date of the painting. Her birthday was a date some time before her baptism on 27th of January 1569, or more correctly 1568/69, remembering that in England, at this time, the year changed on March 25th, Lady Day, and continued so until 1752. (During this time, prior to March 25th, the date would frequently be written - old year/new year ie.1568/69.)

In the Parish register there are just ten baptisms recorded after Emilia, the last being a child named Mary Shingles on March 21st 1568, after which the date is changed, in bold figures in the centre of the page to 1569. Emilia, then, would have celebrated her 25th birthday, and entered her twenty-sixth year (aetatis suae xxvi annis) in January, 1593/94 - spot on! This calculation also dates the painting more accurately, as it must have been painted, assuming the sitter is Emilia, between her twenty-fifth birthday some days before the 27th of January 1593/94, and before the year changed to 1594 on the 25th of March, a period of two months only. Possibly painted for her 25th birthday!

He continued

I'm still working on other possible clues within the painting. She is wearing a four string necklace, on which are visible 25 black beads, or bugles (25 -Her number of birthdays? and black bugles as Phoebe's eyes are likened to in As You Like It?) And each section or unit of her Tire looks like an owl's face, I wonder if there is any significance there? The Southampton portrait by Hilliard is dated 1594 but this could have been just a couple of months after Emilia sat for him. Did Southampton pay for both portraits?

Hilliard's portrait accords with lines 9 and 10 in Sonnet 127

Therefore my Misteress eyes are Rauen blacke,
Her eyes so suted, and they mourners seeme,

and is duplicated in Berowne's descriptions of another promiscuous *Dark Lady*, Rosaline.

A whitly wanton, with a veluet brow.
With two pitch bals stucke in her face for eyes.
I, and by heauen, one that will doe the deede,
Though Argus were her Eunuch and her garde.
(Loues Labour's lost 4.1.934-7)

O if in blacke my Ladies browes be deckt,
It mournes, that painting vsurping haire
Should rauish doters with a false aspect:
And therfore is she borne to make blacke, faire.
Her fauour turnes the fashion of the dayes,
For natiue bloud is counted painting now:
And therefore red that would auoyd dispraise,
Paints it selfe blacke, to imitate her brow.
(Loues Labour's lost 4.3.1500)

Along with others, Peter Jensen believes that *Loues Labour's Lost* is a skit on the Southampton circle with Navarre representing, Southampton, Elizabeth Vernon as the Princess of France, Berowne as Shakepeare and Rosaline as Emilia.

John Hudson has suggested that Alphonso Lanier was younger than Emilia. I don't think he's correct, Alphonso appears to have been born in France in 1563, or earlier, making him at least thirty when he married Emilia.

When they married Emilia shed the surname of one musical dynasty and donned another, which, in time, was to become equally celebrated. Alphonso was the second son of Nicholas Lanier I, not to be confused with his grandson, Nicholas Lanier 2, the first ever *Master of the Kings Musick* a position established by Charles I.

Nicholas Lanier, composer, singer and bass viol player, painter and art expert was to collaborate with Ben Jonson on his masque *Lovers made Men* in which Nicholas also appeared as a singer. It was Nicholas Lanier's portrait, painted in Genoa by Van Dyke, that was so admired by Charles I that led the King to invite Van Dyke to work in England, but that was some half a century on.

I suspect Alphonso was homosexual and chosen by Hunsdon as a marriage partner for Emilia so that their affair might continue after marriage without arousing jealousy in a cuckolded husband. My suspicion over Alphonso's sexual orientation is supported by his connection to two influential associates; Bishop Bancroft, who was a life long bachelor, and Southampton who was known to have homosexual traits.

Alphonso's lack of interest in heterosexual activity may well have given Emilia *carte blanche* to freely indulge in the freedom within marriage that Forman described. Although after the birth of Henry there were other pregnancies - some resulting in still-births - and one full term, producing a daughter, Odillia, who died in infancy, I think it unlikely that Alphonso was the father.

Dr Catherine Hood has written *that if infection is passed from mother to child it can cause premature births, stillbirths and even early infant death.* From Forman's account it would appear that Emilia was beset with these tragic difficulties.

This brand she quenched in a coole Well by,
  Which from loues fire tooke heat perpetuall,
  Growing a bath and healthfull remedy,
  For men diseasd, but I my Mistresse thrall,
    Came there for cure and this by that I proue,
    Loues fire heates water, water cooles not loue. (154.9-14)

There is little doubt that Shakespeare blamed his venereal infection on his Dark Lady, if his verse describes his symptoms, then Chlamydia, would be the most likely modern diagnosis.

Paul Edmundson and Stanley Wells have concluded that Sonnets 154 and 153 are a schoolboy translation of the same Greek epigram. That seems unlikely if Jonson's comment on Shakespeare's linguistic knowledge is correct, *small Latin, less Greek*. Much more likely that it is a rewriting of a later English or Italian translation of Scholasticus' original Greek.

It is line 12 of Sonnet 127

Slandring Creation with a false esteeme that gives the clue that Hunsdon wasn't the father of Emilia's son. Most modern editions print Creation with a lower case c, the first edition uses an upper case C, giving it special significance. Shakespeare may well have had Emilia's new married name of Lanier turning over in his mind as a pun when he chose the word *Slandring*.

Henry was the Christian name of Lord Chamberlain Hunsdon, one of the most *esteemed* and powerful courtiers in the land. It was in Emilia's interests - financial and social, to say nothing of protecting her reputation - to give the world at large, the strongest impression that the baby was Hunsdon's. The most effective way to achieve that was to name her son after him.

There is another aspect to the *false esteem* allegation. If, as has been suggested, Hunsdon was an illegitimate child of King Henry VIII, Henry Lanier would have been the grandson of a late king, and therefore in a murky line of succession to the throne.

It would appear that if Emilia protested the child was his, Hunsdon believed her, or perhaps, as a politician he thought expedient it to go along with the notion, because he settled £40 a year on her and allowed her to keep the jewels and clothes he had bought for her after her marriage.

This would also agree with the concept that a liaison continued between Hunsdon and Emilia after her marriage. I assume that Hunsdon's financial settlement on Emilia ceased on his death, which is why she was hard up when she first visited Forman.

Hunsdon recorded the names, times and dates of birth and godparents of eight of his children in his copy of Froissart's history book *Chroniques*.

It seems that the author of the play *Edward lll* had access to this very book because he quotes *verbatim* some of Hunsdon's marginal annotations. Hunsdon's last recorded birth is of Margaret in 1567. Margaret was to become the wife of Sir Edward Hoby and resident at Bisham Abbey with her mother-in-law, Lady Russell. Not surprisingly, Hunsdon didn't record the names of his several illegitimate children but we know that one of them, Valentine Carey, was born around 1570, when Hunsdon was forty six.

How would Shakespeare know that naming the boy Henry was *slandring Creation with a false esteeme* unless he knew some one else was the father? Emilia might have told him that Hunsdon wasn't the father, but why would she do that if she wanted the world at large to believe that he was? Much more likely that Shakespeare absolutely knew that he was the father and the conception was at Bisham Abbey during the Queen's visit between the 11th and 13th August 1592.

In the next Sonnet (128) The *Dark Lady* is shown to be musical, like the Queen, she plays the clavichord, a different keyboard instrument to the virginals, a similar keyboard technique though:-

HOw oft when thou my musike musike playst,
  Vpon that blessed wood whose motion sounds
  With thy sweet fingers when thou gently swayst,
  The wiry concord that mine ear confounds,
  Do I enuie those Jackes that nimble leape,
  To kisse the tender inward of thy hand,
  Whilst my poore lips which should that haruest reape,
  At the woods boldnes by thee blushing stand.
  To be so tikled they would change their state,
  And situation with those dancing chips,
  Oer whome their fingers walke with gentle gait,
  Making dead wood more blest than liuing lips,
    Since saucie Jackes so happy are in this,
    Giue them their fingers, me thy lips to kisse.

In the British Library copy, someone has inked in commas after both of the words *musike* in line one, and most modern editors have changed *their* to *thy* in lines eleven and fourteen.

Some commentators have suggested that in lines 5 and 6, Shakespeare was confused over keyboard nomenclature mixing up keys for jacks. However, there was an advanced playing technique for the clavichord whereby the left hand was placed inside the case of the instrument to stop the string striking mechanism with the hand creating a muted effect. Because the far end of keys hit the string, by moving the keys ever so slightly sideways, it was possible to create a vibrato that is alluded to in *gently swayst.*

One thing is certain, the *Dark Lady* was a sufficiently compelling keyboard player to hold the world's greatest playwright spellbound in the palm of her hand.

4 Hands of the harpsichordist Carole Cerasi

2. Music in the Family

This Musicke mads me, let it sound no more,
For though it haue holpe madmen to their wits,
In me it seemes, it will make wise-men mad:

The life and death of King Richard the Second (5.4. 2625)

Emilia couldn't have been born into a more musical family, however it was her conduct, rather than music, which drove Shakespeare *frantick madde with euer-more vnrest* (147.10).

Music making went back at least four generations to the end of the C15 starting with Emilia's great grandfather, who repaired and tuned the organs for the Franciscans at the order's church in Crespano del Grappa (part of Venice's mainland territory), and forward thirteen generations to musical Bassanos still performing today.

En route, in the C16 and C17 six generations of the family worked as state employed musicians in Venice and England. After the English Civil War there were two generations of Vicars choral at Lichfield Cathedral including the composer, Christopher Bassano, whose music is similar in style to Henry Purcell. In the following century, the Derbyshire based Joseph Wright, painted a portrait of Mary Bassano, with a recorder in her hand.

A decade or so later, the sisters Louisa and Josephine Bassano, graduates of London's Royal Academy of Music, became professional opera singers. Louisa was sufficiently successful to have worked as a soloist with both Liszt and Mendelssohn. She toured England with Franz Liszt in 1840 and in 1846 sang the recitatives of Mendelssohn's *Elijah* at the first performance at Birmingham Town Hall with the composer conducting.

In 1516, six years after the Bassano family had moved from Bassano del Grappa to Venice, Emilia's grandfather, Jeronimo, faced a serious dilemma because of an edict by the Doge's ruling Council.

The Jews must all live together in the Corte de Case, which are in the Ghetto near San Girolama; and in order to prevent their roaming about at night; let there be built two gates, on the side of the Old Ghetto where there is a little bridge, and likewise on the other side of the bridge, that is one for each of the said two places, which gates shall be opened in the morning at the sound of the Marangona [the main bell of San Marco] and shall be closed at midnight by four Christian guards appointed and paid by the Jews at the rate deemed suitable by our Cabinet

Riccardo Calimani: The Ghetto of Venice

The Ghetto lies in Cannaregio, the most northern sestiere of Venice. The word *Ghetto* is Venetian dialect for *foundry* and has since the Second World War became synonymous with the worst kind of murderous oppression. In 1516 it was less sinister, just a system of keeping a suspect race - as the Venetians perceived the Jews - under control. The terms of the edict, although restrictive to freedom, still allowed the Jews - like Shylock in *The Merchant of Venice* - to continue their money lending, pawn-broking and other mercantile activities.

For Jeronimo de Bassano, sackbut player, member of the Doge's wind band, the *Pifferi*, lay brother of the *Scuola Grandi* and the *Scuola di Santa Maria dei Mercanti*, the edict was of the greatest concern. Jeronoimo was of Jewish descent and as such he was legally ineligible to work for church or state. He lived either as a *converso*, or *marrano* (crypto Jew) conforming to the Catholic religion, or giving the outward impression of conforming, albeit the rather more independent, less prescriptive, version of Catholicism practised by the Venetians.

Adhering to the requirements of the edict meant revealing his ancestry and very likely foregoing his musical employment. Despite severe penalties if discovered, Jeronimo chose to keep his secret and his living.

The north of Italy had become a popular haven for Jews following their expulsion from the Iberian peninsular by Ferdinand and Isabella in the 1490s but it would seem that the Bassano family were resident in the Veneto before this.

In 1481, Emilia's great Grandfather, named Baptista, like her father, was living in Crespano some 10 miles east of Bassano del Grappa, where the family were known as Piva. *Prima face* this would appear to be a name associated with occupation, like Baker, Thatcher or Smith in English, because the word *Piva* in Italian means a *bag pipe*.

However there are two other colloquial meanings, both anti-semitic - *big-nose* and *penis* - which might encourage a Jewish family to consider renaming itself when the opportunity arose. At some time after 1481 the family moved to to Bassano del Grappa where they bought a house in the precinct of Borgo de Lion which remained in the family for many years.

5 Bassano del Grappa

After the War of the League of Cambrai (1509-16) all of the Jews were expelled from Venice's mainland territories but it was before the start of the conflict that Jeronimo and his family to move to Venice where they dropped the dubious name Piva and and instead assumed the name of their last home, Bassano.

In Venice Jeronimo's instrumental expertise allowed him to accept the many musical opportunities offered by the republic under the twenty year rule of Doge Leonardo Loredan.

The family took a house in the parish of San Maurizio in the sestiere of San Marco, easy walking distance to the Doge's Palace and the basilica of St Mark and the *Scuola grande di san Rocco* and other *Scuole* where most of the liturgical services with extensive musical accompaniment took place. One by one, over two decades, Jeronimo's six sons, Alvise, Antonio, Giovanni, Gasparo, Jacopo, Giovanni-Baptista followed their father into Venice's flourishing music profession.

They witnessed the introduction of the pioneering composing techniques of Adrian Willaert appointed *maestro di cappella* at St Mark's by Doge Andrea Gritti and heard first-hand the acoustic differences made to the basilica by Jacopo Sansovino's architectural changes.

By 1539 Edmund Harvel, King Henry Vlll's Venetian ambassador - apparently unaware that four of the Bassanos had already worked in England - wrote to the King about their musical capabilities

all excellent and esteemed above all others in this city in their virtue

Politically, the situation for all *marranos* in Venice was deteriorating. The city was rife with rumours of the introduction of the Inquisition. For Jews living as Christians - but not true converts - and benefitting from the subsequent advantages, this development would have been catastrophic.

Jews wearing the compulsory identifying yellow cap and living in the Ghetto would not have been subject to the Inquisition, but all 'Christians' would have been in danger of being summoned before the Inquisitors of the Holy Office with potentially serious consequences. In the following two decades the Venetian Inquisition appears to have imposed imprisonment or servitude on a galley, rather than the barbaric *auto-da-fé* of Madrid or Seville.

Harvel wrote his testimonial recommending the Bassanos to King Henry Vlll because the King's instruction to seek outstanding instrumentalists who would help achieve ambitious musical plans for his wedding to Anne of Cleves. As a keen amateur musician - both wind player and composer - it was the King's ambition to improve the quality of the *King's Musick*, the court's musical ensemble of wind and strings formed by his father, King Henry Vll.

Harvel was given the diplomatically sensitive job of negotiating with Doge Pietro Lando for the Bassano brothers release in order to recruit them permanently to the *King's Musick*.

The four older Bassano brothers had worked in England in the preceding decade, so knew what benefits were to be found by permanent employment at the Tudor Court. The King realised that he was attracting the best instrumentalists in Europe with extensive knowledge of the visually and orally impressive *cori-spezzati* (separate choirs) performing practice pioneered in Venice, and was prepared to recompense, in both money and conditions in order to secure their services.

For the Bassanos, substantially more pay, free accommodation, commercial incentives and above all, as the King's servants, immunity from arrest, were conditions they found most attractive.

In April of 1540 five of the six brothers were given permanent employment at court, their names semi-anglicised to Lewis, Anthony, John, Jasper, Jacomo and Baptista. The oldest brother Jacopo made instruments for Henry, although he never held a court playing appointment. When he arrived in England the King granted him and his brother, Anthony, a licence to import three hundred tuns of Gascon wine. In Tudor times French wine was a very lucrative commodity.

Henry offered the Charterhouse, the dissolved Carthusian order's London priory, (still standing near the Barbican), as a dwelling-house and instrument making workshop. All of the brothers, with the single exception of Baptista, the youngest brother, were married. The wives of Jacopo and Anthony bore the identical maiden-name, de Nasi, and so were probably sisters. According to Peter Matthews they were daughters of Benedetto de Nasi, a Jewish Venetian banker and silk merchant.

Each brother and their families were allocated former Monks' cells as personal accommodation and instrument making workshops. Lewis was allocated the most living space, the Priors New Cell and Pulpit House, and two further former monks' cells.

The reason for this preference was because he arrived with at least three children - Augustine, Ludovico and Laura - all born in Venice. In maturity, Augustine and Ludovico became composers and have left behind attractive instrumental music for wind consort and lute.

The other four brothers, three with wives, occupied five further cells. The sound of babies crying and children playing was something unheard of before within the walls of this ecclesiastical building. As was secular music, madrigals - an after supper entertainment for the whole family - and the rehearsal of dance music that needed preparation before playing at court with the monarch in close proximity.

Jacopo returned to Venice in 1544 but the remaining Bassanos stayed at the Charterhouse until 1552 when the owner, Sir Edward North, moved to have them evicted so he could develop the buildings into a grand London mansion.

Four of the brothers moved *en masse* to a house called The Bell in Mark Lane in the parish of All Hallows, Barking. The house remained in the ownership of the family for several generations and is mentioned in the 1726 will of Richard Bassano, a deputy herald for Sir William Dugdale. The church, partially destroyed by bombing in World War ll, is now known as All Hallows-by-the-Tower.

Baptista, Emilia's father moved to a separate independent location, Norton Folgate in the parish of St Botolph, Bishopsgate, which lies outside of the jurisdiction of the city and an area popular with actors. It would seem that the location, despite being close to Bedlam, the hospital for the insane, was in a fashionable part of London.

The gardens of the houses to the west side of Bishopsgate backed on to Moor Field and those to the east, to open countryside. The census records don't list Baptista until 1571 when it is said that he has been there *but ten years*. it maybe that he lived somewhere else immediately after leaving the Charterhouse.

It isn't known why Baptista chose to live away from his brothers and their families. They continued to work together and it would seem there was no great family rift because he called his first child Lewis, the anglicised version of Alvise, Baptista's late brother, who had died some ten years earlier.

His marriage, if there was one, is something of a mystery because of a line in his will which says

Margaret Bassanio alias Johnson, my reputed wife

It could be that *reputed wife* means common law wife, however, it may just be a curious turn of phrase for someone whose native language wasn't English.

Because of the dates of birth of Baptista's children - the first in 1554 the last in 1571 - Margaret may have been Baptista's second wife, whether either union was blessed by the sanctity of marriage in church, remains unknown. She is named *Margarett Bassana* in the entry of her burial in the St Botolph's parish register.

Had they all lived, Emilia would have enjoyed the companionship of three siblings; Lewes, who died aged thirteen months in November 1563, Phillip, who died at the age of nearly three in 1573 and Angela, some fifteen years older than Emilia, born in 1554 and died at the age of twenty four in October 1578. Angela's cause of death is unknown but her demise left her son Philip, two years old, without his mother.

Angela had married the lawyer, Joseph Holland, at St Botolph's on 16 May 1575. Holland was a member of the Inner Temple, and active participant in the Elizabethan *Society of Antiquaries* and a prolific writer on English historic subjects. Their son, Philip Holland, survived and from 1619 was a herald, *Portcullis Pursuivant*, until his death in 1625.

Four of the Bassano' brothers; Emilia's uncles, Anthony, Lewis, Jasper and John had already been employed as instrumentalists at court, arriving via Southampton in the autumn of 1531. On this visit they stayed in England for three months. It seems likely that there is a connection between their employment in England and the arrival of Mark Raphael, the apostate Venetian rabbi earlier that year.

Raphael's crucial ruling in favour of the King's wish to separate from Katherine of Aragon so he could wed Anne Boleyn lent biblical authority to the illegality of the the royal partnership leaving the way clear for the King to instruct Archbishop Cranmer to annul the marriage. It was Raphael's opinion which began the tortuous process which was to radically change English history and the final severance of jurisdiction by the Pope.

In May 1532 the Church of England agreed to surrender its legislative independence and canon law to the authority of the monarch. A year later the *Statute in Restraint of Appeals* removed the right of the English clergy and laity to appeal to Rome on matters of matrimony, tithes and oblations.

In 1534 the *Act of Submission of the Clergy* removed the right of all appeals to Rome, effectively ending the Pope's influence. The *first Act of Supremacy* confirmed the King by statute as the *Supreme Head of the Church of England* in 1536. He was later to be renamed as *Supreme Governor of the Church of England.*

Because of Raphael's ruling, the King got his way against widespread opposition, perhaps this influenced him to view all Venetian Jews in a kindly light.

The *Privy Purse Expenses* for September, October and November shows payments to the four Bassano 'sackbuts' for their three months stay in England

September 1531
Itm the [30] daye paied by the kinges comanndet to marke Antony
loyesde Jeronom pylgryn Maiohū Jasp de Jeronimo   John de Jeronimo
£7.17s. 6d.

Itm the [24] daye paid to 4 new mynstrells for ther going to Southampton to fetche ther stuf:
£13. 6s. 8d.

November 1531
Itm the [9] daye paied to Antony the Sagbut for his costes going Southampton wt the new sagbuttes: 53s. 4d.

This doesn't necessarily mean that all four Bassanos brothers - Anthony, Lewis, Jasper and John - played the sackbut, although they probably did. *Sackbut* was used by the court scrivener as generic term for all wind instruments and could have applied to recorders and shawms too.

Shakespeare included instructions for music throughout his plays, often specifiying the instruments he wants. I can only find one mention of the sackbut in the canon and that is in *Coriolanus*.

Trumpets, Hoboyes, Drums beate, altogether.

Messenger
The Trumpets, Sack-buts, Psalteries, and Fifes,
Tabors, and Symboles, and the showting Romans,
Make the Sunne dance. Hearke you.

Coriolanus (5.4.3463-5)

No one knows specifically why the visit to the English court should have occurred at this time, but it is known that the King was hugely impressed by the music performed by the French musicians at the *Field of Cloth-of-Gold* in 1520 and had ever since been working to achieve equally high musical standards at home.

The 1540 decision to settle in England permanently cannot have been an easy one for the Bassano family to make because it meant uprooting wives and children. The King's ruthless inconstancy over women had a fatal outcome for one of his court musicians, the lutenist, Mark Smeaton - who the older Bassanos knew - in 1536 was executed along with Sir Francis, Henry Norris,

William Brereton, George Boleyn and Viscount Rochford for adultery with Queen Anne.

It seems that the public were more scandalised by the accusation of adultery with Smeaton - a commoner and servant - than they were by the allegation of the Queen's adultery with her own brother. Whether all, some, or none of those accused were guilty as charged only they and the Queen can really have known. What must have been obvious is that the English court under King Henry's rule was a potentially dangerous environment for any incautious servant.

Emilia's father, Baptista didn't come to England with his brothers in 1531, he is nearly always listed last in any payments and so it is likely that he was the youngest brother, a *native of Venice* as he described himself in his will, he must have been born there around 1515-20.

The licence issued to Jacomo and Anthony to import Gascon was renewed in 1542, but by November 1544, Jacomo had returned to Venice. Jacomo's grandson, Giovanni Bassano, was destined to become the best known musician in the entire family, excelling as a composer, cornett virtuoso and choir trainer. For some decades Giovanni Bassano worked as an instrumentalist alongside Andrea Gabrieli and later Giovanni Gabrieli, but in 1601 he was appointed *Maestro di Concerti*, musical director of the large instrumental ensemble in St. Mark's Basilica. It was in this building that his great-grandfather and great-uncles had performed regularly from seventy years before.

Giovanni Bassano's musical duties were to collaborate on the all important state occasions with three of the world's greatest Renaissance composers and organists, Andrea and Giovanni Gabrieli and Claudio Monteverdi.

Throughout their time at court, the English branch of the family stayed in contact with their relatives in Venice and retained ownership of a house in Bassano del Grappa.

Baptista made at least three visits to Venice. The first, in March 1545, when Sir Henry Knyvett, the Wiltshire MP and *Gentleman of the Privy Chamber* supported Baptista's application for a passport, £20 in cash and a horse. He visited again in 1546 shortly after the death of his father, so this was very likely in connection with tying up legal matters.

On 9 November 1552 another passport was issued to Baptista

to travel beyond the seas with one servant, one horse and other necessaries.

By this time the Bassanos were achieving great success as instrument makers, exporting a wide range of wind and some string instruments to court ensembles throughout Europe. There is little doubt that Baptista was delivering instruments to clients and taking orders *en route* to Venice and back.

It still remains the matter of some debate whether or not the family were Jewish. The most vocal opponent of the notion that they were Jewish is from Alessio Ruffatti, an Italian musicologist who thinks that Jews wouldn't have been employed by the Fransicans in Crespano because the order was notoriously anti-Semitic. There is more support for the pro-Jewish side.

There is no doubt that when the Bassanos arrived in England, Jews had been legally excluded from the country in 1290 by Edward I, but in mid 1500s there were some exceptions, Mark Raphael, for one. Two of the wind players that they replaced were further exceptions - John de Antonia *alias* Moyses and Pelegryne Simon *alias Maiohn* - were Jews.

It would seem that the Jewish culture was strong in the Bassanos whilst resident in Venice because Jacomo and Anthony married two Jewish sisters, Elina and Julia Nasi. Jewishness is passed down via the matriarchal line and so the children of these two women would definitely have been Jewish. Nasi is the family name of the renowned Portuguese Jewess from the family of bankers, Donna Gracia Mendes-Nasi, who emigrated to Venice from Portugal via Antwerp, albeit, after the Bassano brothers had left.

In Tudor times the silk industry was almost exclusively conducted by Jews. When they arrived in England, the Bassanos maintained connections with the Portuguese Jewish community in London, and later had the College of Arms confirm their Italian coat-of-arms, featuring silk worm moths. Laura Bassano, Lewis's daughter married a Jewish musician, Joseph Lupo.

The name Bassano and its derivatives are strongly associated with Jews, Mordecai Bassani (c.1632–1703) was rabbi of Verona and Isaiah Ben Israel Hezikiah Bassano (d. 1739), rabbi in Cento, Padua, Ferrara, and Reggio Emilia. Georgio Bassani, the Italian writer of the auto-biographical *Garden of the Finzi-Continis*, was a Jew writing about a Jewish family and their Ferrara estate. He survived deportation during World War ll by living in Florence under a pseudonym, showing that using the name Bassani would have alerted the Fascists to his ancestry.

The extensive Bassano family in Malta are all Jewish. The licence to import three hundred tuns of Gascon wine awarded to Jacopo and Anthony Bassano had formerly been held by a Jew, Mark Raphael. Emilia's book *Salve Devs Rex Judæorum* has the Latin word for Jews in its title and her second child was named Odillia - a curious choice after calling her son Henry - is a name with Hebrew origins.

A young cousin of Emilia the son of Nowell and Elizabeth Bassano was given the Jewish name of Abraham. Abraham Bassano had a connection with Oxford University, published a book of herbs and simples, and was the compiler of a common place book which included two of the Shakespeare sonnets, numbers 32 and 74.

Even though it has some liturgical independence from Rome, Christian migrants from Venice, would still have been most likely to have been Catholic. So shortly after Henry Vlll had severed connections with the Church of Rome, Catholics would have had more than second thoughts about moving to a country whose state rejection of their religion would have made for a less than comfortable stay.

The Charterhouse by the time of the Bassanos' arrival had been the scene of the most horrific deaths of its former occupants, the Prior and monks of the Carthusian order. Catholics would surely have felt uncomfortable living in accommodation haunted by such a recent tragic history?

On the balance of probabilities, it would seem that the Bassano family were of Jewish origin, but had conformed outwardly as Christians in Venice and continued to do the same, albeit as Protestants, when they arrived in London.

6 The Charterhouse

3. Emilia's Life

Pedro
You embrace your charge too willingly: I thinke this is your daughter.
Leonato
Her mother hath many times told me so.
Benedicke
Were you in doubt that you askt her?
Leonato
Signior Benedicke, no, for then were you a childe.

(Much adoe about Nothing 1.3.94)

In the tenth year of Queen Elizabeth's reign, on 27 January 1569, Emilia was baptised at the family parish church of St Botolph, Bishopsgate. By this date the Bassano family had been a highly visible feature of the Tudor court for three and half decades, recognised by their physical appearance and known by their names to all members of the royal family and its courtiers.

The church scribe noted the child's name as *Emillia Baptist.* Unlike other entries of birth, above and below Emilia's, surnames are written, but she isn't called by her father's family name of Bassano. It is possible that there was some discussion over what should be recorded, because although they cohabited, Emilia's parents probably weren't married.

Because of the extensive number of Bassano appointments as royal musicians, the family was considered to belong to the social class known as minor gentry. Emilia's father, Baptista, seems to have developed a special relationship with the Queen, either introducing her to playing the lute, or assisting her to improve her technique. This began when, as Princess Elizabeth, the only surviving child of the reigning King and executed Queen Anne, she was confined to a solitary life at Hatfield House, some twenty three miles from the Palace of Whitehall, and even further from the other court buildings of Richmond, Windsor and Greenwich. At Hatfield self-amusement was the main option.

On 22nd November 1552 Baptista was paid the substantial sum of 74s.8p (worth more than £1,000 in today's money) plus another 30s (equivalent of £400 today) *in reward* for a visit he made to Hatfield. A later Hatfield payment, but with no date given, was for 17s in payment *for lute stringes for her grace.*

The first 74s 8d may well have been his payment for supplying a lute to the future queen. If so, this would have meant Baptista being presented to Elizabeth and either introducing her to elementary lute playing technique or offering advice on further improvement.

The amount of 30s payment *in reward* was equal to about twelve day's pay for a court musician so I think it highly likely that he stayed at Hatfield for a week or more in order to give Elizabeth daily lute lessons, instilling a daily practise regime, something musicians recognise as essential to achieve competence on an instrument.

Around 1580 Nicholas Hilliard painted a miniature of Elizabeth I playing the lute. At the time of its creation the Queen was approaching fifty, playing the instrument had begun three decades, earlier but remained a pastime well into maturity. The Queen also played the virginals. In 1564 Sir James Melville, emissary for Mary Queen of Scots, mentions hearing her play. These are the two instruments that were also played by Emilia giving her something in common with Elizabeth I.

Nicholas Hilliard
Queen Elizabeth I

Musicians in church, court and theatre occupy a prominent visual position, therefore they get noticed. In 1547, Baptista along with his four older brothers played at the funeral of Henry Vlll, Elizabeth's father. The same five musicians also played at the funeral of Elizabeth's half-sister, Queen Mary in 1558, and then at the coronation of Queen Elizabeth in the following year when Baptista's brothers, John, Anthony and Jasper along with his nephew, Augustine also played.

On these important state occasions, the ever watchful Elizabeth would have recognised Baptista as a regular performer at court but also acknowledged him as the musician who helped her with her lute studies and on two occasions visited Hatfield.

There are contemporary reports of instruments accompanying voices in England, as in Venice, so it is likely that the wind players doubled vocal parts, or accompanied solo voices as well as providing processional music.

In 1564 reaffirming the symbolism of the lute as an association between monarch and servant, Baptista gave the Queen a Venetian lute at the annual exchange of New Year's gifts. Venetian lutes were prized by aristocratic families, the instrument features as a status symbol in many Tudor portraits.

Six were imported on the Venetian ship the *Santa Maria de Gracia* along with a consignment of 54 butts of sweet wine to Emilia's father and her uncle Jasper's son-in-law, Innocent Locutello. Augustine Bassano's 1596 will bequeathed

two of my best lutes & all my music books to his brother-in-law, Thomas Lupo.

Not only did the Bassanos play the lute but they wrote music for it too. Attractive and ingenious pieces for the instrument - written in lute tablature rather than standard music notation - exist by Augustine and Ludovico in the Trumbell and Matthew Holmes Lute Books.

Hardly surprising then that in 1588, or thereabouts, when Emilia first appeared at court as the attractive young mistress of her cousin, Henry Carey, Lord Hunsdon, the ageing Queen took more than a passing interest in her.

Forman noted

She hath been favored much of her mati [Majesty]

In 1563 Baptista was the intended victim of a failed assassination attempt about which little is know. Sir Thomas Egerton, Lord Keeper and Lord Chancellor, entered in the Council and Star Chamber notes

Henry Dingeley, Mark Anthony, et al, to be whipped, to stand on the pillory, and lose their ears, and bide for ever in Bridewell, and Mark Anthony banished for ever for conspiring the murder of Baptist Bassano, Italian

Presumably Dingeley and *et al* were native Englishmen and so were sentenced to life imprisonment, Mark Anthony, a foreigner, banished.

In 1570 Baptista became the owner of property in the parish of St Botolph's Bishopsgate

a messuage, a garden and a parcel of land (21 feet long by 18 feet wide).

It would appear that this was an addition to an existing property portfolio because his will mentions

my three messuages or tenements..situate..in the parish of St Botolph's

An *inquisitio post mortem* held at the Guildhall in 1584 showed that he had also owned a property in the parish of St Christopher-le-Stocks.

For a commoner, Emilia's life is well documented for the Elizabethan/Jacobean period through information in her poetry and other writing, her medical records, and some legal records. Forman's professional diary and casebooks are crucial and they were the single source of Rowse's confidence in his nomination of Emilia as the *Dark Lady*.

His discovery propelled the historian in pursuit of her only known book of published poetry, *Salve Devs Rex Judæorum* .

Emilia visited Forman several times in 1597 for consultations that incorporated astrological readings, which was usual practice for Forman. Forman was sexually aroused by her, and if his account is correct, she encouraged intimacy by inviting him to dine and stay the night whilst her husband was away. On the first occasion, she allowed Forman to kiss her and feel all parts of her body but stopped short of consenting to copulation.

Some thirty years earlier, in September 1568 when Emilia's mother was five months pregnant with her daughter a petition was presented to the Queen in Italian from *the poor musician brothers of Your Majesty* [the Bassanos] *complain that Alvise, their eldest brother, died:-*

leaving his foreign wife with many sons and daughters at our expense; now being in old age and great poverty, always educating our sons in virtue to enable them to serve Her Majesty, as they have done and continue to do, and at the end of so much and such long service we are troubled and seriously oppressed by Mr. Lichfield, who is trying by various means to make us pay back the salary of our dead brother, we having petitioned for it immediately after his death to Queen Mary, who replied to us that nothing would be taken away, as in fact has always been paid to us, all of us being under one patent, never being asked by our payer for any further warrant or discharge for its payment, him knowing very well about the death of our brother; we have therefore always believed until now that he had sufficient discharge, and we not having enough funds either to pay back or to make litigation to defend ourselves in front of the law, humbly implore your Grace together with her Majesty to consider our poor state and long service and our extreme old age - besides, the son has always served in the place of his dead father.

This letter shows that the remaining brothers were justifying claiming Lewis's court duty fees after his death and explaining that it was anticipated that the family would fill the place of a musician who had died with a younger son who they had trained musically.

The text demonstrates that they remained a close-knit family, maintaining financial responsible for family dependants, a charitable commitment that may well have benefitted Emilia and her mother.

Eight years later, in April 1576, Baptista died when Emilia was just seven years old, a traumatic experience for the young girl. Baptista's will left Emilia a dowry of £100, to be given to her either when she turned twenty one or when she married, whichever came first.

When Emilia visited Forman he noted that

she hath hard fortune in her youth. Her father died when she was yonge; the wealth of her father failed before he died, and he began to be miserable in his estate

Presumably the *hard fortune* relates to the sequence of deaths of close relatives between 1573 and 1578. Emilia's first bereavement was the loss of her two year old brother Phillip when she was only four, her Uncle Anthony, who was head of the family, followed a year later, her father two years after that, her Uncle Jasper in 1577 and her half sister Angela in 1578.

When Emilia first consulted Forman on 13th May 1597 it was on medical grounds, she was suffering from pain in her left side, was this a symptom of Chlamydia she had already transmitted to Shakespeare?

Forman noted her name as *Millia Lanier of 24 years* - in fact, she was 28 - and her residence as *Longditch at westmester.* Longditch was a fashionable area of London, home to various noblemen, including the MP Sir Edward Hoby and his wife Margaret, Lord Hunsdon's daughter.

8 Simon Forman

When she returned on 17th May Forman recorded her by her maiden name *Emilia Bussana,* and amended her age to 27 - still a year out - and noted that she was the daughter of *Baptista* and *Margaret Bassana* and wife of Alfonso Lanier. Forman noted

she hath many false conceptions

It seems she was susceptible to miscarriage - a danger with Chlamydia - or perhaps she had subjected herself to abortions, which had exacerbated the condition.

Her subsequent visits were much more concerned with her seeking information, via astrological predictions about her future life, both financial and within society. The second visit a fortnight later, on 3rd June, she wanted Forman to cast a horoscope to see if her husband would be successful in obtaining the suit they hoped for. No details of the suit were given, but since Alphonso had already joined the Essex-Raleigh Island Expedition in was doubtless to discover if Alphonso would share in the Spanish booty.

Forman noted she had been brought up by the Countess of Kent and had been married four years, but the old Lord Chamberlain had kept her long.

On 16th June her consultation was to enquire, again by the casting of a horoscope, whether her husband Alphonso would return from the Azores with any preferment and wealthy, or indeed if he would return at all? Three months later on 2nd September she returns to enquire whether she shall be a lady? By this she wants Forman to predict whether her husband will be knighted by his commander, the Earl of Essex. This would have given the couple the title Sir Alphonso and Lady Lanier.

Forman noted

She hath been favored much of her mati [majesty] *and of mani noblemen*

We know about Hunsdon and Southampton but *many* - perhaps a case of the *Bay where all* [noble]*men ride?* (137.6)

Forman's reference to a nobleman that is dead relates to Hunsdon, who had been dead for over a year but *Loved her well & kept her longe* arouses suspicion that the affair with the Lord Chamberlain may have continued after her marriage.

Forman's horoscope unreliably predicts

She shalbe a ladie or attain some great dignity. He [Alphonso] *shall speed well and be knighted hardly* [with difficulty], *but shall get little substance. The time shall come she shall rise two degrees, but hardly by this man; it seems he will not live two years after he come home And yet there shall some good fortune fall on her in short time*

In fact, Alphonso wasn't knighted, an unlikely ambition, anyway, since he was trained as a musician, not a soldier. None-the-less he was commissioned as a Captain by the Earl of Essex and lived for another fifteen years after returning from the Azores.

Unfortunately the good fortune predicted for Emilia never materialised, her social status and income declined and she was to end her days in litigation and poverty.

A further account during Emilia's consultation about Alphonso's ambition comments

whose husband has gone to sea with the Earl of Essex in hope to be knighted - though there is little cause why he should

and she sought a prediction whether *she should be a ladie or noe*

Forman later added

he [Alphonso] *was not knighted nor yet worthy thereof*

The diary shows that Forman's sexual interest in Emilia has been aroused and intends using Alphonso's absence to initiate some intimacy between them, which she appears to have actively encouraged.

On 11th September Forman begins the page with a question to himself:-

Beste to do A thing or noe

Forman writes in the third person, but is clearly referring to himself

A certain man longed to see A gentlewoman whom he loved & desired to halek with. and because he could not tell howe to com to her & whether he shoulds be welcom to her or noe, Moved this question wh[ether]er yt were best to send to her to knowe howe she did. and therbi to tri wh[eth]er she wold byd the messaunger byd his mrs round to him or noe. Thinking therby what he myght goodlye bolden therby to see her

Halek is Forman's code word for intercourse, it appears frequently in his notebooks. Two astrological predictions appear under this entry, one with the title Lanier, the other left untitled, but could be a prediction for himself, with the later date *1597 20 Sept.*

Under which he wrote

The partie sent his servaunte by who she sente word that if his mr came he should be welcom. & he wente and supped with her and staid all night. and she was familiar & friendlie to him in all thinges. But only she wold not halek. Yet he tolde all parts of her body wilingly. & kyssed her often but she wold not doe in any wise. Whereupon...he departed friendes

to which he further remarked

but yet they were frendes again afterwards but he never obtayned his purpose & she was a hore and delt evill with him after

Perhaps Emilia took Forman's money but refused him sex. Six days later on 17th September Emilia sent for Forman, but for no obvious reason he chose not to go, Forman asked himself

Best to goe to Laniere todae or noe

but

next daie at after non she sent her maid to me & I went with her to her

Forman appears to have possessed a robust sex drive because, seven weeks later, on October 24 he went to watch the royal procession for the state opening of parliament where he picked up a fellow member of the crowd - Jone Harington - by late afternoon they had *haleked*. His diary entry the same afternoon questioned

to go to Lanier this night or noe

She sent a man and a maidservant

I went with them and stayed al night

Since he makes no comment about sexual rejection, it seems he was more successful in his desire to *halek* this time, than seven weeks earlier.

At the end of 1597 Forman reminds himself in Latin to question Emilia over her tales of the invocation of spirits - whether or not an incuba. This would appear to suggest some kind of incubus suspicion, a concept completely in the realms of fantasy to the modern mind, but not so in 1597.

It was precisely at this time, that King James whilst he was King of Scotland, but before he was crowned successor to Elizabeth wrote a dissertation entitled *Daemonologie*, in which *incubi* and *succubi* are included in his classification of demons.

Before any words are uttered the stage directions for the beginning of *Macbeth* say *Thunder and lightening. Enter three witches.* There are references to exocism in *King Lear* and *The Comedie of Errors* and mock exorcism of Malvolio in *Twelth Night*.

We have become a generation of cynics when it comes to the belief in the supernatural and any such reference in an academic paper these days are likely to devalue its scholarly acceptance.

In the reminiscences of her husband Gustav, Alma Mahler describes a highly disturbing séance that the couple attended in Oyster Bay which culminated in a mandolin levitating and hitting the composer on the head. Mahler is one of the few C20 composers to write for mandolin (in the 7th Symphony and *Das Lied von der Erde*).

In *Macbeth* and *The Tempest* Shakespeare shows his interest in witches and ghosts make appearanced in *Hamlet, Macbeth, Richard lll*, and *Julius Caeser* demonstrate that he knew his audience believed in the existance of such manifestations.

Two of the later sonnets show that the poet associates his love for Emilia as a madding fever brought on by magic potions:-

> *WHat potions haue I drunk of Syren teares Distil'd from Lymbecks foule as hell within........In the disatraction of this madding fever?* (119:1/2 & 8)

and with her dabbling in the dark arts:-

For I have sworne thee faire, and thought thee bright, Who art as black as hell, as darke as night (147.13/14)

In the late 1597 entry Forman contemplates his relationship with Emilia, whether *I shall end it or noe*. The last phrase would appear to mean that their affair had developed and Forman was thinking of putting an end to it.

Emilia disappears from Forman's case books for two years. He begins his new case-books in January, rather than starting the year on Lady day, the 25th March, the conventional beginning of the Elizabethan year.

An entry on 7th January 1600 shows that they had kept in touch, albeit in a volatile relationship. Forman wants to know

whi Mrs Lanier sent for me

and in Latin

what will follow, and whe[the]r she Entend any mor villani or noe

What villainy? Had Emilia accused Forman of being the father of her late daughter, Odillia, christened in December 1598 and buried nine months later? Villainy is another characteristic of the *Dark Lady* lines in the sonnets.

THou art as tiranous, so as thou art, As those whose beauties proudly make them cruell (131.1/2)

and

In nothing art thou blacke saue in thy deeds (131.13)

The next month, on 25 February, Forman writes

Henri wresly he is 27 yers old Elizab va\r/ney of 29 years

On this occasion Forman has recorded the ages of his clients correctly.

By this date, Henry Writhiosley and Elizabeth Vernon had been married for eighteen months and were entitled to be called the Earl and Countess of Southampton. Why Forman chooses to note their names so informally is unclear, but intriguing.

The husband, as dedicatee of *Venvs* and *Lucrece* is of course, closely associated with Shakespeare, and the joint consultations of Southampton and Emilia with Forman so close together indicates a connection. Perhaps Emilia, as a long standing client of Forman, recommended him.

At this date, the Southamptons are parents of a one year old daughter, Penelope, conceived out of wedlock and born in the Fleet Prison where the couple were briefly imprisoned for marrying without the Queen's consent. Presumably Southampton and the Countess would be seething about their harsh treatment by the Queen.

Why the Southamptons consulted Forman isn't clear because the hand writing that follows their names is written in code. The date is less than a year before the abortive Earl of Essex rebellion, in which Southampton was deeply involved and re-incarcerated, this time, in the Tower of London. Southampton's appearance at Forman's consulting room begs the question was he seeking a prediction on the outcome of the planned coup against the Queen?

A number of feminist academics have sprung to the defence of Emilia's reputation besmirched in Forman's note-books, suggesting that Forman's account of his sexual relationship with his married client was unreliable, exaggerated and a fantasy. They point to the fact that Emilia wouldn't *halek* as evidence of her reluctant promiscuity and provided evidence of an underlying virtuous intent.

In my chivalrous hat, I too instinctively want to defend my poor cousin's tarnished reputation. However, few people can really think that a married woman who allows her medical practitioner to spend the night with her shortly after she first consulted him, and then on at least two further occasions is entirely chaste. In her defence, Emilia's forced and desperately unhappy marriage, with her comfortable £40 a year gone, a spend-thrift husband who had no interest in her, gives every reason for seeking solace in another's arms.

I doubt Forman ever cast a horoscope that predicted that an Oxford professor would be pouring over his private professional papers four centuries later and publicly disclosing such intimate stuff. In the prologue to Morgan Lloyd Malcolm's play *Emilia,* the protagonist is reading Forman's words from a book:-

She was a whore and dealt evil with him

she throws the book to the floor in high dudgeon. I have little doubt if the real Emilia had read this, she too would have responded in a similar fashion.

Coming as she did from a Venetian family, Emilia's view of giving herself for money, or favours from noblemen, was open to less approbation than if she had possessed solely English ancestry. Her behaviour would have been much more acceptable in Venetian society.

Bernardo Strozzi is well known for his c.1630 portrait of Claudio Monteverdi - Giovanni Bassano's musical colleague - but his celebrated portrait of a young woman with a viola da gamba, thought to be the Venetian musician and composer, Barbara Strozzi shows how little Venetian society was concerned with female modesty. It is not known how closely Barbara was related to the artist, but the surname would indicate that they were from the same extended family.

The most famous Venetian *cortogiana onesta* - the intellectual courtesan - was Veronica Franco, some twenty years older than Emilia but with un-

9 Bernardo Strozzi: Claudio Monteverdi

mistakable similarities. Veronica was a poet, she was musical, she had been made much of by many noblemen - including Henry lll, King of France, to whom she composed two sonnets - she was suspected of witchcraft and was a proto-feminist. A letter from Veronica shows that her views on men are close to Emilia's, revealed in *Salve Devs*:-

When we too are armed and trained, we can convince men that we have hands, feet, and a heart like yours; and although we may be delicate and soft, some men who are delicate are also strong; and others, coarse and harsh, are cowards. Women have not yet realized this, for if they should decide to do so, they would be able to fight you until death; and to prove that I speak the truth, amongst so many women, I will be the first to act, setting an example for them to follow

Bernardo Strozzi - Venetian gamba player

Forman's records show that after the death of her father, in 1576, Emilia went to live with Susan Bertie, Countess of Kent. In *Salve Devs*, Emilia gives her readers the same information in her dedication to Susan Bertie

Come you that were the Mistris of my youth, The noble guide of my vngouern'd days

Some scholars have questioned whether Emilia went as a servant to Bertie rather than live as part of the family, but there is no conclusive evidence to confirm this one way or the other. If the Countess were her *mistress* then of course, Emilia could have been employed as her servant, however I think the auto-biographical

noble guide of my ungouvern'd days

means that Susan Bertie, who at the time was a childless young widow, was acting in *loco parentis*. Emilia was effectively a ward of Susan Bertie.

Emilia's life, from the time of her moving in with Susan Bertie, up until the publication of **Shakespeare's Sonnets**, was socially ambivalent. She enjoyed an intimate association with the aristocracy, without being of noble birth herself. She lived a life of daily familiarity with aristocratic mothers and daughters, who were literary, musical, feminists and staunch protestants and the regular interaction rubbed off.

In 1555 Susan's mother, the dowager duchess and her second husband, went into exile in Europe with their two children for the remainder of the Catholic Queen Mary's reign. They returned when the danger to Protestants had passed after the death of Queen Mary and the accession of Queen Elizabeth in 1559.

When the family returned they lived at the countess's elaborate manor house of Grimsthorpe in Lincolnshire. When the family resettled in England Susan was five, her brother, Peregrine, later to become Lord Willoughby, was a year younger. Her life just over a decade later was to be touched by tragedy.

Susan Bertie was married, when she was just sixteen, to Reginald Grey of Wrest, the nephew of Bess of Hardwick, who was shortly afterwards to become Earl of Kent, a redundant title, restored by the queen. Three years later, in 1572, the Earl died in his thirties, leaving Susan a young widow without children.

After her husband's death she lived part of of the time in Greenwich and rest with Lord Willoughby her brother at Willoughby House, his London home, near the Barbican. Emilia may have lived in both houses, affectively as part of the family.

Willoughby also played host to his mother, Catherine Duchess of Suffolk, known as an active Protestant philosopher and advocate of feminism. It was under Susan's supervision at Willoughby House - conveniently positioned for Emilia to walk to visit her mother in Norton Folgate - that Emilia was given a humanist education and continued the family tradition of musical performance with a regular daily practise instilled in her early on by her father.

She became schooled in the opinions of a Protestant leaning household, which may have been the very start of the process of conversion from her father's family Judaism, which was finally achieved in Cookham and acknowledged in *Salve, Deus*.

Farewell (sweet Cooke-ham) where I first obtain'd Grace from that Grace where perfit Grace remain'd (The Description of Cooke-ham 1-2).

Emilia was fond of using the word *grace*, it appears in her text for William Byrd in *Songs of sundrie natures* and over eighty times in *Salve Devs*, this is hardly surprising since *Gratia dirige nos* (Grace me Guide) was the Bassano family motto, accompanying its coat-of-arms. It was also the name chosen by Beatrice Nasi (Mendes), Emilia's heroic cousin, the saviour and benefactor of many Jewish refugees expelled from the Iberian peninsular. By 1553 Beatrice had fled Venice and at the invitation of Suleiman the Magnificent, taken up residence in Constantinople, where she chose to call herself Donna Gracia.

Despite Susan Bertie's strong Protestant faith, Latin and probably Greek remained on Emilia's educational syllabus. Emilia was already an Italian speaker and, in the views of John Hudson and Peter Matthews, had knowledge of Hebrew too.

Florence Amit points out Shakespeare's use of Hebrew phrases in *All's Well that Ends Well:*

First Soldier

Boskos vauvado [In bravery, like boldness], *I vnderstand thee, & can speake thy tongue. Kerelybonto* [I ama aware of his deception] *sir, betake thee to thy Faith or seuenteene ponyards are at they bosome.*

Influenced by her mother's feminist stand, Bertie greatly valued and emphasised the importance of girls receiving the same level of education as boys.

In 1581 Susan Bertie earned the displeasure of the Queen by marrying Sir John Wingfield a nephew of Bess of Hardwick. One assumes that at this stage Emilia, at the age of twelve, could either have returned home to her mother, just down the road, or remained at Willoughby House but with less of Bertie's personal attention.

John Hudson has suggested that in 1582 Lord Willoughby, as Ambassador to Denmark, took her with him on his sea voyage to Elsinore, during which they encountered a ferocious storm. This suggestion has been made to give credence to Hudson's view that Emilia was the author of the Shakespeare plays and experience of the storm at sea and knowledge of the Castle at Elsinore provided enough detail to write scenes for *The Tempest* and *Hamlet.*

A visit to Denmark does seem like a strong possibility and Emilia may well have gained the knowledge that Hudson suggests, however she could also have passed on that first hand experience to Shakespeare who possessed an actor's memory to be regurgitated in his future plays.

I don't agree with Hudson's next suggestion, that it was at the age of thirteen - the age of consent under Elizabethan law - when Emilia became Hunsdon's mistress.

He suggests that Willoughby knew that Hunsdon was lonely and that a thirteen year old, highly educated and musically talented girl would alleviate his loneliness. He thinks that the Bassano family concurred with this mis-match - Emilia, 13, Hunsdon, 56 - because it would be in their professional interests.

Although there are examples of marriage with the bride being only thirteen years old, viginity was held to be a piceless commodity to achieving any advantageous marriage. Emilia's stock in the marriage market would nosedive if she were sexualy exploited in this way. Emilia's mother was still alive, would she have had anything to say on the matter? Susan Bertie, too, would surely have disapproved of the sexual enslavement of such a young girl?

There is no doubt that she did become sexually exploited by Hunsdon but I think that was some five years later, when she was eighteen, and the experience taught her how to use her sexuality to personal advantage, a skill which is succinctly retold in the Sonnets and *Venvs and Adonis* too.

4. The Sonnets, an autobiography

It was a Louer, and his lasse,
With a hey, and a ho, and a hey nonino,
That o're the greene corne feild did passe,
In the spring time, the onely pretty rang time.
When Birds do sing, hey ding a ding, ding.
Sweet Louers loue the spring

(As you Like it 5.3.2467)

The word sonnet comes from the Italian word *sonetto*, little song. It was first used in English by the playwright and poet, Robert Greene, Shakespeare's detractor, who with his last gasp accused Shakespeare of stealing other playwright's ideas. There's more than an element of truth in Greene's accusation.

Shakespeare, the magpie, adapted ideas from many earlier writers; Holinshed, Ovid, Plautus, Plutarch, Seneca, and Terence and, as Greene complains - an *vpstart Crow, beautified with our feathers* - contemporary authors too.

The little song, *It was a lover and his lass,* was delightfully set to music by Thomas Morley, probably at the suggestion of the author. Morley and Shakespeare were neighbours in the Parish of St Helen's, Bishopsgate, towards the eastern end of the City of London, both lived there for three years from 1596. In 1598, their names appeared together in a list of defaulters in a moderate tax assessment.

As you Like it is believed to have been written in 1599 and the four verses of *It was a louer* published by Morley in 1600 in his collection, *First Booke of Ayres,* which were lute songs with additional bass viol accompaniment.

An earlier publication, Nicholas Yonge's 1588 *Musica Transalpina,* is a collection of madrigals, mainly by Italian and English composers, some of them with personal connections to the Bassanos. One major contributor to the collection was Alfonso Ferrabosco the Elder, whose son was a court musician with the Bassano family from 1592.

In January 1612 Ferrabosco the younger married Ellen Lanier, daughter of Nicholas Lanier and his second wife, Lucretia neé Bassano. The 1588 collection, also included a madrigal by William Byrd, the Queen's favourite composer who, the following year, set some of Emilia's texts to music in his *Songs of sundrie natures.*

Shakespeare and Morley, if not friends, must have been acquainted with one another. Parishioners were obliged by law to worship at the parish church, and so each Sunday, Morley - unless his job as organist at St Paul's exclusively precluded it - and Shakespeare would have been together in a church that saw a congregation of around two hundred.

Both were active as professional public performers - Morley at the organ console, Shakespeare on stage - and both had experience of having to prepare their manuscripts for publication. Morley's unique *A Plaine and Easie Introduction to Practicall Musicke* was published 1597 with a dedication to William Byrd.

There are three rhyming commendations for the book after the dedication page. The first, a sonnet by the composer Anthony Holborne, the second and third writers identified only by their initials; A.B. and I.W. Since it is a book on music the assumption is that the initials belong to well known musicians. I.W. could be either John Ward or John Wilbey. Apart from the Bassanos there are no other acknowledged Elizabethan composers who bear the initials A.B. The initials could belong to any three of the second generation of Bassano musicians; Augustine, Arthur or Andrea, all of them active performers at the time Morley published. However, as far as we know, only Augustine was a composer, so he is the most likely owner of the A.B. initials.

For a tuition manual it is unusually presented with lessons structured as witty dialogue between two music students. Setting an effective text is something that Morley might have sought assistance with from his playwright neighbour. Perhaps it was in recompense for this textual advice that Morley set *It was a lover* to music. This celebrated setting is one of two cases of contemporary composers writing songs from text in the Shakespeare plays.

It isn't known whether Morley's setting *It was a lover* was ever heard in a contemporary performance of *As you Like it,* unlike the vocal and instrumental music of Robert Johnson the other composer who wrote specifically for set Shakespeare performances. Johnson composed the music for at least eighteen songs, including *Where the bee sucks* and *Hark, hark! the lark* his setting of *Woods, rocks, and mountains* is thought to be from the Fletcher/Shakespeare play *Cardenio* perhaps revived in Lewis Theobold's *Double Falsehood,* although the song *Woods, rocks and mountains* doesn't feature.

In addition to the songs there are ten dances for lute and keyboard. Robert Johnson was a putative relative of Emilia's mother, Margaret Johnson, most likely her nephew. Johnson also set words by Ben Jonson, Shakespeare's friend, colleague and fellow playwright. These connections link Shakespeare to musicians at court, of which the Bassanos made the largest family group.

In 1599 the year that *As you Like it* was written, the court recorder consort

- very much a quiet, indoor ensemble, which performed in close proximity to the monarch - consisted of six players, four of them were Bassanos, another was Alphonso Lanier, Emilia's husband. Robert Johnson was the son of John Johnson, who along with Emilia's father and her cousins Augustine and Ludovico was one of the Queen's lutenists

It was a lover could well be a snippet of late-teens auto-biography. Shakespeare recalling the bucolic walk with Anne Hathaway along the footpath through fields between Stratford and Shottery, where Anne's home, her parent's farm, was located. The pair indulging in *hey nonino* in the field, in the spring at first, as the song suggests, but certainly by August 1582. The agricultural caresses leading to Anne's pregnancy and the couples' shotgun wedding - rushed through by special licence - in November 1582, when he was 18 and she was 26.

Just six months after the wedding, Susanna, the Shakespeare's first born child was baptised on 26 May 1583. By the time the Shakespeare sonnets were published in 1609 the poet had spectacularly broken his marriage vows and the *sweet lovers* relationship had turned sour.

11 title page SHAKE-SPEARES Sonnets

A decade after Morley and Shakespeare collaborated, Thomas Thorpe, who had never before published anything by Shakespeare, registered *a booke called Shakespeares sonnettes* is how it was recorded on the Stationer's Register on 20th May 1609. The registration of books was required by law under a Tudor royal charter. Thorpe, and every other Jacobean publisher registered their books, which may then have been subjected to censorship. The collection, printed by George Eld and sold at the bookshop of William Aspley in St Paul's Churchyard, was a collection of one hundred and fifty four sonnets in a single volume, each sonnet, generally accepted to have been composed by Shakespeare.

There are four protagonists in the sonnets, they are commonly called the *Fair Youth*, the *Rival Poet*, and the *Dark Lady*, the fourth is Shakespeare himself. All of the sonnets are written in the first person, it is the voice of Shakespeare we hear.

In their book, *All the Sonnets of Shakespeare,* Paul Edmundson and Stanley Wells have tried to overturn this long established interpretation by suggesting that some of the Fair Youth sonnets might have been written for other men and women.

This proposition is unconvincing for one very good reason. Shakespeare himself tells us there were only two loves in his life.

Two loues I have of comfort and dispaire,
Which like two spirits do sugiest me still,
The better angell is a man rightman right faire:
The worser spirit a woman collour'd il. (144.1-4)

He admires the *Fair Youth's* beauty and tries to persuade him to marry and have children just as the young man's parents did to produce him. The relationship between author and *Fair Youth* becomes closer, more intimate, perhaps sexual even. The poet has a turbulent adulterous affair with a *Dark Musical Lady* - they are both married - which starts passionately but later drives him

frantick madde with euer-more vnrest (147.10).

The *Fair Youth* also has an affair with the *Dark Lady*, which Shakespeare confesses to have authorised. This was perhaps with the intention of persuading the young man that procreation was a good idea. Despite proposing the idea, Shakespeare still regards himself as betrayed, by both friend and mistress.

The poet is downcast by the perception that the *worthier pen* (79.6) of the *Rival Poet* enjoys a more favourable relationship with the *Fair Youth*. Suddenly the *Rival Poet* is referred to in the past tense, as if he's died. The complete sequence of sonnets contains an intimate account revealing personal secrets that no-one identified is likely to want made public.

The 1609 publication has left a legacy of unresolved and intriguing questions which have occupied some of the greatest literary minds for centuries. Some of the questions thrown up are

1. When were they written and were they published chronolgically and were they numbered by the poet?

2. Did Shakespeare authorise and oversee publication?

3. Who was the dedicatee?

4. Who was the *Fair Friend*?

5. Who was tbe *Rival Poet*?

6. Who was the *Dark Lady*?

7. Who was the father of the *Dark Lady's* child? (127.4)

Finding convincing answers to these questions relies heavily on getting the dates of composition correct; about that alone there is huge controversy.

As an appendix to the collection of sonnets there is a narrative poem entitled *A Lover's Complaint*. This runs to some three hundred and thirty five lines in Rhyme Royal (seven line stanzas in ABABBCC rhyme) a structure first used by Chaucer. Its story is one of the seduction of a *fickle-maid* who relates her confession to a *Reverend Man*.

Although *A Lover's Complaint* has similarities to *The Rape of Lucrece*, published in 1593, the question over its authorship has provoked historic critical debate, which still continues today.

I think that this work's publication as a companion to the Sonnets is authentic, appropriate and significant. It is an example of Shakespeare parodying Emilia's poetry, not just her writing, but her delivery of speech and her inherited Italianate temperament too.

The *Sonnets*, are all authentically by Shakespeare, unlike an earlier collection, *The Passionate Pilgrime*, the complete contents of which were advertised as being by Shakespeare, when in fact, many of the poems were by others. *The Passionate Pilgrime* was published by William Jaggard in 1599, by which time Shakespeare was something of a best selling author, hence it was an enhanced profit motive that emboldened Jaggard's unauthorised use of his name.

Jaggard was also employed by John Hemings and Henry Condell to produce the first folio edition of the plays in 1623, seven years after Shakespeare had died.

The anthology of twenty poems attributed them all to "*W. Shakespeare*" on the title page, but it seems only half, or even less, are genuinely by Shakespeare. Appended to *The Pasionate Pilgrime* are a further are a further six poems with a separate title page called *SONNETS. To sundry notes of Musicke.* There is no music, only one poem is a sonnet and none are by Shakespeare.

Two that are by Shakespeare in the main body of *The Passionate Pilgrime* are *If Loue make me forsworne, how shall I sweare to loue?* (*LLl* 4.3.1176) and *Did not the heauenly Rhetoricke of thine eye* (*LLl* 4.3.1297) authenticated because they were included in *Loues Labour's lost*, which had been published in 1594/5.

Another two are authentic because they are a slightly different version of the late numbered Sonnet 138 - *When my loue sweares that she is made of truth* - and an identical version of the even later numbered Sonnet, 144 - *Two loues I have, of comfort and dispaire* - from the 1609 edition.

The Passionate Pilgrime versions of these sonnets have changes in both words and meanings, seven lines in Sonnet 138 and minor changes in three lines of Sonnet 144. It is not known which of these versions was written first, they could be contemporaneous, a first, second, or perhaps subsequent draft, or revisions edited over months, or years, even.

Given the late numberings, I think this demonstrates that all of them, must have been written before 1599, the publication date of *The Passionate Pilgrime*.

There are a number of highly regarded scholars who date some of the sonnets later and others who date at least one sonnet - no 145 *Those lips that Loues owne hand did make, Breath'd forth the sound that said I hate* (145,1/2) - as early as 1582.

Despite the late numbering, the argument is that

I hate, from hate away she threw, And sau'd my life saying not you (145.13-14)

contains an intentional homonym on Hathaway (*hate away*) and Anne (*And*) and so relates to the balmy spring of the couples' relationship.

It is likely that *hate away* does refer to Anne Hathaway but coming immediately after an obvious Dark Lady sonnet

The worser spirit a women colour'd il (144.4)

such an early dating makes it a *non sequitur*. Much more likely that its dating is 1593/4 and that the *I hate, from hate away* sounds very much like Emilia's Latin temperament and could well be an expression of her *hatred* of the other woman in Shakespeare's life, bizarrely exacerbated in her mind, because Anne was his legally wedded wife.

My conclusion is that the sonnets were written over five years 1590-94, with a gap of some time after completion of the first seventeen. The numbering has been very misleading to anyone trying to sort out an accurate chronology. An easy but erronious assumption to make is that the poet wrote a number at the top of each sonnet which the publisher adhered to.

This cannot be the case because of a single event - the betrayal of Shakespeare by the *Fair Youth* and the *Dark Lady* - referred to in numerically separate sonnet sections.

There is a logic to the numbering but I think they are in reality four sonnet sequences, partially overlapping and written contemporaneously.

I don't think that Shakespeare authorised publication, if his permission had been sought, I think he would have demurred because of the personal trouble for him that would be caused by public disemination.

Had he agreed to publish and overseen the editing, the numbering, if used, would have been quite different, probably four sequences, with independent numbering. The 1609 sequence of one hundred and fifty four sonnets are certainly not published chronologically and the numbering of each sonnet, with the possible exception of the first seventeen, was, most likely, added by the publisher.

I believe that Southampton is the *Fair Friend*, that Christopher Marlowe is the

Rival Poet and that Emilia Bassano is the *Dark Lady* and that Shakespeare was the father of her son, Henry.

Anyone who already has an interest in this subject will recognise that I have accepted A. L. Rowse's nominations and general overall dating. During his lifetime, Rowse was regarded as the pre-eminent historian on the Elizabethan period, and was passionate about the works of Shakespeare and idolised the man.

Rowse was irascible and blunt to the point of rudeness in print about the work of some of his fellow academics. I met him at his house in Cornwall and we corresponded - despite his undiplomatic outspokenness, of which I too was the recipient - I held his opinions on Tudor England in the highest esteem. In one of his letters, Professor Rowse urged me to use his ideas and words, I am following his advice.

I believe though that I am the first to suggest that Emilia's son, Henry, wasn't as generally accepted, sired by Lord Hunsdon, but by Shakespeare.

I believe that Shakespeare's affair with Emilia began two months before she was married off to Alphonso Lanier and continued after her wedding and after the birth of her son, Henry. It was at a later date - probably the winter of 1593 - that the affair with Southampton occurred. I will put forward my theory and such evidence that exists, in the sure and certain knowledge that I am entering a mine-field.

There is an undeniable logic to the sonnet sequence as published by Thomas Thorpe. Attempts to re-arrange the first edition order, including John Benson's 1540 attempt in the second edition - but most notably Sir Denys Bray's 1925 *The Original Order of Shakespeare's Sonnets* - are less than convincing.

There are two sequences that can be proven to overlap one another in terms of dating - Sonnets 40 and 133 are contemporaneous - so it is clear that the 1609 numberings cannot have been written on the top of each sonnet at the time of their composition.

Since the cycle was written in an instalment sequence for a readership of one, Southampton - who may have shown or read some to a few private friends - it included arcane allusions, insults, personal topics, sexual in-jokes and innuendoes, it was very difficult, if not impossible to fully understand for any but the *cognoscenti.*

For a best-selling author, sales of the first sonnet publication were surprisingly disappointing, there was no pressing demand for an early print-run of a second edition. It is possible though, that sales of the first edition and the publication of a second edition were suppressed by someone who was motivated and in a position to do so. If suppression took place, perhaps it was Lord Southampton who exerted his influence.

It wasn't until 1640, when all the identifiable characters - with the single exception of Emilia - were dead, that a second edition was published.

There are only thirteen copies of the first edition still extant. One of these was originally thought to be owned by the actor Edward Alleyn who supposedly bought his copy in June 1609, but an entry on the letter from which this information was gleaned, is now thought to be a forgery by John Payne Collier.

The quotes from the sonnets in this book have been copied from the first edition owned by the British Library and made available on-line.

The reader may well have some initial difficulty reading the unconventional and inconsistent spelling - 'v's for 'u's and 'e's at the ends of words for example - capitalisation, lack of apostrophes and other punctuation inconsistencies from modern conventions, but fluency will occur quickly. I have used the first edition rather than a modern one, because it is the closest we can get to the words Shakespeare used and how he wrote them.

The Petrarchan sonnet, with its fourteen line format was imported into Elizabethan England from Italy. The genre was enthusiastically adopted by English poets, notably Drayton, Daniel and Sidney as well as Shakespeare. Its brief structure, traditionally written in iambic pentameter, lent itself to thematic or narrative sequence and an individual sonnet was quick to copy and easy to memorise.

The general view of most scholars - but by no means all - is that Shakespeare's sonnets are broadly autobiographical. A very few commentators take the view that they are an artistic and literary invention. There is another theory that they are a mixture of biography and invention.

Shakespeare, who in the sequence refers to *Will* - a word, in all its connotations he uses seventy times - often printed with a capital W when he is probably refer to himself. He introduces three further unidentified characters; an aristocratic young man of great beauty, a rival poet who would seem to be endeavouring to attract the young aristocrat's largesse, and a musical and promiscuous mistress, whom he calls black (in colouring and deed).

It is unfortunate for us that posterity has given the slightly misleading title, *Dark Lady* to Shakespeare's mistress. Although he refers to her in Sonnet 147 as being *darke as night*, it is the single occasion that he uses the word *dark*. In the last twenty seven sonnets, the so called *Dark Lady* sonnets he uses the word *black* nine times to describe her appearance and her conduct, including the damning insult *black as hell* (147.14)

The narrative of the first seventeen sonnets - which may well have been numbered by Shakespeare - is written in avuncular fashion to a young man of great attractiveness

From fairest creatures we desire increase (1,1)

persisting in urging him to marry and have children

You had a Father, let your Son say so (13,14)

Hidden in the text are cryptic references to masturbation, probably obvious to the addressee, but less obvious, one would hope, to others.

Unthrifty louelinesse why dost thou spend, Vpon thy selfe thy beauties legacy? (4.1/2)

Make sweet some viall; treasure thou some place, With beautis treasure ere it be selfe kil'd: That vse is not forbidden vsury (6.3/5)

No loue toward others in that bosome sits That on himselfe such murdrous shame commits (9.13/14)

There is an obvious reference to the addressee's mother

Thou art thy mothers glasse and she in thee Calls back the louely Aprill of her prime (3.9/10)

Although children often do look like their mothers or fathers, comparison of portraits of mother and son show a remarkable resemblance.

12 de Critz Lord Southampton - 13 Countess of Southampton his mother

With Sonnet 18 comes a new and significant change of approach:-

SHall I compare thee to a summers day?
  Thou art more louely and more temperate:
  Rough windes do shake the darling buds of Maie,
  And Sommers lease hath all too short a date:

Sometime too hot the eye of heauen shines,
And often is his gold complexion dimm'd,
And euery faire from faire some-time declines,
By chance, or natures changing course vntrim'd:
But thy eternall Sommer shall not fade,
Nor loose possession of that fairr thou ow'st,
Nor shall death brag thou wandr'st in his shade,
When in eternal lines to time thou grow'st,
   So long as men can breathe or eyes can see,
   So long liues this, and this giues life to thee.

When read by itself, most people have assumed that in this famous sonnet, Shakespeare is addressing a woman, but astonishingly, he isn't. It is a young man that he is amorously flattering. This is particularly odd for a married poet whose wife, by the time it was written, had borne him three children. It is Henry Writhiosley, 3rd Earl of Southampton, that is the subject of Shakespeare's compliments.

In *Romeo and Juliet,* Juliet asks

What ? in a names that which we call a Rose, By any other word would smell as sweete (2.2.808)

Here's another example of the first folio being different to the edited version of this much quoted phrase. Ian Steere has suggested Southampton was called *Rosely,* an affectionate nickname. The rose is a renowned English symbol and specifically associated with the Tudors.

Southampton came from a family of heralds, his great-grandfather, John Wrythe (an alternative spelling of Writhiosley) was *Garter King at Arms* from 1478 - 1504, his great uncle William Wrythe was appointed *Rouge Croix* around 1505 and *York Herald* in 1509, he died in 1513 and another uncle, Sir Thomas Wrythe, *Garter King at Arms* from 1505 - 1534. Hardly surprising, then in the very first sonnet that Shakespeare refers to *herald* in line 10.

Apart from the occasional enigmatic reference to the adolescent tendency to masturbate, nothing sexually deviant can be read into the first 17 sonnets - the so-called *procreation sonnets.*

Four centuries on, Elizabethan pronunciation cannot be infallibly reproduced. "Risley", is the commonly held way to pronounce the Earl's surname. Ian Steere's suggestion of "Rosely" is a theory which would appear to be supported by the frequent use of the word rose in the sequence.

At the outset in Sonnet 1 line 2, *Rose* is spelt with a capital R and printed in Italics. It appears in the same format, in Sonnets 35, 54, 67, 95, 98, 99, 109 and 130, giving the word a special significance, which must have been obvious in the autograph manuscript for the type-setter to emulate it in print.

There are other words associated with roses; seven uses of the word *bud*, five of the word *canker* and three of the word *thorns* indicate a symbolic association between roses and the young man.

Sonnet 109 demonstrates that Shakespeare thinks of Southampton as his Rose in its final two lines

For nothing this wide Vniverse I call, Save thou my Rose, in it thou art my all

In the final quatrain of Sonnet 18 there is an epitaph predicting a perpetual memorial. Shakespeare confidently predicts that his *lines* will prove *eternal*, in this he has proved prophetic.

Henry Writhiosley inherited his title, 3rd Earl of Southampton, on the death of his father, the 2nd Earl, when he was still a boy. His portrait, probably painted in 1590 shows an androgynous subject, easily mistaken for a young woman.

Shakespeare's obsession with the young man continues through the next 107 sonnets, although the other protagonists - the *Rival Poet* and *Dark Lady* - appear within this sequence too. The sonnets can be grouped in sub-sections.

Sonnets 19 to 126 shows a much warmer relationship has developed between poet and subject since the first seventeen; less avuncular, more affectionate, intimate and some would say, sexual. The poetry expresses *love* for the young man and the related subjects are cover a very wide range.

It is this major part of the sequence that has led some to speculate on Shakespeare's sexuality, whether there was some ambiguity? Was there a physical sexual relationship between Shakespeare and Southampton accompanied by emotional passion?

At the beginning of Shakespeare's sexual journey, the impetus was initiated by heterosexual urges. The Hathaway's farm in Shottery lay about two miles from Shakespeare's family home, a thirty minute cross-country walk from Stratford.

Anne was twenty six and already pregnant when she married the eighteen year old Shakespeare in November 1582. William was almost certainly the father, although no one can be completely sure. Might some of the couple's prenuptial love-making have taken place in the fields between their two homes.

I wonder about the significance of the third verse of the *lover and his lass* song

Betweene the acres of the Rie, With a hey, and a ho, & a hey nonino: These prettie Country folks would lie (*As you Like it 5.3.2477*)

Was Susanna, William and Anne's oldest child, conceived in a field of rye which by the summer would have grown tall enough to conceal a copulating couple?

William and Anne went on to have further children, the twins, Judith and Hamnet (another version of the name Hamlet) named after a Stratford friend, Hamnet Sadler, a baker, who witnessed Shakespeare's will.

If Shakespeare possessed homosexual tendencies, it seems unlikely that he practised exclusivity in that persuasion, but might he have been bisexual? In the four centuries since Shakespeare's active sex life there have been a number of well known bisexuals of both genders identified. Many of these have been professional writers, musicians, dancers and actors; Lord Byron, Leonard Bernstein and Sir Laurence Olivier, Rudolph Nureyev are four examples. Nureyev and Byron's peccadillos are well documented, Bernstein's and Olivier's less well publicised.

Joan Plowright, an acclaimed actress and Maggie Smith's successor as *Beatrice* in the Zeffirelli production of *Much adoe about Nothing*, was married to Olivier, his third wife, for 28 years. She commented on suggestions of homosexual liaisons in the great actor's life

If a man is touched by genius, he is not an ordinary person, he doesn't lead an ordinary life. He has extremes of behaviour which you understand and you just find a way not to be swept overboard by his demons. You kind of stand apart.

Might this assessment of an exceptional sexual orientation be true of Shakespeare too, might Anne Hathaway, have had suspicions, but been a less understanding wife than Lady Olivier?

A. L. Rowse - who was himself openly homosexual, and may have more reason than most to 'out' Shakespeare - expressed no doubts about the poet's sexual orientation:-

Everything in his life and work shows that Shakespeare was an enthusiastic heterosexual

Is he correct?

I am saddened by the literary establishment's rejection of much Rowse's work and his vilification as a scholar since his death. Anyone with an interest in Shakespeare should be deeply indebted to him, not just for his discovery that Emilia was the *Dark Lady* - no matter how hard that might be for some to accept - but also unearthing Emilia's long poem on the crucifixion, *Salve Devs Rex Judæorum.*

The first edition was published in 1611 under her married name of Æmilia Lanyer, the world had to wait nearly four hundred years for Rowse to arrange for the book's second edition.

Never one for compromise, Rowse, entitled his edition *The Poems of Shakespeare's Dark Lady.* He suggested that *Salve Devs* with feminist tone and its numerous dedications to female aristocrats was written by Emilia as a retaliatory response to the defamatory portrait of her revealed in the Sonnets.

Emiia's own words on the title page guarantees the reader that her book contains

diuers other things not ufit to be read

could be interpreted that the Sonnets weren't fit to be read.

Rowse's edition has now been superseded by Susanne Woods' scholarly edition for Oxford University Press.

Rowse's explanation of the terms of endearment offered to the young man in the Sonnets was simply a different way of carrying on in time separated by more than four centuries. The word *love* used between men in Elizabethan England had completely different connotations to its use today; *the love I bear for you* simply the way educated men spoke to one another in the 16th century.

There are hundreds of examples of this kind of affectionate language between men in Elizabethan plays and contemporary private letters. It was an expression of platonic love, an emotional affection between men that stopped short of sexual relationships. In fact, any hint of sexual intimacy would have been considered destructive to genuine platonic principles.

There is no doubt that this common use of language by Elizabethan men has been expunged from England between the administrations of Cromwell and Victoria, and means that it is almost impossible for us to recreate this allusive concept. I suppose the closest we come to it is the expression of *love* between relatives, a father and son, brothers, or uncle and nephew.

No-one has ever questioned that Sonnets 1-126 are addressed to the patron or *Fair Friend*, although it isn't beyond the realms of possibility that this general universal assumption may not be exclusively the case and that some of the 126 sonnets may, in fact be addressed to a woman.

The jury is still out on whether there was any plurality in Shakespeare's sex life, but were I a betting man - I'm not, by the way - I would say that he was bisexual.

Sonnets 19-39 continue to address ageing and looks

et doe thy worst, ould Time (19,13)

stage-fright

as an vnperfect actor (23,1)

patronage and duty

Lord of my loue, to whome in vassalage (26,1)

touring

How far I toyle, still farther off from thee" (28,8)

exhaustion

Weary with toyle I hast me to my bed (27,1)

separation

Let me confesse that we two must be twaine (36,1)

infirmity, poverty and hatred

I make my love ingrafted to this store: So then I am not lame, poore, nor dispis'd (37,8-9)

Sonnets 34 to 42 acknowledge the sexual betrayal of Emilia with Southampton and the poet's forgiveness of Southampton's role in the affair - Hobson's choice if Shakespeare was reliant on the young earl's patronage

I doe forgiue thy robb'rie gentle theefe (40,9)

Thou doost loue her, because thou know't I loue her (42,6).

These nine sonnets date from the same time as sonnet 133.

Sonnet 40 - addressed to the young friend

TAke all my loues,my loue, yea, take them all,
What hast thou then more then thou hadst before?
No loue, my loue, that thou maist true loue call,
All mine was thine before thou hadst this more:
Then if for my love thou my love receivest,
I cannot blame thee for my loue thou vsest,
But yet be blam'd,if thou thyself deceivest
By wilful taste of what thy selfe refusest.
I doe forgiue thy robb'rie, gentle theefe,
Although thou steale thee all my pouerty:
And yet, loue knowes, it is a greater griefe
To beare loues wrong, then hates knowne iniury.
   Lasciuious grace in whom all il wel showes
    Kill me with spights yet we must not be foes.

Sonnet 133 - addressed to his mistress

BEshrew that heart that makes my heart to groane
For that deepe wound it giues my friend and me;
Is't not ynough to torture me alone,
But slaue to slauery my sweet'st friend must be.
Me from my selfe thy cruell eye hath taken,

And my next selfe thou harder hast ingrossed,
Of him, my selfe, and thee, I am forsaken,
A torment thrice three-fold thus to be crossed:
Prison my heart in thy steele bosomes warde,
But then my friends heart let my poore heart bale,
Who ere keepes me, let my heart be his garde,
Thou canst not then vse rigor in my Iaile.
   And yet thou wilt, for I, being pent in thee,
   Perforce am thine and all that is in me.

It is possible to read bawdy connotations in lines 2 and 6.

In addressing his aristocratic young friend

All mine was thine before thou hadst this more (40.4)

there is a pun on the word *more*, since Shakespeare refers to his dark mistress as a *moor*.

posing a rhetorical question to his mistress

Is't not ynough to torture me alone, But slaue to slauery my sweet'st friend must be? (133,3-4)

intimates that Shakespeare's *Fair Friend* and his mistress have engaged in sex, probably whilst Shakespeare was away from London.

Othello and Aaron in *Titus Andronicus* are both Moors. *Moor* was the Queen's nickname for Francis Walsingham, because of his preference for dark clothes. Another example of Shakespeare punning on the word is in Lorenzo's accus-ation in *The Merchant* that he has impregnated Portia's African maid

the Moore is with childe by you Launcelet?

and Launcelot's reply:

It is much that the Moore should be more then reason: but if she be lesse then an honest woman, shee is indeed more then I tooke her for (3.5.1785-9)

Might this be Shakespeare admitting paternity of his *more's* child?

Two other characters in *Titus* are worthy of consideration. Æmilius and Bas-sianus, the names conjoined give us the name of the subject of this book.

Shakespeare's use of the grapheme Æ in the spelling of Æmilius - the Roman aristocrat - was later used by Emilia to spell her name in print as the author of *Salve Devs*; Æmilia.

An early manuscript at the College of Arms showed that the tree in the base of the Bassano coat-of-arms wasn't a laurel tree, as originally noted in more re-cent genealogical publications, but a mulberry tree, and that the insects were silk worm moths. This discovery made more sense of the heraldic drawing, because silk worms feed on mulberry leaves.

The Italian word *moro* stands for both a moor and a mulberry tree. When I told Roger Prior about my discovery he immediately understood the significance, revealing to me that Shakespeare refers to his mistress as a *moor* and quoted lines 9 and 10 of Sonnet 150.

Sonnet 150 addressed to his mistress

> *O from what powre hast thou this powrefull might,*
> *With insufficiency my heart to sway,*
> *To make me giue the lie to my true sight,*
> *And swere that brightnesse doth not grace the day?*
> *Whence hast thou this becomming of things il,*
> *That in the very refuse of thy deeds,*
> *There is such strength and warrantise of skill,*
> *That in my minde thy worst all best exceeds?*
> *Who taught thee how to make me loue thee <u>more</u>,*
> *The <u>more</u> I heare and see iust cause of hate?*
> *O though I loue what others doe abhor,*
> *With others thou shouldst not abhor my state.*
>   *If thy unworthinesse raisd loue in me,*
>   *<u>More</u> worthy I to be belou'd of thee.*

(my underlining)

The two uses of the word *abhor* in lines 11 and 12 can also be perceived as a pun - *ab-whore* - another insult. Shakespeare famously planted a Mulberry tree in the gardens of his home New Place in Stratford following a command from King James in 1609 that all landowners should plant them in the hope of promoting a native silk industry.

The assumption is that Shakespeare was merely obeying a royal decree, and that may be so, but there is no doubt he would have associated the tree with his former lover.

The Rev Francis Gastrell who owned New Place in the 1750s became irritated by the constant requests to see the tree and take cuttings from it, in order to grow a tree themselves, had it felled.

In October 1987 Roger Prior wrote an article for the *Financial Times* based on my discovery entitled *More (Moor? Moro?) Light on the Dark Lady*. This article argued that the heraldic revelation showed that in the *more* sonnets, Shakespeare indulged in a triple pun. The article is regarded as important by some, significantly those that realise how pivotal to Elizabthean life heraldry was. Sir Anthony Wagner, Garter King at Arms admitted to me at his Aldeburgh home that Rowse's identification of Emilia as the *Dark Lady* "was right, after all".

There is a fourth *moor* connection. Emilia lived for a great deal of her early life in the parish of St Botolph, Bishopsgate where the gardens of the house owned by her parents backed on to Moor Field. The 1562 Agas map shows a large L shaped field with its southernmost access through Moor Gate of the city wall. Shakespeare's mind would never have missed such an association.

The following eighteen sonnets (43-60) touch on obsessive love and separation (again)

All dayes are nights to see till I see thee, And nights bright dais when dreams do shew thee me (43.13-14)

Unhappiness

My greef lies onward and my ioy behind (50.14)

Monuments and posterity

Not marble, nor the gilded monument, Of princes shall outliue this powrefull rime (55.1-2)

Servitude

That God forbid, that made me first your slaue (58.1)

Sonnets 61-88 refer to images

Is it thy wil, thy Image should keepe open My heavy eie'ids to the weary night? (61.1-2)

ageing

With lines and wrincles, when his youthfull morne Hath trauaild on to Ages steepie night (63.4-5).

The sequence from 78 to 86 is dominated by concern over the rival poet, who Shakespeare modestly admits possesses a superior talent

And my sick muse doth give an other place I grant (sweet love) thy lovely argument Deserves the travail of a worthier pen (79.4-6).

The death of the rival poet shown by the use of the past tense

Was it the proud full sail of his great verse (86.1)

If the rival poet was Christopher Marlowe, as many believe then Sonnet 86 dates from after Marlowe's death in a Deptford tavern brawl. The inquest verdict was that it was an accident in Ingram Frizer's self-defence because of an argument over the bill. However there is a strong argument that, because of Marlowe's activity as a spy, that it was a state-murder.

If *The coward conquest of a wretches knife* (74.11) also refers to the death of

Marlowe this shows that Sonnet 74 was written after or at the same time as Sonnet 86. Shakespeare alluded to the death of Marlowe in Touchstone's much quoted line

it *strikes a man more dead then a great reckoning in a little roome* (*As you Like it* 3.4.1574)

The greek word for touchstone is βάσανο, it is pronouced Basanos.

I think that first eight of these nine sonnets were written some time before the death of Marlow on 30th May 1593, the ninth shortly after Marlow's fatal stabbing, together making a separate sequence.

Sonnets 89-103 touch on abandonment and lameness

 Say that thou didst forsake me for some falt, And I will comment vpon that offence, Speake of my lamenesse, and I straight will halt: Against thy reasons making no defence (89.1-4)

Was the poet lame from birth or because of an injury, or is this just an expression of his state of mind? As well as this sonnet he refers to being *made lame by Fortunes dearest spight* (37.3)

John Eddowes has suggested that Shakespeare's leg was broken on the orders of Lord Hunsdon who discovered his infidelity with Emilia, whilst she was still his mistress.

Hatred

Then hate me when thou wilt (90.1)

Ancestry, skill, possessions, physical strength

Some glory in their birth, some in their skill, Some in their wealth, some in their bodies force (91.1-2)

Fidelity

So shall I liue, supposing thou art true, Like a deceiued husband.(93.1-2)

It has taken until the introduction of same-sex marriage for male homosexual couples to openly acknowledge a "husband and wife" role in their relationship.

Faults

Oh what a mansion haue those vices got, Which for their habitation chose out thee (95.9-10)

An elusive muse

Where art thou Muse that thou forgetst so long, To speake of that which giues thee all thy might? (100.1-2)

The seasons

Our loue was new, and then but in the spring, When I was wont to greet it with my laies, As Philomell in summers front doth singe (102.5-7)

Sonnets 104-126 deal with aging

To me faire friend you neuer can be old (104.1)

Love

Let not my loue be called Idolatrie (105.1),

Acting and touring

Alas 'tis true, I haue gone here and there, And made my selfe a motley to the view (110.1-2)

Absence (again)

Since I left you, mine eye is in my minde (113.1)

Writing

those lines that I before have writ do lie (115.1)

Marriage

Let me not to the marriage of true mindes Admit impediments (116.1)

This famous sonnet - erroneously numbered 119 in the first edition - uses the words of Archbishop Cranmer's marriage service as a template.

Travel abroad

That I have hoisted sail to all the winds Which should transport me farthest from your sight (117.7-8)

Appetite and food

Like as to make our appetite more keen With eager compounds we our palate urge (118.1-2)

Alchemy

What potions have I drunk of Siren tears Distilled from limbecks foul as hell within (119.1-2)

Unkindness

That you were once unkind befriends me now (120.1)

Reputation

Tis better to be vile than vile esteemed (121.1)

A valedictictory farewell

*O thou my lovely boy who in thy power, Dost hold Time's fickle glass his fickle hour:
Who hast by waning grown, and therein show'st, Thy lovers withering, as thy sweet
self grow'st* (126.1-4)

The 25 Sonnets, numbered 127-152, deal with the appearance, character,
skills, promiscuity and behaviour of Shakespeare's mistress. Katherine Duncan-Jones thinks that the number of sonnets is significant, representing the
25 days of the human female menstrual cycle.

Shakespeare refers to his mistress's black hair and eyebrows, her use of cosmetics, her musicality, her illegitimate child, her duplicity, the power she
holds over him and her immorality and unrestrained sex life.

the bay where all men ride (137.6)

Since some of the sonnets are highly insulting, only a few of the *Dark Lady*
sonnets - significantly the early ones - could have been conceived as suitable
for her to read. I think that the majority of poems in this sequence were conceived exclusively for Southampton's eyes.

When Shakespeare began writing the *Dark Lady* sonnets Emilia had already
given birth to her son, Henry, although born in wedlock, we know her husband wasn't the father. So does Shakespeare

And beauty slandered with a bastard shame (127.4)

No baptismal record can be found for Henry Lanier, but his likely date of birth
is May 1593. Were it to have been towards the end of the month, the boy could
have been born on Susanna Shakespeare's tenth birthday, or a few days later it
would have coincided with the death of Kit Marlowe.

The marriage to Alphonso was hastily arranged by Hunsdon. My feeling is
that Alphonso was homosexual, and since he predeceased Emilia by thirty
two years probably in his thirties or even forties, when Hunsdon - who commanded court musicians - ordered him to wed Emilia.

It is possible that in this choice of a husband, Hunsdon intended to remain
intimate with Emilia, after her marriage. A sexless, as well as a loveless, relationship with her husband would facilitate that ambition.

After the marriage Alphonso was frequently away from home, either at court,
or on the annual progress of the monarch, or on active service with the Earl of
Essex. Emilia confessed to Simon Forman that her marriage was an unhappy
one, that she was hard up, because of her husband's reckless spending, and
Forman notes that he thinks she would grant sex for money.

She certainly appeared to grant sexual favours to Forman whilst Alphonso
was away from home.

On the 11th September 1597 Forman dined and stayed the night with her
when he

felte all p[ar]tes of her body willingly .& kyssed her often

although she wouldn't allow intercourse.

Sonnets 151 (8-14) and 152 (1-6) graphically demonstrate that there was a physical sexual relationship between the poet and his *Dark Lady* phallically expressed in

.....flesh staies no farther reason,
But rysing at thy name doth point out thee,
As his triumphant prize, proud of this pride,
He is contented thy poore drudge to be
To stand in thy affaires, fall by thy side.
*   No want of conscience hold it that I call,*
*   Her loue, for whose deare loue I rise and fall*

and emotionally in

IN louing me thou know'st I am forsworne,
But thou art twice forsworne to me love swearing,
In act thy bed-vow broake and new faith torne,
In vowing new hate after new loue bearing:
But why of two othes breach doe I accuse thee,
When I breake twenty: I am periur'd most,

For both of them, love and sex means breaking marriage vows. Perhaps the *bed-vow* was Emilia swearing fidelity to William.

The final two sonnets are versions of a single Greek epigram making reference to the little love-god, Cupid, although the text is developed to suit Shakespeare's predicament.

But at my mistres eie loues brand new fired,
The boy for triall needes would touch my brest,
I sick withall the helpe of bath desired,
And thether hied a sad distemperd guest.
*   But found no cure, the bath for my helpe lies*
*   Where Cupid got new fire; my mistres eye*
(153.11-14).

This confession shows that Shakespeare was suffering from a sexually transmitted disease. Bath was the city where Elizabethan gentlemen suffering from such ailments went to seek a cure in the city's rich mineral waters, unsuccessfully for Shakespeare it appears.

Note the two uses of the phrase *mistres eye* quoted in line 9 of the first Dark Lady sonnet (no.127) and the opening words of Sonnet 130, clearly his mistress's eyes were of some significance to him. These last two sonnets would indicate that Shakespeare was still in love.

Shortly after the start of Emilia's affair with the elderly Henry Carey, Lord Hunsdon, she collaborated with the Catholic composer William Byrd, furnishing the text for several of his 1589 *Songs of sundrie natures*. These included paraphrases of verses from several Psalms, a song, *Susanna Fair*, and significantly, a sonnet *Of Gold all Burnisht and brighter than sunne beames*.

Byrd ostentatiously dedicated the collection to Lord Hunsdon with an acknowledgement that music had recently become more significant in Hunsdon's life.

Having observed (Right Honorable) that since the publishing in print, of my last labors in Musicke, divers persons of great honor and worship, have more esteemed & delighted in the exercise of that Art, then before. And being perswaded that the same hath the rather encreased, through their good acceptation of my former endevors: it hath especially moved and encouraged me to take further paines to gratifie theyr curteous diospositions thereunto, konwing that the varietie and choyse of songs, is both a prayse of the Art, and a pleasure to the delighted therein. And finding no person to whome the dedication thereof so fitly and properly belonged, as unto your Lordship, by whome (through the honorable office which you exercise about her Maiesties person) both myselfe (for my place of service) & all other her highnesse Musicians are to be commanded, and under your high authoritie to be protected. And for many favours to me shewed, being most deepely bound unto your Honor, having not in me any other powre of servicable thank fulnesse then in notes & tunes of Musicke.

Although known for his interest in writers and poets, Hunsdon had no known connection with musicians until this dedication. Byrd's careful wording shows that Hunsdon has recently become more interested in music. 1588 is precisely the time that Emilia's affair with Hunsdon began. Byrd's observation that *more estemed & delighted in the exercise of that Art, then before* is in recognition of Emilia's musical skills employed to entertain Hundson.

Byrd's *last labors in Musicke* were the 1588 collection of songs *Liber primus sacrarum cantionum*. It isn't until two years later in November of 1590 that Byrd's name appears again on the list of payments made to the *Gentlemen of the Chappell* following his suspension and virtual house arrest because of his association with Catholic conspirators in 1584, and yet the title page of *Songs of Sundrie Natures* proclaims *William Byrd, one of the Gentlemen of the Queenes Maiesties honorable Chappell*

How is it that during the five years when more Catholic plots were discovered Byrd had enough confidence to publish his reappointment before he appears to have been paid anything for singing a note?

It would have been foolhardy for Byrd to have written as he did without some prior assurance from Hunsdon, who was in charge of all court appointments, that his reappointment to the *Gentlemen of the Chappell* was a foregone conclusion. I imagine that Byrd used the good offices of Emilia to put in a word for him with Hunsdon to assure his reappointment.

In the line from his autumnal Sonnet No. 73

Bare rn'wd quiers, where late the sweet birds sang (73.4)

Shakespeare may have been making reference to the Byrd family of musician - as boys, William's two brothers were choristers at St Paul's Cathedral. The *bare ruined choirs* obvious to the country dwellers near abandoned, neglected and vandalised ecclesiastical buildings like the abbeys of Tintern and Rievaulx.

14 Steven van Herwijck: Lord Hunsdon

Hunsdon was born Henry Carey, the son of Anne Boleyn's older sister Mary, who had been a mistress of Henry Vlll prior to the Kin's liaison with Anne. By 1520 the King appears to have tired of Mary and had her married off to William Carey, a young gentleman of the Royal household. Anthony Hoskins in the Society of Genealogists journal argues that a sexual relationship between Henry VIII and Mary continued after her marriage to William Carey and that both children, Henry, and his older sister Catherine were in fact illegitimate children of the King. Hoskins wasn't the first to suggest that Henry Carey was the son of Henry Vlll.

In evidence to the Council in 1535, John Hale, vicar of Isleworth - finally executed for his opposition to the King's divorce - stated

Morever, Mr. Skydmore dyd show to me yongge Master Care, saying that he was our suffren Lord the Kynge's son by our suffren Lady the Qwyen's syster, whom the Qwyen's grace might not suffer to be yn the Cowrte

Hale would have known Henry Carey personally because as a child Hunsdon lived in Isleworth.

The payment of Royal grants to William Carey from February 1522 to May 1526 indicate the time scale of king's affair with Mary Boleyn after her marriage.

The shared paternity with Elizabeth I gave Hunsdon a complex and close consanguinity with the Queen, making him both her cousin, and half-brother.

William Carey died in 1528 when Henry was only two. His mother was considered unsuitable to raise him alone and so his aunt, Anne Boleyn, who at the time was engaged to Henry VIII was given custody. Henry still maintained regular contact with his mother until her clandestine elopement with William Stafford an impecunious soldier in 1535.

Anne Boleyn and Henry VIII raised the boy, providing him with a Cistercian education. His lifelong interest in poetry was aroused by his lessons with the French poet, Nicholas Bourbon, and continued with his patronage of the poet, William Warner, author of *Albion's England* and finally led to the position for which he is best remembered today as Patron of Shakespeare's company of actors, *The Lord Chamberlain's Men*.

Hunsdon's very early life can't have been entirely without music because it was of importance to his mother. She was known as a singer and excelled at playing several instruments, including harp, lute, viol, and virginals. Might Hunsdon's very earliest memories of his mother have been rekindled by Emilia's musicality?

On the death of William Carey, Mary's husband, Hugh Aston composed the melancholy keyboard piece, *My Lady Carey's Dompe*, in sympathy with the new widow's grief. The work has become a favourite recital item in the repertoire of many modern harpsichordists.

When he was nineteen, a few years after the execution of his aunt and the death of his mother, Henry married Anne Morgan the daughter of Sir Thomas Morgan of Arkestone in Hertfordshire by whom he had seven sons and three daughters. Throughout this marriage Hunsdon maintained a number of mistresses - of which Emilia was probably the last - and fathered illegitimate children too.

One of Emilia's texts in Byrd's *Songs of sundrie natures*, is the sonnet *Of Gold all Burnisht and brighter than sunne beames*, which was parodied by Shakespeare in *My mistres'eyes are nothing like the Sunne* (130)

In fourteen lines these sonnets share nine concordances 1) eyes 2) sun 3) lips 4) red 5) white 6) damask 7) head 8) breath 9) heaven. The part by part praise of a woman's body, known as a blason, was commonly used in Elizabethan love sonnets, so those same words could just be a coincidence. However comparing subject lines shows extreme contradictory comparisons in lines 1-1, 4-2, 5/6-5, 2-8 and 8-9 are unlikely to be a coincidence. Emilia used a solar analogy in *Salve Devs* too *Thy beauty shining brighter than the Sunne* (1401)

Shakespeare frequently uses just such quick witted ripostes between his courting couples; Petruccio and Katharina and Beatrice and Benedick for example. I think the revelation of Emilia's authorship of *Of gold all burnisht* helps make more sense of Shakespeare's notoriously difficult sonnet. Irony also offers an explanation for writing in so curiously defamatory a fashion about a woman that you love.

This wasn't the only occasion on which the poet was mischievously motivated to parody Emilia's writing.

Sonnet 130

MY Mistres eyes are nothing like the Sunne,
Curraal is farre more red,then her lips red,
If snow be white, why then her brests are dun:
If haires be wiers, black wiers grow on her head:
I haue seen Roses damaskt, red and white,
But no such Roses see I in her cheekes;
And in some perfumes is there more delight
Then in the breath that from my Mistres reekes.
I loue to hear her speake, yet well I know
That Musicke hath a farre more pleasing sound:
I graunt I neuer saw a goddesse goe,
My Mistres when shee walkes treads on the ground.
  And yet, by heauen, I thinke my loue as rare,
  As any she beli'd with false compare.

Songs of sundrie natures
XXXVl
The first part
OF gold all burnisht, and brighter then sunne beames,
were those curles lockes vppon her noble head,
from whose deepe conceits, my true deseruings flead,
wherfore these mine eyes, such store of teares out streames,
Her eyes are faire starrs, heer red like damaske rose,
her white siluer shyne of Moone, on Chris-tall streame,
her beauty perfext, wheron my fancies dreame,
her lipps are rubies, her teeth of pearle two rowes,

The second part
HEr breath is more sweet then perfect Amber is,
her yeeres are in prime, and nothing doth she want,
that might drawe Angells from Heauen to further blisse,
of all things per-fect, this do I most complaine,
her hart is a rock made all of Adamant,
which guifts all delight, the last doth one-ly paine.

5. The Lovely Boy - Henry Wriothesley, 3rd Earl of Southampton

When that I was and a little tine boy,
with hey, ho, the winde and the raine:
A foolish thing was but a toy,
for the raine it raineth euery day

Twelfe Night, or, What you will (5.1.2467)

One cannot help but feel great sympathy for the *lovely boy* and his unfortunate early life. For Henry Wriothesley, the little tiny boy, *the rain it raineth every day*.

He was born on the 6th October 1573, a date of significance to the composition of the sonnets. His birthplace was Cowdray House, near Midhurst in Sussex, a house grand enough, with a family significant enough, to have been honoured with three visits from Henry Vlll, some decades earlier.

Cowdray was one of a number of houses with estates in the country owned by the Wriothesley Family. Southampton House, on the south side of Holborn, east of Chancery Lane, was the family's London home. Titchfield Abbey in Hampshire, is now a ruin, but in its day, as the Southampton's main residence it was spectacular. Before the Reformation, the Abbey was the home of a community of Premonstratensian canons.

The building and estate were given to the 1st Earl, Henry's grandfather, by Henry Vlll for his assistance in achieving the Suppression of the Monasteries, something of an irony since the 2nd Earl, also called Henry, was to remain staunchly Catholic throughout his life.

The 3rd Earl was the only son of the 2nd Earl and his wife, Mary, neé Browne, the only daughter of Anthony Browne, 1st Viscount Montague, and his first wife, Jane. Henry's parents had two previous children, both girls, Jane, who died young, before Henry's birth, and Mary who was about six when her brother was born.

Following his paternal grand-mother's death in 1574, Henry's father began the realisation of a long held ambition, the building of a great new house near the village of Dogmersfield in Hampshire. Henry's parent's marriage was an affectionate one until Henry was four, at which point his father was given reason to be suspicious over his wife's relationship with a man named Donesame, described as "a common person". After Mary's perceived infidelity, cordiality between the couple evaporated, replaced by enmity.

Mary vehemently denied adultery and accused a servant, Thomas Dymock, of maliciously inventing the cause of the jealousy which tormented her husband. In 1580 Henry's father was told that Mary had again been seen at Dogmersfield with Donesame which provoked him into initiating a forced separation. This required his wife to live under virtual house arrest on one of his Hampshire estates. She was additionally put under constant surveillance by her husband's trusted servants who were instructed to report any untoward behaviour.

Not surprisingly, Viscount Montagu was unhappy over the 2nd Earl's treatment of his daughter. Lord Montagu wrote to Mary seeking her version of events. In response she sent him a copy of a letter that she had sent to her husband, which she learnt her husband had refused to read. This was despite the fact that Mary had entrusted their young son, Henry, with delivery of the letter. In a desperate postscript to the copied letter, Mary Wriothesley wrote:-

That yowr Lordship shalbe witnes of my desier to wyn my Lorde by all such meanes as resteth in me, I have sent yowe what I sent him by my little boye. Butt his harte was too greate to bestowe the reading of it, coming from me. Yett will I do my parte so longe as I am with him, but good my Lorde, procure so soone as conveniently yowe may, some end to my miserie for I am tyred with this life.

Some years later, the English Jesuit, Robert Parsons blamed the intrigue that created the rift between the couple on Charles Paget, one of the Catholic conspirators in the Babington Plot against Elizabeth I.

For nearly four years after his mother's anguished use of him as a postboy, Henry didn't see her again until after the death of his father on 4 October 1581. Two days later, the *lovely boy* suffered a miserable eighth birthday. Perhaps his mother - whose love for her son had further deepened following their enforced separation - became determined that Henry's future birthdays would only be a cause for celebration.

At his father's death, Henry, as the only son, inherited the title, 3rd Earl of Southampton. Southampton inherited a yearly income from estate property of £1,097.6s the equivalent of about £250,000 in 2020. Dymock and Paget were named executors, not surprisingly the will was contested by the Dowager Countess and a compromise settlement reached. Dymock retained the Earl's generous bequests, but relinquished his executorship. Southampton's wardship, and with it, his future marriage, were sold by the Queen to her cousin, Charles, Lord Howard of Effingham for £1000.

Howard appears to have entered into a further agreement which transferred to Lord Burghley the custody and marriage of the young Earl, but left Howard holding income from his land. Late in 1581, or early 1582, Southampton, still only eight years of age, went to live in Burleigh's household, pergrinating between Cecil House in the Strand and Theobalds in Cheshunt, where his guardian could supervise his education and keep a close eye on him.

Burghley - often thought of as the model for Polonius in *Hamlet* - had held the lucrative office of Master of the Court of Wards and Liveries since January 1561.

The concept of wardships is alien to modern life, but in Elizabethan times it was common for aristocratic heirs and heiresses under the age of legal maturity, whose mothers lived, but whose fathers had died, to be made wards of a great personage for a financial consideration at the time of the ward's marriage. This was a mercantile activity to which the child friendly Burghley was attracted. Burghley effectively took charge of his wards' estates, ensuring good maintenance of buildings and lands, maximising profitablity and yield by modestly raising the rents of good tenants and evicting those who fell behind with rent.

It wasn't just Southampton who was made his ward, but several others including Burghley's grand-daughter, Elizabeth de Vere, Robert Devereux - the future Earl of Essex - and young Roger Manners the 5th Earl of Rutland. Two decades later all three of the boys were to feature together as conspiritors in the Essex Rebellion.

Burghley, who possessed unshakeable allegiance to the Queen and a belief in the divine right of monarchs, would have been horrified had he lived to see it.

Burghley provided an intense and broad based private education for all of the wards in his care, an investment which paid off, when the time for an arranged marriage occurred.

When he was twelve, in October 1585, Southampton entered St John's College, Cambridge, graduating as a Master of Arts on 6 June 1589. His name was entered in the Gray's Inn legal society register before he left university, on 29 February 1588.

Most commentators believe that *A Midsommer Nights Dreame* was written as a commission for the wedding of an aristocratic bride and groom between 1592 and 1594. In his edition of the play for Oxford University Press, Peter Holland has suggested eleven possible marriages for which it may have been written.

The marriage of Elizabeth Carey to Sir Thomas Berkeley on 19 February 1596 is one possibility. Elizabeth was the grand daughter of Lord Hunsdon who at the time of her marriage was Patron of the *Lord Chamberlain's Men*, Shakespeare's company of actors created in 1594. However the February wedding date is far away from mid-summer suggested by the play's title and 1596 outside of the 1592-94 time scale.

Another possibility is the marriage of Southampton to Elizabeth Verney on

30 August 1598, but again the month is much later than mid-summer and the year is outside of the general view of the time of writing 1592-1594.

For almost fourteen years Southampton's mother remained unmarried but on 2 May 1594, a year after the publication of Shakespeare's *Venvs and Adonis* and one week before the registration of *the Ravyshement of Lucrece* now more often referred to as *The Rape of Lucrece* (both dedicated to her son), she married the courtier Sir Thomas Heneage, Vice Chamberlain of the Queen's Household. It is therefore most likely that *A Midsommer Nights Dreame* was written for and first performed at the marriage celebrations for the Heneage/Southampton union on 2nd May 1594.

Now vntill the breake of day,
Through this house each Fairy stray.
To the best Bride-bed will we,
Which by vs shall blessed be:
And the issue there create,
Euer shall be fortunate:

A Midsommer Nights Dreame (5.1.2087)

Line three is of interest, the playwright's sole bequest to his wife in his will, was the second-best bed.

Oberon's blessing was to prove as impotent as the bride. Mary was forty one at the time of her marriage to Heanage. In Elizabethan times she would have been past child bearing age. For both partners this was their second marriage. The union was destined to be a very brief one, five months later, at the age of sixty one, Heneage suffered a fatal stroke. Robert Cecil, Bughley's son commented on Sir Thomas's health and appearance

Yesterday there was great hope, but today as great despair, for his looks are again very ghastly and his speech fails

Before the stroke, in a letter to Sir Robert Cecil, Heanage described Southampton as *an unkind and injurious son-in-law*. Whatever the quality of their relationship, with Heanage's death, Southampton, at the age of twenty one, had lost his second father-figure, and his mother, her second husband.

Among the Elizabethan aristocracy, arranged marriages were the norm. The union of two great families strengthened the political potency and financial resilience of both. With the boy's marriage in mind on the 6 October 1589, Burghley noted Southampton's 16th birthday in his diary. Burghley then began negotiations with Southampton's grandfather, Viscount Montague, and his mother, Mary, to arrange a marriage between Southampton and Elizabeth de Vere, a child of Burghley's daughter, Anne Cecil, and Edward de Vere, 17th Earl of Oxford.

In our time Edward de Vere is regarded as the strongest contender as an alternative author for the Shakespeare canon. Elizabeth was two years younger than Southampton, and considered to be a very suitable wife for the young man. She was attractive, the daughter of a courtier, who was also a playwright, a lyric poet and a generous patron of the arts. Elizabeth inheriting her father's love of poetry and literature bestowing on her much in common with Southampton. The achievement of a marriage between Elizabeth and Southampton would have been a lucrative and consolidating outcome for Burghley.

The earliest portrait we have of Southampton (see chapter four) has been dated circa 1590-93. I would suggest the early dating of 1590 is correct and coincides with Sonnets 1-17. It is attributed to the Flemish painter, John de Critz who was to paint a later portrait of an incarcerated Southampton.

The portrait was in the possession of the Cobbe Family, descendants of the Wriothesleys, but not until relatively recently identified as the 3rd Earl. As you can see, he appears to be an effeminate young man with *rosy lips* (116:9) his right hand sensually caressing his *browny locks* [that] *did hang in crooked curls* (*A Lover's Complaint* 85) and a choice of earring more appropriate to a young lady than a young man.

For three centuries it was thought to be of a young woman, Lady Norton, identified as her by a C18 hand-written label on the back of the painting. In 2002, Alastair Laing, the National Trust's adviser on art and sculpture, told Alec Cobbe, the portrait's owner, that he believed the portrait was not of a woman, but of a young man. Cobbe investigated further and discovered how his Anglo/Irish family, descended from the Writhiosleys, came to inherit the portrait. He compared the sitters with the Hilliard portrait of Southampton with his portrait of Lady Norton and found them to be the identical subject. In fact Elizabeth, Lady Norton was Southampton's great-grand-daughter, which would explain why the writer of the identifying label might have been confused.

Hilliard's miniature of Southampton held at the Fitzwilliam Museum in Cambridge has been dated 1594, when he was in his twenty first year. Still sporting the curled locks but the four year gap shows that Southampton has matured from a boy to a man, none-the-less there is still the gender ambiguity about his appearance.

Even if his mother wasn't over concerned about Southampton's sexual orientation, you can be sure that Burghley was, since he had a personal and financial interest in getting him married. Might the seventeen procreation sonnets have been a commission for Shakespeare from Burghley and/or Lady Southampton to be presented to the boy as a present on his seventeenth birthday? As old Adam - a role putively acted by Shakespeare - points out to the young Orlando *At seauenteene yeeres, many their fortunes seeke* (*As you Like it* 2.4.753)

Perhaps the Cobbe portrait was another birthday present? *Much liker then your painted counterfeit* (16:8) would make it appear that there was already a portrait of Southampton in existence when Sonnet 16 was written, perhaps Shakespeare had seen it before it was presented.

There is flattery for the mother early on in Sonnet 3

Thou art thy mothers glasse and she in thee Calls backe the louely Aprill of her prime (3:9-10)

What more significant a present for a poetry lover and a narcissistic art love than the poet should present the autograph manuscript and the painter his portrait in person on his seventeenth birthday?

This might explain the very beginning of the friendship between Shakespeare and Southampton and how it was that two individuals from such extremes of society - actors in Elizabethan times were categorised as vagabonds - should become so close. If I'm correct, this would date the completion of the first seventeen sonnets to some time before 6 October 1590. Sonnet 104 ends with a reference to Southampton's October birthday with the line *Ere you were borne was beauties summer dead*

15 Nicholas Hilliard: Lord Southampton

There is no evidence that Shakespeare had arrived in London as early as 1590, but it is likely that it would have taken time before he would have been considered for such a commission. It would have taken even longer for his reputation as a playwright to have grown sufficiently to provoke the jealous deathbed riposte against him from Robert Greene.

In September 1592 Greene's *Groats-worth of witte* was published posthumouslygiving advice to fellow university educated playwrights. This was in the form of a tirade against Shakespeare, the *upstart crow*, who dared to enter the arena of drama playwright without a university education instead plagiarising the work of graduates. The intended recipients of Green's advice are thought to be Marlowe, Nashe and Peele.

Greene's text was almost exclusively printed in Gothic type but with occasional phrases printed in Roman type. It isn't clear why, except perhaps to give the two phrases - *Tygers hart.....*and *Johannes fac totum* - some addional emphasis.

there is an vpstart Crow, beautified with our feathers, that with his Tygers hart wrapt in a Players hyde, supposes he is as well able to bombast out a blanke verse as the best of you: and being an absolute Iohannes fac totum, is in his owne conceit the onely Shake-scene in a countrey

The idea of an *upstart crow* is lifted from Aesop's fable of a crow that borrowed the feathers of more beautiful birds and attached them to his own. The *Tygers hart* quote is a line from Shakespeare's *Henry VI*, Part 3, *Oh Tygres Heart, wrapt in a Womans Hide.* (1.4.552) *Shake-scene in a country* is a reference to Shakespeare's rural upbringing, no doubt he still had a Warwickshire accent.

Later Greene refers to Shake-scene as a *rude groom* and a *peasant.* There is a C18 anecdote reported by Samuel Schoenbaum that places Shakespeare tethering horses owned by members of the audience outside of the Globe Theatre.

When the attack on Shakespeare appeared in the autumn of 1592, it was rumoured that it was Thomas Nashe who had in fact written the pamphlet. Nashe vehemently denied the accusation in October when he prefaced *Pierce Penilesse* with these words:

Other newes I am aduertised of, that a scald triviall lying Pamphlet, called greens groats-worth of wit, is given out to be my doing. God neuer have care of my soule, but utterly renounce me, if the least word or syllable in it proceeded from my penne, or if I were in any way priuie to the writing or printing of it

The nature of the language shows the Nashe was anxious about the rumour that he was the author of the pamphlet. Commentators have assumed that it was because of what was written against Shakespeare that Nashe was concerned, but might there have been far more for him to worry about?

Lamilia, Greene's courtesan, the seductive singer and lutenist, has to be a reference to Emilia, she certainly would have thought so. In the autumn of 1592, albeit a month or so before her marriage to Alphonso Lanier, she was to all intents and purposes, still the mistress of Hunsdon and by naming her child Henry was announcing to the world - albeit equivocally - that Hunsdon was the father.

It has been suggested that it was in pursuit of Southampton's patronage that Nashe decided to distance himself from the publication. There may be some merit to this argument, but were Hunsdon to have believed that it was Nashe who wrote the *Groatsworth* pamphlet it would be more than potential patronage that Nashe was in danger of losing. My argument would be true for Greene too, but at the time *Groatsworth* was written he didn't care, because he knew he was dying.

Might the well-known reputation of Venetian courtesans like Veronica Franco - paramour to Venetian aristocracy - that made Emilia, with her Venetian ancestry, as well as her association with Hunsdon, an object of suspicion as a courtesan?

By 1594, a year after Emilia's open affair with Hunsdon had ended, Nashe felt emboldened to write about another Aemilia, also a courtesan, like Green's Lamilia. Emilia wasn't a common name in Elizabethan London, so there is no doubt that our Emilia would have thought that in their writing, both Nashe and Greene, were referring to her.

The Unfortunate Traveller, with a dedication to Southampton, describes his life-threatening encounter

There was a delicate wench called Flauia Aemilia lodging in S. Markes streete at a Goldsmiths, which I would faine haue had to the grand test, to trie whether she were currant in alcumie or no. Aie me, shee was but a counterfeit slip, for she not only gaue me the slip, but had welnie made me a slipstring. To her I sent my gold to beg an hour of grace, ah gracelesse fornicatresse, my hostesse & she wer confederate, who hauing gotten but one piece of my ill golde into their handes, deuised the meanes to make me immortall

Flavia in Latin means blond, perhaps used satirically by Nashe to distinguish her the from Dark Lady? The Bell, a house on the east side of [St] Mark Lane, at the southern boundary of the city, close to the Thames, was the Bassano family home for generations, from October 1552 when it was in the ownership Sir Walter Devereux the first Earl of Essex, father of the executed 2nd Earl. It was still in the family's ownership two centuries later.

There would appear to be connections observed by both Simon Forman and Shakespeare with Nashe's Aemilia and our Emilia. Forman notes that Emilia

was wealthy to him that married her, in money and jewels

and continues in Latin concerning Emilia's tales of the invocation of spirits and in Sonnet 119 suggesting practice of alchemy

WHat potions haue I drunk of Syren teares Distil'd from Lymbecks foule as hell within (119.1-2)

The decade after Southampton's seventeenth birthday leading up to his misguided entanglement in the Essex rebellion in 1601 was a significant one for him, and for Shakespeare too.

In 1591 the poet John Clapham, who also happened to be Burghley's Clerk in Chancery, dedicated a poem in Latin to Southampton. The ode, *Narcissus,* recounts Ovid's *Metamorphosis* story of the attractive young man obsessed with his own beauty, who drowns admiring his image reflected in water. This poetic mythgives a different take on the theme of the seventeen procreation Sonnets.

LOoke in thy glasse and tell the face thou vewest, Now is the time that face should

forme an other (3:1-2)

She caru'd thee for her seale, and ment therby, Thou shouldst print more, not let that coppy die (11:13-14)

Might Clapham's poem have been another Burghley/Lady Southampton commission made in an effort to get Southampton suitably wed in order to continue the Writhiosley line?

In 1593 Shakespeare dedicated his narrative poem *Venvs and Adonis* to Southampton Adonis, like Southampton, was an attractive and desirable young man. This was followed in 1594 by *Lucrece* also dedicated to Southampton.

The dedication of *Venvs and Adonis* is restrained, reflecting a more cautious deferential approach to an aristocrat. The dedication of *Lucrece* is couched in extravagant and affectionate terms:

THE loue I dedicate to your Lordship is without end ... VVhat I haue done is yours, what I have to do is yours, being part in all I haue, devoted yours

This would indicate that a cordial, friendly and devoted relationship had developed over time. The kind of progress of intimate friendship, albeit with bouts of turbulence in the relationship, suggested in the passage of time in Sonnets 18-126.

When Viscount Montague, died in October 1592, not only did Southampton lose his maternal grandfather, Burghley lost one of the main advocates of marriage to Elizabeth de Vere. If thje motivation of Sonnets 1-17, Chapman's *Narcissus* and perhaps *Venvs* and *Lucrece* was to stimulate heterosexual desires in Southampton and achieve his agreement to marry Elizabeth de Vere, it was totally unsuccessful. Southampton demurred to the match so carefully and tenaciously arranged by the ambitious Burghley.

This proved to be an expensive decision for Southampton, resulting in a huge fine payable to Burghley. In a letter written in November 1594, about six weeks after Southampton had turned twenty one, the Jesuit, Henry Garnet reported that

The young Erle of Southampton refusing the Lady Veere payeth £5000 of present payment

This was a massive sum, close on £1m today. The payment of the fine is indicative of how little appetite Southampton had for marriage - at least to Burghley's grand-daughter - at that time. This is despite my suggestion that Southampton had lost his 'heterosexual' virginity to Emilia, a female sexual predator, that started about a year before

And when a woman woes, what womans sonne Will sourely leaue her till he haue preuailed (41.7-8)

It is possible that Southampton's affair with Emilia was still on-going when he rejected Elizabeth's hand in marriage.

Southampton was now spending much of his time at court, where his flamboyant dress and attention-seeking demeanour was noticed by the ever observant Queen. Royal progresses were an annual event; where the Queen went, so did her courtiers and servants, including musicians. Southampton was included in the entourage when Queen Elizabeth visited Oxford in late September 1592, and he was lauded in the Latin poem written by John Sanford, chaplain of Magdalen College to commemorate the visit.

Post hunc insequitur clara de stirpe Dynasta. Lure suo dives quem South-Hamptonia magnum Vendicat heroem. After him [the Earl of Essex] followed a Prince of a distinguished race, whom, rich in her right, Southampton blazons as a great hero (translated by Charlotte Stropes).

Since the court moved with the monarch on the 1592 progress of the Queen, I think it safe to assume that Southampton was present at Bisham Abbey, the home of the dowager Lady Russell, for the Queen's visit some six weeks earlier in August 11-13 as well. More of the significance of the Bisham Abbey visit later.

There is an anecdote that tells of a gift of a £1000 by Southampton to Shakespeare *go through with a purchase.* G.P.V.Akrigg notes

Not for nothing does our word 'generous' derive from the Latin generosus, designating one of noble birth. A lord who was truly noble was expected to pour forth bounty. Southampton in his youthful prodigality may have allowed that bounty to far outstrip his means, but we can respect the ideal

If word had got out about Southampton's generosity towards Shakespeare, no wonder so many writers decided to dedicate publications to him.

In 1593, Barnabe Barnes published *Parthenophil and Parthenope,* a collection of verse with cringingly self-denigrating dedicatory sonnets to six aristocrats, one of which was to Southampton.

TO THE RIGHT NOBLE AND VER|tuous Lord, Henry Earle of Southampton.

*Receaue (sweet Lord) with thy thrise-sacred hande
Which sacred muses make their instrument,
These worthlesse leaues, which I to thee present
Sprong from a rude and vnmanured lande:
That with your countenance grac'de, they may withstande
Hundred ey'de enuies rough encounterment,
Whose patronage can giue encouragement
To scorne back-wounding Zoilus his bande.
Voutch-safe (right vertuous Lord) with gracious eyes
Those heauenly lampes, which giue the muses light,
Which giue, and take in course (that holy fier)*

To vewe my muse with your iudiciall sight,
Whom when time shall haue taught by flight to rise,
Shall to thy vertues of much worth aspyer.

On 27 June 1593 Thomas Nashe completed his novel, *The Unfortunate Traveller*, relating his life-threatening encounter with Flavia Aemilia. It wasn't published until a year later and in the dedication to Southampton Nashe employs some bizarre turns of phrase.

To the right Honorable Lord Henrie Wriothsley, Earle of South-hampton, and Baron of Tichfeeld.

INgenuous honorable Lord, I know not what blinde custome methodicall antiquity hath thrust vponvs, to dedicate such books as we publish, to one great man or other ; In which respect, least anie man should challenge these my papers as goods vncustomd, and so extend vppon them as forfeite to contempt, to the seale of your excellent censure loe here I present them to bee scene and allowed. Prize them as high or as low as you list : if you set anie price on them, I hold my labor well satisfide. IvOng haue I desired to approoue my wit vnto you. My reuerent duetifull thoughts (euen from their infancie) haue been retayners to your glorie. Now at last I haue enforst an opportunitie to plead my denoted minde. All that in this phantasticall Treatise I can promise, is some reasonable conueyance of historic, & varietie of mirth. By diuers of my good frends haue I been dealt with to employ my dul pen in this kinde, it being a cleane different vaine from other my former courses of writing. How wel or ill I haue done in it, I am ignorant : (the eye that sees round about it selfe, sees not into it selfe) : only your Honours applauding encouragement hath power to make mee arrogant. Incomprehensible is the heigh of your spirit both in heroical resolution and matters of conceit. Vnrepriueably perisheth that booke whatsoeuer to wast paper, which on the diamond rocke of your iudgement disasterly chanceth to be ship-wrackt. A dere louer and cherisher you are, as well of the louers of Poets, as of Poets themselues. Amongst their sacred number I dare not ascribe my selfe, though now and then I speak English : that smal braine I haue.to no further vse I conuert, saue to be kinde to my frends, and fatall to my enemies. A new brain, a new wit, a new stile, a new soule will I get mee, to canonize your name to posteritie, if in this my first attempt I be not taxed of presumption. Of your gracious fauor I despaire not, for I am not altogether Fames out-cast. This handfull of leaues I offer to your view, to the leaues on trees I compare, which as they cannot grow of themselues except they haue some branches or boughes to cleaue too, & with whose iuice and sap they be euermore recreated & nourisht : so except these vnpolisht leaues of mine haue some braunch of Nobilitie whereon to depend and cleaue, and with the vigorous nutriment of whose authorized commendation they may be continually fosterd and refresht, neuer wil they grow to the worlds good liking, but forthwith fade and die on the first houre of their birth. Your I/ordship is the large spreading branch of renown, from whence these my idle leaues seeke to deriue their whole nourishing : it resteth you either scornfully shake them off, as worm-eaten & worthies, or in pity preserue them and cherish them, for some litle summer frute you hope to finde amongst them.

Your Honors in all humble seruice :
Tho : Nashe.

....if you set any price on them. I hold my labour well satisfied could be seen as a request for payment.

A dear lover and cherisher you are, as well of the lovers of poets as of poets them-
selves. Amongst their sacred number I dare not ascribe myself, though now and
then I speak English

Is a statement worthy of exploration.

Who are these poets and lovers of poets that Nashe is referring to, some of whom prefer to speak or write in foreign languages, rather than English?

One has to be Shakespeare, whose English version of *Venvs and Adonis* - published on 18 April 1593 - was originally written by Ovid in Latin. Clapham's 1591 *Narcissus* was written in Latin. When John Florio published his Italian/English Dictionary the dedication to Southampton spoke of being in the Lord's *pay and patronage* for some years. Emilia was a poet too, by this time she had been William Byrd's librettist, translating from Italian and Latin in a number of his *Songs of sundrie natures* printed in 1589.

Would it though not be too close to the bone for Nashe to suggest that Southampton as a *dear lover and cherisher...of poets themselves*, meant a real sexual relationship along the lines of his own amorous aims towards Flavia Aemilia?

When Nashe wrote his dedication, drinking water was hazardous, and neither tea nor coffee were the ubiquitous drink of today, a couple more centuries had to elapse before that happened. Perhaps Nashe's diplomatic judgement was clouded by two much alcohol in his daytime tipple?

In *The Unfortunate Traveler*, as well as his reference to the courtesan Flavia Aemilia, Nashe rather outspokenly says of Italy, that one only learns

the art of atheism, the art of epicurizing, the art of whoring, the art of poisoning,
the art of sodomitry.

When you consider that Italy was a country whose language was loved and eloquently practised by Southampton, the works dedicatee, this would seem a foolhardy comment for someone seeking patronage.

Emilia and her extended family remained fluent in Italian, twice petitioning the Queen - also an Italian speaker - in their native language in 1568 and 1576.

Nashe's pornographic poem *The Choise of Valentines or the Merie Ballad of Nash his Dildo* only contemporaneously existing in manuscript, was also dedicated to Lord Southampton.

Pardon, sweete flower of Matchles poetrie,
And fairest bud the red rose euer bare;
Although my Muse, devorst from deeper care,
*   Presents thee with a wanton Elegie.*
Ne blame my verse of loose unchastitie
For painting forth the things that hidden are,
Since all men acte what I in speache declare,
* Onlie induced with varietie.*
Complants and praises euery one can write,
And passion out their pangu's in statlie rimes;
But of loues pleasures none did euer write,
That have succeeded in theis latter times.
Accept of it, Deare Lord, in gentle gree,
And better lynes, ere long, shall honor thee.

The second line gives another example of another writer using Southampton's nickname, *Rose*.

Publication of this particular piece of literature, following on from *Venvs* and *Lucrece*, begs the question why were so many salacious works dedicated to Southampton? Was it well-known amongst those in pursuit of patronage that Southampton was taken with the subject? Not everything dedicated to Southampton was was of a sexual nature.

In 1595 Gervase Markham included a dedicatory sonnet to Southampton in *The Most Honorable Tragedy of Richard Grinvile, Knight.*

On 2 March 1596 John Florio's Italian/English dictionary was entered in the Stationers' Register. There were three dedicatees, the Earls of Rutland and Southampton and Lucie Countess of Bedford one of Emilia's dedicatees in *Salve Devs.* Florio, who, like Emilia was of Anglo Italian descent, was for some years employed as a tutor by the Earl. In his dedication he complimented Southampton on his fluency in Italian, saying he

had become so complete a master of Italian as to have no need of travel abroad to
perfect his mastery of that tongue

In 1597 Henry Lok included a sonnet to Southampton among the sixty dedicatory sonnets in his *Sundry Christian Passions.* In the same year William Burton dedicated a translation of Achilles Tatius's *Clitophon and Leucippe.* There seems little doubt that poets and writers saw Southampton as a potential source of generous patronage.

On 17 November 1595, Southampton jousted in Queen's accession day tournament, earning a mention in George Peele's *Anglorum Feriae* as *gentle and debonaire.* It would appear that from this date Southampton declined in favour with the Queen, mainly due to his own uncontrolled behaviour.

In April 1596 the Queen's displeasure with Southampton had developed sufficiently for her to forbid Essex to take him on an expedition for the relief of Calais, neither did he accompany Essex on the Cadiz expedition in the summer. In February 1597 Southampton challenged the Earl of Northumberland to a duel with rapiers, requiring intervention by the queen and Privy Council.

In the summer of that year Southampton was with Essex on the ill-fated voyage to the Azores, Alphonso Lanier, was with them too, his wife taking advantage of his absence by inviting Forman to dine and stay overnight. We learn from Forman's records of her consultations that Alphonso had gone in the hope of sharing in Spanish bounty and receiving a knighthood from Essex.

According to Rowland Whyte, the Elizabethan official, businessman and letter writer reported that

My Lord of Southampton fought with one of the Kings [of Spain] *great Men of Warre, and suncke her*

On his return Southampton made his first appearance in the House of Lords on 5 November, and was appointed a member of several committees, but seldom attended meetings. By this time he was in serious financial difficulties, and had turned over administration of his estates to two trustees, who by the end of the year had sold off tracts of estate land.

In 1598 Southampton was involved in a brawl at court with Ambrose Willoughby, one of the Queen's *esquires of the body,* who had ordered him to leave the presence chamber where he was gambling at cards after the queen had retired for the evening. Courtiers were well aware that one of the Queen's prerequisites, both in royal palaces and for her lodging in country houses on her annual progress through the realm, was silence, once she had retired.

Southampton struck Willoughby, and *Willoughby puld of some of his locke,* Southampton's portraits show this must have been a strongtemptation for any adversary. The Queen thanked Willoughby for his actions, saying *he had done better yf he had sent hym to the porters lodge, to see who durst have fetcht hym out.* The altercation was rumoured to be initiated because of a remark that Willoughby had made about Elizabeth Vernon, Southampton's future wife, who at the time was one of the Queen's *maids of honour.*

Southampton's behaviour had him banished from court, although he appears to have been permitted to return, but not enjoying the queen's earlier cordiality. Whyte reported *My Lord of Southampton is much troubled at her Majesties straungest Usage of hym*

Faced with serious financial difficulties and the Queen's ongoing disfavour, Southampton determined to live abroad for a time, and seized the opportunity of accompanying Sir Robert Cecil, Lord Burghley's son as envoy to Henri IV of France. By March he and Cecil were in Angers, where Southampton was presented to the French King.

When Cecil returned to England, Southampton remained at the French court, planning to travel to Italy with Sir Charles Danvers and Sir Henry Danvers, whom he had helped to escape from England in 1594. The Danvers family were involved in the death of Henry Long, the youngest son of their neighbours in a feud that had developed out of hand. Southampton's unshakeable loyalty to his friends often resulted in his own disadvantage.

The Queen pardoned the Danvers brothers and they returned to England by 30 August 1598, at which time Southampton was also in London and clandestinely married his pregnant mistress, Elizabeth Vernon. He left for the continent almost immediately afterwards but by 3 September the Queen had learned of the marriage and consigned the new Countess to the Fleet Prison for marrying without her consent.

The Queen ordered Southampton to return to England forthwith, but he disobeyed, remaining in Paris for another two months, losing large sums in gambling. By the beginning of November he was back in England, where he was also confined in the Fleet. He remained in prison with his wife for a month, during which time she gave birth to their daughter, Penelope.

To add to his difficulties, Southampton was at this time involved in a dispute with his mother over her prospective marriage to Sir William Hervey. Lord Henry Howard was brought in as a mediator to smooth matters between mother and son. He was unsuccessful and the Countess and Hervey were wed - without Southampton's blessing - in early January 1599.

The Queen had been troubled over the choice of a military commander for Ireland, at a time when two factions dominated her court. One faction was led by Essex, the other by her principal secretary, Sir Robert Cecil, Burghley's son. Essex offered his services to take on the Irish problem, the Queen accepted.

Essex departed London on 27 March 1599. Prayers were offered in the churches for his success, and he was cheered on for four miles in the sunshine by a crowd of well-wishers. A change in the weather sent the public in search of shelter. With Essex were Southampton and Sir Christopher Blount both of whom had been decommissioned by the Queen and were now attending on Essex in a private capacity.

In September, on his return from Ireland, Southampton attracted notice as a playgoer. In 1599 Whyte wrote to Sir Robert Sydney

My Lord Southampton and Lord Rutland come not to the court: the one doth but very seldom. They pass away the time in London merely in going to plays every day

At the beginning of the following year Southampton and his wife are to be found in Forman's consulting room. Forman's coded entry makes it difficult to learn the reason for the couple's visit but Southampton was clearly disenchanted with his treatment by the Queen and her ministers because over the next year he was motivated to openly put his family in harm's way in Essex's reckless and foolhardy enterprise.

I think it unlikely that Southampton kept his views on the Queen to himself, whether Shakespeare suggested caution, or not, who knows. It is though possible that Shakespeare felt his friend had a good reason for being disgruntled.

Essex used his London residence, Essex House, as a meeting place for those who were unhappy with Elizabeth's government and wanted to force change. On 3 February 1601, five of the main conspirators met at Drury House, Southampton's home. Essex himself was not present but this was simply in order to allay suspicion.

There were discussions over Essex's proposal for a coup which included seizure of strategic sites, the court, the Tower of London and the city. The aim was to force the Queen to change the leaders in her government, particularly Robert Cecil, Southampton's recent companion in France.

Four days later some of the conspirators visited the *Globe* to commission the *Lord Chamberlain's Men* to stage a special performance of *Richard ll* with the deposition scene included. The players were reluctant to perform such a controversial play, but agreed once they were promised a modest payment of 40 shillings (less than £300 in 2020).

On the same day, the council summoned Essex to appear before them, but he refused. He had lost his chance to take the court by surprise, so he fell back on his scheme to rouse the city of London in his favour with the claim that Elizabeth's government had planned to murder him and had sold out England to Spain.

Essex and his followers hastily planned the uprising. At 10 o'clock on the morning of 8 February, the judge and friend of Essex, Thomas Egerton, the Lord Keeper and three others came to Essex in the name of the Queen. Essex held the four messengers captive keeping them hostage while he and his two hundred or so followers made their way to the city. Their arrival was timed to coincide with the end of the sermon at open air pulpit of St. Paul's Cross because they anticipated that the Lord Mayor would be there.

Unbeknown to Essex, Robert Cecil had sent a warning to the Lord Mayor and instructed the heralds to publicly denounce Essex as a traitor. Once the word traitor was used, fearing the consequences,many of Essex's followers took fright and fled, and none of the citizens - who had so enthusistically acclaimed him on his departure for Ireland - joined him as he had hoped. Essex and his few remaining followers found themselves in a desperate position and decided to return to Essex House. When they arrived the hostages had been released.

Lord High Admiral Howard with a detachment of armed men had laid siege to the house. By that evening, after burning incriminating evidence, Essex surrendered. He and Southampton and the other remaining rebels were placed under arrest.

Along with Essex and the other conspirators Southampton was sentenced to death. Cecil urged the Queen to show the greatest possible degree of clemency and over time obtained the commutation of his penalty to life imprisonment. During this time the young widow, Frances Howard, who earlier had harboured marital ambitions for Southampton was consulting Forman to predict whether or not he would be executed.

16 John de Critz: Southampton in the Tower of London

There is another portrait of Southampton, dating from the end of his incarceration, with his pet cat sharing his accommodation. It was painted by the same artist, the court painter, John de Critz, who painted his seventeenth birthday portrait.

A small depiction of the Tower of London is shown in the top-right background, above it the Latin words: *In vinculis invictus* (in chains unconquered) *Februa 8 1600; 601; 602; 603 Apri.*

The Wriothesley coat-of-arms (*Azure, a cross or between four hawks close argent*) are shown on the cover of a book lying on the windowsill before the curiously questioning cat. The artist has captured the toll that life had taken on the Earl but seems to have been instructed to show to the world that although he's "down", he's not yet "out".

On the accession of James I in 1603, Southampton was released from captivity and resumed his place at court, receiving numerous honours from the new king and resuming his connection with the stage. In spite of his earlier effeminate appearance, Southampton quickly entered arenas of conflict and engaged in more than one serious quarrel, one in the presence of Queen Anne, with Lord Grey of Wilton.

Grey had been an enemy since the Ireland campaign, this particular argument resulted with another spell in prison for Southampton. He appears to have been the recipient of royal clemency because in January 1605 he organised the entertainment for Queen Anne with a performance of *Loues Labour's lost,* played by Burbage and his company, to which Shakespeare belonged, at Southampton House.

Probably poet and patron were delighted to reaffirm their friendship. The choice of *Loues Labour's lost* as late as 1605 when there were a huge number of plays to choose from is of significance. The play was written as a skit based on members of Southampton's circle and parodied other Elizabethan courtiers too.

Two of the characters, Berowne and Rosaline, have been suggested as aliases for Shakespeare and his *Dark Lady*. Ian Steere has argued that the name Rosaline was an invention by the poet with reference to Emilia's seduction of Southampton and can be taken to mean *Rose-besmircher*

The King comments on Rosaline

O paradoxe, Blacke is the badge of hell,
The hue of dungeons, and the Schoole of night:
And beauties crest becomes the heauens well.
(Loues Labour's lost 2.1. 1495-7)

Another character in *Loues Labour's lost* is Moth.

Three moths are an heraldic feature in the Bassano coat-of-arms, the playwright would have known that.

Among the Jacobean aristocrats, Southampton led the way as a captain of industry. He pioneered modern investment practices, modernising the management of estates, overseas trade and colonisation. He financed the first tinplate mill in the country, and founded an ironworks at Titchfield. He developed his properties in London, Bloomsbury and Holborn and revamped his country estates. He participated in the efforts of the East India Company and the New England Company, and backed Henry Hudson's search for the Northwest Passage.

A significant artistic patron throughout his life, as well as Shakespeare, Southampton promoted the work of George Chapman, Samuel Daniel and Thomas Heywood. Heywood's popular dramas reflected Southampton's maritime and colonial interests.

Another beneficiary of Southampton's patronage was the composer and court musician, Alfonso Ferrabosco the younger. This gives us a definite link to Emilia - albeit later than her affairs with Southampton and Shakespeare - since in 1612 Ferrabosco married Ellen Lanier, the daughter of Lucretia Lanier neé Bassano, Emilia's cousin once removed.

The New World Tapestry was begun in the 1980s, Henry Wriothesley's name, his coat-of-arms and next to it a white rose is included in the 1605 panel commemorating the expedition to Maine. Southampton took a considerable share in promoting the colonial enterprises of the time, and was an active member of the Virginia Company's governing council.

Southampton's name is thought by many to be the origin of the naming of the harbour of Hampton Roads and the Hampton River. Although named at later dates, similar attribution may involve the town (and later city) of Hampton, Virginia, as well as Southampton County, Virginia and Northampton County.

In 1613 the day after the *Globe Theatre* was burned to the ground Thomas Lorkin noted that Southampton was peeved that he hadn't been appointed to the Privy Council

My Lord of South-Hampton hath lately gott lycense to make a voyage over to Spaine, whether he is ether allready gone, or means to goe very shortly. He pretends to seeke remedy against I knowe not what maladie: but his greatest sicknes is supposed to be, a distontentment conceyved, [for] that he can not [be] compasse to be made one of ye Privy council; which not able to [digest] brooke heer well at home; he will try if he can better digest it abroad.

Southampton's disappointment at home pointed him across the Atlantic to Virginia. Although the Virginia Company was never hugely profitable, his vision for an English Colony at Jamestown was fulfilled. He and Sir Edwin Sandys, who eventually became the Treasurer, united forces within the company, and worked tirelessly to support the struggling venture.

In addition to profits, Southampton sought to establish a permanent colony which would enlarge British territory, relieve the nation's overpopulation, and expand the market for English goods. Unexpectedly, profits largely eluded the Virginia Company, and it ceased trading in 1624.

As one interest evaporatd another appeared. Southampton was one of four Englishmen appointed to command troops fighting in the Low Countries against the Spanish. Shortly after their arrival at Rosendael, the earl's eldest son, James Wriothesley, succumbed to a fever. Five days later, on 10 November 1624, Southampton died of a similar infection at Bergen-op-Zoom, aged 51. Both their bodies were repatriated to be buried in the parish church of Titchfield, Hampshire.

The National Portrait Gallery has identified eleven images of Southampton, in which he is depicted with dark auburn hair and blue eyes, compatible with Shakespeare's description of *a man right faire.*

We don't know if Southampton ever met John Shakespeare, or whether William related details of the uncomfortable job John was ordered to complete. At some time after the injunction of 1559 to remove

all signs of superstition and idolatry from places of worship

John Shakespeare was paid two shillings for

defasyng ymages in ye chapel.

The wall paintings in the Guild Chapel, which had been commissioned by Hugh Clopton, former owner of New Place, Shakespeare's final home in Stratford, had remained hidden for two hundred and fifty years.

Who knows why John chose not to deface the images as instructed, instead he just applied a coat of lime wash over the paintings. In 1802 the lime wash was cleaned off it revealed a fearful *Doom for Sinners*, an *Allegory of Death* and the *Life of Adam.* Only the face of the Archangel Michael in the *Allegory of Death* painting can be seen to have been clearly 'defaced', literally scratched away.

The lime washing actually served to protect the paintings, many of them in very fine detail. Since the images were covered some five years before Shakespeare was born, he would never have seen them himself. Had he done so there was one image that would have resonated with him, that of *St George Slaying the Dragon.* St George, patron saint of England and the poet sharing the same name day, 23 April.

There was another image associated with Southampton that was revealed in 2008. Art historians from Bristol University were preparing paintings for an exhibition to be held at Montacute House in Somerset.

A portrait of Elizabeth Vernon, dressed in black and wearing ruby ear-rings was subjected to X-ray. Underneath the surface was a man with flamboyant appearance and long auburn hair. It was Henry Wriothesley, the third Earl of Southampton, Shakespeare's *Young Friend*, the *Lovely Boy*.

6. Never resting time - Dating the Sonnets

THose howers that with gentle worke did frame,
The louely gaze where every eye doth dwell
Will play the tirants to the very same,
And that unfaire which fairely doth excel:
For never resting time leads Summer on.
To hidious winter and confounds him there
(*Sonnet 5.1-6*)

There is no doubt that establishing an exact dating for the Sonnets has confounded many that have considered it. The American academic and writer Peter Jensen, sees numerical significance, codes and cryptic anagrams in many of the sonnets and poems and has argued that the first seventeen sonnets - the so-called procreation sonnets - which make a single cogent whole, were commissioned from Shakespeare by the dowager Lady Southampton as a birthday present for her son's seventeenth birthday.

I think he's correct, but I wonder if Robert Cecil, Lord Burghley might also have been involved in the commission. We know that in 1590 Burghley had Elizabeth de Vere, his fifteen year old grand-daughter, in mind to marry Southampton. Elizabeth and her sisters had been residents of Cecil House after Southampton had left for Cambridge. If Jensen is correct the seventeen poem 'present' would need to have been completed by the 6 October 1590, in time for the Earl's seventeenth birthday celebrations.

The word *time* makes seventy eight appearances in Sonnets 1-126 and not once from Sonnets 127, the first Dark Lady Sonnet, to the end of the sequence. Sonnet 12 begins

WHen I doe count the clock that tels the time

there are, of course, twelve hours on a clock. Shakespeare's preoccupation with time, appears to be with its progressing the devastation of youth and beauty.

I have come to the conclusion that there are four parallel sonnet sequences within the publication, with the second third and fourth sequences overlapping in their time of composition.

The first 126 Sonnets, with the exception of the Rival Poet sonnets, are most likely chronologically written and the *Dark Lady* sonnets are written in a part parallel chronology, with Sonnet 133 being written around the same date as

Sonnet 40.

This is the moment when the poet has it confirmed that the two people dearest to him, have conspired together to sexually betray him, even though in order to bring an heir to the Southampton household, he may have suggested the liaison himself.

This questionable act of altruism is mirrored in the *Two Gentlemen of Verona* when Valentine gives his love Silvia to Proteus.

The authority to trespass is admitted in Sonnet 35

All men make faults, and euen I in this,
Authorizing thy trespas with compare,
My selfe corrupting saluing thy amisse,
Excusing thy sins more than thy sins are:
For to thy sensuall fault I bring in sense,
Thy aduerse party is thy Aduocate,
And gainst my selfe a lawfull plea commence:
Such ciuill war is in my loue and hate,
*   That I an accessary needs must be,*
*   To that sweet theef which sourely robs from me*

(35.5-14 my underlining)

To complicate matters further there is a strong possibility that the numbered sequence was Thorpe's guess and there may be several, or many sonnets in the wrong order. We know that there are at least two sonnet sequences written contemporaneously, so why not more, with the Rival Poet sequence Nos 78-86 written independently too?

Notwithstanding the difficulties, the dating of the writing of the sonnets is crucial if we to give certainty to the identities of the Young Friend, the Rival Poet and the Dark Lady, as well as identifying historic events referred to within the poems. Nominating absolutely certain dates is not without its problems and has been the subject of great controversy.

Scholars generally think that it was the closure of the London theatres, mainly because of plague, that gave Shakespeare the opportunity, away from the daily grind of acting and fulfilling the completion of plays, to concentrate on writing poetry. Plague struck London on three separate occasions during Shakespeare's residence there, and the authorities - believing that the disease spread from person to person - closed down the theatres in an attempt to limit the contagion. It wasn't though just plague that closed playhouses.

The Privy Council closed the theatres - because of concerns over escalation of the apprentice riots - in June 1592 until Michaelmas (the end of September) but before this period was over plague broke out and the actors were warned not to commence performances again until December. The theatres opened again in January 1593 but closed again in February. The theatres were more or less permanently closed from June 1592 until May 1594, then again in the 1603 and 1608 outbreaks.

During these enforced acting bans in London the acting companies took to the road touring provincial towns and cities, it seems that Shakespeare chose not to join them, but remained in London to shift the emphasis of his writing from plays towards poetry.

Of course, there is absolutely no reason why Shakespeare couldn't write poetry when the theatres were open and to limit consideration of the likely dates exclusively to plague years might be misleading. In fact, the putative dating of the first seventeen sonnets to the Autumn of 1590 was a time when the theatres were open. If the early sonnets, were a commission from Lady Southampton and/or Burleigh, then a substantial payment might have been made and Shakespeare would have given a well paid commission priority over play writing. It goes without saying, that all 154 sonnets need to have been written before the date of publication, that is before 1609, and so any of these plague periods should be considered a possibility.

Francis Meres' *Paladis Tamia: Wit's Treasury Being the Second Part of Wits Commonwealth* was printed in 1598 the same year as *Loues Labour's lost* Quarto and is important to the dating of many of Shakespeare's works. Meres, a Cambridge graduate, mentions twelve plays

for comedy *Getleme of Verona, Errors, Loues labours Lost, Loue Labours Wonne, Midsummers night dreame, Merchant of Venice*, for tragedy *Richard the 2, Richard the 3, Henry the 4, King Iohn, Titus Andronicus*, and *Romeo and Iuliet*

this establishes the creation of these plays to before 1598.

Meres observed:-

so the sweete wittie soule of Ouid liues in mellifluous & hony tongued Shakespeare, witnes his Venus and Adonis, his Lucrece, his sugred sonnets among his priuate friends, &c.

Of course, as well as telling us that Ovid was Shakespeare's poetic Latin influence, this helps us narrow down the time-scale, and it would appear that pre-1598, the sonnets were not intended for publication but to be circulated *among his private friends, &c.*

Who were those friends and what about the &c? Might some of the later sonnets have been written in 1603 or 1608, or indeed, outside of the plague years entirely? Yes, of course they could, but were they? I can't with any certainty say one way or the other? Does Meres' sequential linking of the three anthologies: *Venvs, Lucrece* and the *Sonnets* indeed indicate a closely related time to the process of composition? I think it does.

There are a number of sonnets that indicate potential dates but these are all speculative and therefore open to interpretation. If the first seventeen sonnets, were written in time for Lord Southampton's seventeenth birthday this gives a completion date of 6th October 1590. I think there may be something of an interregnum between the completion of Sonnet 17 and the sequence of Sonnets beginning with Sonnet 18 *SHall I compare thee to a Summers day?*

A period long enough for Shakespeare and Southampton to get to know one another personally for the intimacy revealed by the writing to have developed, not only in the Sonnets, but also in the dedications of *Venvs* and *Lucrece*. The time of year providing the inspiration for the opening line, which would mean the summer of 1591 a break of some eight months or might the break be even longer, twenty months, suggesting June 1592? I think that this may be the case.

The sonnets which give dating indicators are mainly cryptic so there are aways alternative theories, one of the first to point us to a historic event is Sonnet 25.

Great Princes fauorites their faire leaues spread
But as the Marigold at the suns eye,
And in them-selues their pride lies buried,
For at a frowne they in their glory die.
The painfull warrier famosed for worth,
After a thousand victories once foild,
Is from the booke of honour rased quite,
And all the rest forgot for which he toild:

(25.5-12)

Sir Walter Raleigh had a catastrophic fall from favour with the Queen after she refused permission for him to sail against the Spanish fleet in 1591 and after her discovery that he had, without her permission, secretly married one of her *ladies-in-waiting*, the pregnant Elizabeth Throckmorton. The couple were imprisoned for some months in the Tower of London from June 1592.

There is no necessity for Raleigh's demise to have been written about immediately but if it were it would make the month of June 1592, a productive one for the poet with the writing of six sonnets.

Sonnet 53, Line 5:

Describe Adonis, and the counterfet Is poorely immitated after you

suggests a time contemporaneous with the writing of *Venvs and Adonis*, shortly before April 1593, when it was published.

TO me faire friend, you neuer can be old,
For as you were when first your eye I eyde,
Such seemes your beautie still: Three Winters colde,

Haue from the forrests shooke three summers pride,
Three beautious springs to yellow Autumne turn'd,
In processe of the seasons haue I seene,
Three Aprill perfumes in three hot Iunes burn'd,
Since first I saw you fresh, which yet are greene.
(104.1-8)

I believe the three years of seasons referred to means exactly what it says, literally three years, since the poet was first introduced to Southampton at his seventeenth birthday party October 1590. Three winters, Aprils, springs and autumns suggests a date of second half of 1593. Others, notably Katherine Duncan-Jones, have given instances of 'poetic' time scales by other Elizabethan and later poets that are not a literal three years.

If the time scale of the end of the sonnet writing is after the death of Elizabeth 1, as many believe, then a poetic *three years* is the only way the late dating stacks up. The poetic *three years* which according to the proponents could in reality be nine, twelve, or more years is suggested in order to give credence to their *Lovely Boy* candidate, William Herbert, the W.H.of Thorpe's dedication.

I am much more inclined to believe that the three years time scale is a literal one and from the completion of Sonnet 17 to Sonnet 104 was some three years.

NOt mine owne feares, nor the prophetick soule,
Of the wide world, dreaming on things to come,
Can yet the lease of my true loue controule,
Supposde as forfeit to a confin'd doome.
The mortall Moone hath her eclipse indur'de,
And the sad Augurs mock their owne presage,
Incertenties now crowne them-selues assur'de,
And peace proclaimes Oliues of endlesse age,
Now with the drops of this most balmie time,
My loue looks fresh, and death to me subscribes,
Since spight of him Ill liue in this poore rime,
While he insults oer dull and speachlesse tribes.
   And thou in this shalt finde thy monument,
   When tyrants crests and tombs of brasse are spent
   (107.1-14)

Sidney Lee was the first to suggest that Sonnet 107 was written in 1603, and refers to the death of Elizabeth 1 and the release of Southampton from prison on the accession of James. The *mortal moon* of the sonnet is undoubtably the Queen. One of her recognised poetic names was Cynthia (the moon) and her death is more than once described as an *eclipse*. Lee's dating suggestion has been adopted by many scholars.

I have to say that it is dating this particular sonnet which gives me the most trouble because I see very clearly the reasons for dating Sonnet 107 to 1603/4 .

Peter Jensen lays out his argument:-

If you focus on one word "endured" and worry about it in isolation, you create a crux. Others have done that with this word, and they are full of doubt about what Shakespeare meant. But a Sonnet is a 14 line little world, and the little globe environment of Sonnet 107 dates it at the death of Queen Elizabeth in 1603, the regime changer to the new King, peace with Spain, and the release of Southampton from the Tower.

Line 1 "Mine own fears" QEI has no heir = her death will lead to civil war / everyone else is worried too "Prophetic soul" quote from Hamlet (1601) the play after the Essex rebellion trial and execution

Lines 2--4 everyone worried/ my true love in the Tower "confined doom"

Line 5 "mortal moon" Elizabeth I is mortal and she has been eclipsed by death. That is what she "endured."

Lines 6-7 all the sad predictions of what her death would cause are replaced with a new King "crown ... assured"

Lines 8 and 9 "Peace / olives" King James I makes peace with Spain an "endless age" this "balmy time"

Lines 10--12 "My love looks fresh" Henry is released from the Tower. We have defeated death, and I and you will live forever in these lines with people who can read, not the illiterates.

Couplet This poem is your monument compared to all the crests and tombs of tyrants (Elizabeth and Cecil over Essex and Henry:) Tomb for Elizabeth

The poem proves its date, 1603, with all its content.

This is a pretty difficult argument to overturn, but if it is true that Sonnet 107 was written in 1603 and that Marlowe was the rival poet who died in 1593 and his death referred to in Sonnet 86 then that gives an unlikely time-scale of ten years to write only twenty sonnets. Of course, that just may be the case.

A.L.Rowse gives the historian's argument for dating Sonnet 107 to 1594:-

This sonnet rewards analysis, though all commentators have found its difficulties insurmountable. To the historian they are not; their solution affords confirmatory evidence for the dating of the Sonnets. The convergence of the two historical events referred to in ll. 5-8 pinpoints the dating and makes it certain. To take ll. 7-8 first: these refer to the the end of the long religious wars in France with the submission of Paris to Henri lV in March 1594 and the achievement of peace. In ll 5-6 all Elizabethan scholars of any judgement recognise that 'the mortal moon' refers to Queen

Elizabeth. She has come through an eclipse, a threat to her: as I indeed she had this winter for 1593-4 with the Lopez conspiracy. Dr Lopez, her personal physician was found to be in touch with Spain with the idea of poisoning her, and he was executed in June 1594. These events made a great impression on Shakespeare's mind as on other people's. The first contributed something to Love's Labour's lost with the theme of Navarre's oath-breaking; the second to the Merchant of Venice with its portrait of Shylock. We are then in the 1594.

The amount of nonsense written about this famous sonnet, in the absence of precise dating, is ludicrous. Nor is there the slightest reason, let alone a compelling one, for removing it from its place in the sequence; it is in its proper place

17 Esalas van Hulsen: engraving Lopez conspiring to poison the Queen

I prefer to take the view that line five refers to the public perception that the allegation of an attempt to poison the Queen by Rodrigo Lopez was a genuine attempt on her life. A dark shadow that had threatened to kill the Queen that had been unsuccessful, she had *endured*. Am I certain that this is correct? No I'm not

Lopez, was probably innocent, even though he was involved in some foolhardy Spanish intrigue. Lopez was a Portuguese Jew banished from his home- and for secretly practising his faith.

A member of the Manasseh Tribe, who at one stage had lived in the Venetian Ghetto, where Jewish doctors were forbidden to treat Christian patients. When in London he had, like the Bassanos openly converted to Christianity, rising sufficiently high in English society to be granted a coat-of-arms.

The Earl of Essex had Lopez arrested on January 1, 1594, tried and convicted a month later, and finally on June 7 hanged, drawn and quartered after the Queen's long reluctance to agree to sign the death warrant. This dating gives us a much less difficult sonnet writing chronology - twenty one sonnets in the numbered sequence - from Sonnet 86 with its reference to the death of Marlowe in May 1593 to the arrest of Lopez eight months later and his execution six months after that.

It was the Lopez affair, which saw Marlowe's *Jew of Malta,* with Barabas, its Jewish stereotype villain, revived to great public acclaim that in turn prompted Shakespeare to write *The Merchant of Venice,* with its two Jewish *conversos,* Antonio and Bassanio.

It is an interesting common perception that because the character of Shylock is so powerful a stage presence that it is assumed that it is he who is the *Merchant,* when of course it is Antonio who is really the *Merchant of Venice.*

My view is that Shakespeare's affair with Emilia, albeit after her fling with Southampton, was still emotionally and physically active at this time.

ACcuse me thus, that I haue scanted all,
  Wherein I should your great deserts repay,
  Forgot vpon your dearest loue to call,
  Whereto al bonds do tie me day by day,
  That I haue frequent binne with vnknown mindes,
  And giuen to time your owne deare purchas'd right,
  That I haue hoysted saile to al the windes
  Which should transport me farthest from your sight.
  Booke both my wilfulnesse and errors downe,
  And on iust proofe surmise, accumilate,
  Bring me within the leuel of your frowne,
  But shoote not at me in your wakened hate:
    Since my appeale saies I did striue to prooue
    The constancy and virtue of your loue.
  (117.1-14)

Taken literally this sonnet seems to show that Shakespeare has travelled abroad *been with unknown minds* and languages, has neglected his duty to his patron, has travelled extensively by sea and now returned home - lines 5-8.

Roger Prior has suggested that Shakespeare visited Italy with three Bassano brothers, cousins of Emilia's in the autumn of 1593 returning before Christmas.

The Merchant of Venice and *Romeo and Juliet* set in Verona date from 1594.

YF my deare loue were but the childe of state,
It might for fortunes basterd be vnfathered,
As subiect to times loue, or to times hate,
Weeds among weeds, or flowers with flowers gatherd.
No it was buylded far from accident,
It suffers not in smilinge pomp, nor falls
Vnder the blow of thralled discontent,
Whereto th'inuiting time our fashion calls:
It feares not policy, that Hereticke,
Which workes on leases of short numbred howers,
But all alone stands hugely pollitick,
That it nor growes with heat nor drownes with showres.
  To this I witnes call the foles of time,
  Which die for goodnes, who have liu'd for crime.

(124.1-14)

Southampton as a former ward of Bughley, was effectively a child of state. The 1593 legislation Act, 35 Eliz. Cap.11 was passed because of worries about fresh threats of invasion from Spain and Popish plots. It mentions

wicked and seditious persons who, terming themselves Catholics and being indeed spies and intelligencers not only for her Majesty's foreign enemies but also for rebellious and traitorous subjects born within her Highness's dominions, and hiding their most detestable and devilish purposes under a false pretext of religion and conscience...

At the dissolution of the 1593 Parliament Queen Elizabeth scolded the Commons for *irreverence* shown towards privy councillors, and cautioned members against discussing politics outside the House, saying that she

would not have her people feared with reporte of great danger, but rather encoraged to boldenesse against the enemyes of this state

The campaign against Jesuit conspirators after the passing of the Act resulted in more executions than at any other time in Elizabeth's reign.

In 1594, Ferdinando Stanley, Fifth Earl of Derby died in suspicious circumstancestwo weeks after an encounter with a witch-like woman on 1st April, April Fool's Day. Although witchcraft was rumoured to be the cause of Derby's death, a Catholic poisoner is more likely to blame.

The main suspect, Richard Hesketh, a religious refugee had been recruited by Jesuits in Prague to visit Derby and suggest that his ancestry entitled him to became a contender for the throne. Derby rejected the idea out of hand and very swiftly informed the authoities about the plot.

Burghley whose spies had learned of the intrigue in Rome would have known about the approach to Stanley and if he hadn't revealed Hesketh's plot, he would be put under suspicion as a fellow conspirator. Hesketh was arrcstcd and executed.

He is said to have told Derby at their meeting, that if he didn't agree to the plan he would find himself dead soon afterwards, the poisoner was very likely one of Ferdinando's servants. This episode points us the meaning of the final lines *the* [April] *fools of time, Which die for goodness, who have lived for crime*

18 Anon: Ferdinando Stanley

Some commentators have rejected the 1594 dating because they feel that the clampdown on Jesuits wasn't significant enough and have argued instead, that this sonnet refers to the Gun-powder plot of 1605. 1605 wasn't a plague year and again if we consider a 1605 dating the conflict of numbering again arises with dating from Sonnet 86 shortly after Christopher Marlowe's suspicious death.

This would give a time span of twelve years for the writing of thirty six sonnets, and if Sonnet 107 dates from the death of the Queen the death in 1603 November 1605 only seventeen sonnets in two years. I think if Shakespeare had an overall structure for the sonnets planned that he would of necessity work much quicker than the fifteen year period - 1590-1605 - suggested by many academics.

There are further reasons for believing that sonnets 107 and 117 creation dates belong to 1593 and 1594 and not 1603 and 1605. Southampton's thirtieth birthday was only months after the Queen's death, he can hardly a *lovely boy* (126.1) having achieved the maturity that for an Elizabethan that was regarded as middle-aged. His image captured by John de Critz in the Tower of London portrait doesn't depict a *lovely boy* either.

If Sonnet 107 was written after the death of the Queen, then all of the *Fair Youth* sonnets after it would have to have been written to Southampton after his marriage, five years before. Many of the sonnets after 107 continue to display endearing and affectionate terms as before

my loue ......sweet boy (108.5)

such cherubines as your sweet selfe resemble? (114.6)

Now I loue you best (115.10)

Loue is not loue (116.2) etc.

What was Southampton's wife, Elizabeth, to make of these sonnets delivered by messenger, or by Shakespeare himself?

I can find nothing in the sonnets that could be said to refer to the birth of Southampton's daughter, Penelope, nor to his marriage to Elizabeth Vernon. Most significantly if, as has been suggested, the dating of Sonnet 117 is after the Gun-powder plot of November 1605, Southampton's wife had borne her husband their first son, James eight months before.

Since the first seventeen sonnets are written with the express intention of persuading the young Southampton to marry and produce an heir, it would surely be unthinkable for the poet not to have made some celebratory comment to mark the success of his early argument? There is nothing in these later sonnets to suggest Southampton has married and had children.

The official version of Marlowe's death, was that it was because of an argument about the bill at an inn in Deptford on 30 May 1593. Shakespeare refers to this event in *As you Like it*

When a mans verses cannot be vnderstood, nor a mans good wit seconded with the forward childe, understanding: it strikes a man more dead then a great reckoning in a little roome: (3.2.1573)

VVAs it the proud full saile of his great verse,
Bound for the prize of (all to precious) you,
That did my ripe thoughts in my braine inhearce,
Making their tombe the wombe wherein they grew?
Was it his spirit, by spirits taught to write,
Aboue a mortall pitch, that struck me dead?
No, neither he, nor his compiers by night
Giuing him ayde, my verse astonished.
He, nor that affable familiar ghost
Which nightly gulls him with intelligence,
As victors of my silence cannot boast,
I was not sick of any feare from thence,
  But when your countinance fild vp his line,
  Then lackt I matter, that infeebled mine.
  (86,1-14)

Lines 9 and 10 of this sonnet echo Marlowe's personal interest in necromancy - echoes of Forman's Latin note about Emilia's invocation of spirits - transported to the stage in his 1589-92 play, *Doctor Faustus*.

The play traces the last twenty four years of Faustus' life after he has made a pact with the Satan. Faustus, a renowned German scholar, is frustrated by the limits of traditional forms of knowledge and enlists the services of his friends, Valdes and Cornelius, to instruct him in the black arts.

He begins by summoning up Mephistophilis, a devil. Despite Mephistophilis's warnings about the horrors of hell, Faustus tells the devil to return to his master, Lucifer, with an offer that Faustus will surrender his soul in exchange for twenty-four years of service from Mephistophilis. There is little doubt that Shakespeare admired Marlowe's writing - *a worthier pen* - and the death of the *Rival Poet* left the way clear for Shakespeare to monopolise Southampton's generosity.

19 Anon: thought to be Christopher Marlowe

When Marlowe died, he left unfinished a poem *Hero and Leander,* not dissimilar in genre to *Venvs and Adonis* which Shakespeare was working on at the same time. If Marlowe had lived to complete *Hero* might he have dedicated it to Southampton?

Venvs and Adonis was printed in April 1593 and *The Rupe of Lucrece* printed just over a year later, in May 1594, both dedicated to Southampton are also a good indication that 1592-4 theatre closure period gave Shakespeare the time to write pure poetry.

These important long poems were both published by Richard Field, a fellow Stratfordian, whose home was close to Shakespeare's, so they would have been acquainted from childhood. The notion of writing without the hope of payment would have been unthinkable for impoverished Elizabethan poets and so Shakespeare wrote his sonnets in the pursuit of income.

It is unlikely that the poet Richard Barnfield was in such acute need of money since he was brought up by an aunt in the Manor House. the most imposing property in the village of Edgmond, Shropshire. Although the following sonnet has been long attributed to Barnfield, an associate of Derby. I would suggest that the author was strongly influenced by his reading of Shakespeare's sonnets and therefore we should add Sonnet Vlll from *The Passionate Pilgrime* for our consideration as another sonnet written about a musical lady, perhaps Emilia:-

IF Musicke and sweet Poetrie agree,
As they must needs (the sister and the brother)
Then must the loue be great twixt thee and me,
Because thou lou'st the one, and I the other,
Dowland to thee is deere, whose heauenly tuch
Vpon the Lute, dooth rauish human sense;
Spenser to me, whose deepe Conceit is such,
As, passing all conceit, needs no defence.
Thou lou st to heare the sweet melodious sound,
That Phœbus Lute (the Queene of Musicke) makes;
And I in deep Delight am chiefly drownd
When as himself to singing he betakes.
   One God is God of both (as Poets faine)
   One Knight loues Both, and both in thee remaine.

I detect an element of triangular bawdy in the final two lines, although South-ampton couldn't be described as a Knight. Perhaps another anonymous notch on Emilia's gun?

As well as a poet, the *Dark Lady* was an active musician, a keyboard player (see Sonnet 128) a lutenist and singer - the three musical disciplines went together.

Robert Greene's Groatsworth quotes Lamilia's (Emilia's?) alluring musical technique:-

No soner come they within ken, but Mistris Lamilia like a cunning angler made readye her change of baytes that shee might effect Lucanios bane: and to begin she discouered from her window her beauteous enticing face, and taking a lute in her hand that shee might the rather allure, shee sung this sonnet with a delicious voyce

Shakespeare borrows the angling metaphor:-

Why of eyes falsehood hast thou forged hookes, Whereto the iudgment of my heart is tide? (137.7-8)

The lute is mentioned in no less than eleven Shakespeare plays. His interest in the subject of the lute combined with poetry is shown in *The Two Gentlemen of Verona*

For Orpheus Lute, was strung with Poets sinewews (4.1.1491)

and the lute is referred to in Sonnet 8 (8.9-10)

Marke how one string sweet husband to an other, Strikes each in each by mutuall ordering

It seems to me that *If music and sweet poetry agree*, whether by Shakespeare or Barnfield, must have been written shortly after Sonnets 127 and 128.

Leo Daugherty, Professor of literature and linguistics at Evergreen State College and the University of Virginia argues that the effeminate Ganymede of Barnfield's *The Affectionate Shepheard Concerning the Complaint of Ganymede* was meant to represent, William Stanley, younger brother of Ferdinando who inherited the title Earl of Derby on his brother's death.

He also offers evidence that Barnfield's published poems from 1594, including over 20 homoerotic love sonnets, were in dialogue with some of Shakespeare's own homoerotic sonnets to his *Fair Youth*. He suggests that Barnfield was the *Rival Poet* and that Stanley was the beloved male pastoral addressee of both poets.

Professor Daugherty's theory is an interesting one but is diametrically opposed to mine. However his research reveals a strong link between the sonnet writing subjects of Barnfield and Shakespeare.

Many scholars tyhat I admire are convinced that the sonnets were written and revised over a time scale of twenty three years with Sonnet 145 written in 1582, 107 completed after the death of Elizabeth 1 in March 1603 and Sonnet 117 after the Gun-powder plot of November 1605.

In the autumn of 2020 the pre-eminent Shakespeare scholars, Paul Edmondson and Stanley Wells published their intriguing book *All the Sonnets of Shakespeare*, which included not only the 154 sonnets from the 1609 edition but also all the sonnets from the plays printed in their perceived chronological order.

Since it is only the 1609 sonnets which concern me here, it is fascinating to see how randomly the numbering of the sonnets have been placed by Edmondson and Wells. The earliest pre-1582 Nos. 152 and 154, 1582 No. 145, 1590-95 127-144 and 146-152, 1594-95 61-77 and 87-103, 1595-97 1-60, 1598-1600 78-86. 1600-1604 104-126.

Although I'm pleased that all of the *Dark Lady* sonnets loosely accord with my time scale, if their conclusions are correct this rules out Marlowe being the *Rival Poet* and effectively precludes Southampton from being the *Young Friend*.

Despite reading their book with great interest I was not persuaded to change my mind. I believe that all 154 sonnets were written between 1590 and 1594 and that there are in reality four sonnet sequences; 1) Sonnets 1-17, the so called procreation sonnets completed before October 1590

2) Sonnets 18-77 and 87-126 the *Fair Friend* sonnets begun in June 1592 finished after April 1594)

3) Sonnets 78-86 the *Rival Poet* sonnets begun before May 1593 and

4) Sonnets 127-154 the Dark Lady sonnets, with sequences 2, 3 and 4 overlapping in the dates of writing between June 1592 to a date after April 1594.

7. The Elusive Mr Shakespeare

This Figure, that thou here seest put,
It was for gentle Shakespeare cut;
Wherein the Graver had a strife
with Nature, to out-doo the life:
O, could he but have drawn his wit
As well in brasse, as he hath hit
His face; the Print would then surpasse
All that was ever writ in brasse.
But, since he cannot, Reader, looke
Not on his Picture, but his Booke.

Ben Jonson (First Folio Preface)

The Shakespeare authorship question has been abbreviated to the acronym SAQ. These initials represent the large and growing body of people who don't think that the *man from Stratford* wrote anything much at all. Four and a half thousand individuals have signed the *Declaration of Reasonable Doubt* over the Identity of William Shakespeare first published in 2007. This includes the signatures of one hundred notable individuals.

An authorship question hangs over the famous etching of Shakespeare by the Dutchman Martin Droeshout which appeared on the frontispiece of the First Folio printed in 1623. There were two Martin Droeshouts, father and son, as well as another relative who specialised in engraving and academics cannot agree which of them worked on the etching. Since it was done posthumously the assumption is that an existing painting was used as a template.

The poor modelling and the clumsy proportions between the head and the body have led many critics to see the image as a poor representation of the poet. Sidney Lee wrote that

The face is long and the forehead high; the one ear which is visible is shapeless; the top of the head is bald, but the hair falls in abundance over the ears

Samuel Schoenbaum was equally dismissive

a huge head, placed against a starched ruff, surmounts an absurdly small tunic with oversized shoulder-wings ... Light comes from several directions simultaneously: it falls on the bulbous protuberance of forehead – that "horrible hydrocephalous development", as it has   been called – creates an odd crescent under the right eye and (in the second state) illuminates the edge of the hair on the right side.

John Hudson has suggested that the engraving was an intentionally "satirical" portrait, tipping the wink to the *cognoscenti* that the image wasn't the person who wrote the plays.

From a technical perspective some of the art criticism is valid, but needless to say, none of these commentators ever set eyes on the living Shakespeare. Ben Jonson, without any perceivable hint of satire and who knew Shakespeare well, thought that the engraver has *hit his face*. Perhaps the bulbous protuberance of forehead of Schoenbaum's critique housed a larger than average sized brain.

Confusion over Shakespeare portraiture exists at the highest of level of scholarship. The *Explore Shakespeare* page of the Shakespeare Birthplace Trust website has this image purporting to be of Shakespeare. The same image has been used on the cover page of the University of Alexandria's edition of *The Merchant of Venice*.

20 Droeshout engraving: Shakespeare

21 Shakespeare?: Shakespeare Birthplace Trust

The Bodleian Library owns a portrait of what looks like the same sitter.

Painted on the front of it are the words *D.D. Tho. Overbury Arinr. de Barton in Com. Warw.* Thomas Overbury was another poet born in Warwickshire.

22 Sir Thomas Overbury

Another well known and genuine image of Shakespeare is the memorial bust in Holy Trinity Church, Stratford by another Dutch artist, Gheerart Janssen, whose name is sometimes anglicised to Gerard Johnson. This image of Shakespeare, which was restored in 1748/49, meets with little universal approval either. Dover Wilson said he looked like a *self-satisfied pork butcher.*

There are connections between Janssen, Shakespeare and Southampton. The Janssen's workshop in London was in close proximity to *The Globe.* The Janssens sculptors had worked for the Southampton family at Titchfield erecting a monument to the 1st Earl in which Southampton, appears as a young man kneeling in prayer attired in armour. Janssen and Markus Gheeraerts, portrait painter of Hunsdon and his grand-daughter knew one another.

Having a portrait painted is a lengthy business, with the sitter forced to remain immobile, unable to read even, conversations between artist and sitter invariable ensue. The Low Countries circle of painters and sculptors employed by the better off London playwrights and actors and their aristocratic patrons would have known some detail of the lives of its subjects.

Sir William Dugdale's 1634 sketch of the original monument to Shakespeare erected before 1623, depicted Shakespeare retaining a sack of grain on his lap, no sign of a quill pen.

This is an engraving made by Wenzel Hollar, it closely resembles Dugdale's original sketch.

23 Gheerart Janssen; Shakespeare bust

24 Shakespeare bust sketched by Dugdale

This detail is questioned, because some think that Dugdale was an unreliable artist and may have made the sketch from memory.

Looking at Dugdales's original book, *The Antiquities of Warwickshire illustrated: from records, leiger-books, manuscripts, charters, evidences, tombes, and armes: beautified with maps, prospects, and portraictures,* to give it its full title, it's clear that Dugdale was pretty thorough in accurately recording every detail of the churches he visited.

The text he quotes is precisely what remains inscribed on the Shakespeare memorial and tomb today. I think he would have been equally precise in his drawing. Dugdale who was later appointed *Norroy King of Arms,* was a Warwickshire man himself and so was especially careful with Shakespeare's memorial; he drew what he saw.

Underneath the memorial bust of Shakespearc in Holy Trinity there are engraved a Latin epitaph and a poem in English.

IVDICIO PYLIVM, GENIO SOCRATEM, ARTE MARONEM, TERRA TEGIT, POPV-
LVS MÆRET, OLYMPVS HABET

The phrase translates as *A Pylian in judgement, a Socrates in genius, a Maro in art*, comparing Shakespeare to Nestor the wise King of Pylus, to the Greek philosopher Socrates, and to the Roman poet Virgil (whose last name, or *cognomen* was Maro). The second phrase reads *The earth buries him, the people mourn him, Olympus possesses him* referring to Mount Olympus, the home of the Greek gods.

The English poem reads:

STAY PASSENGER, WHY GOEST THOV BY SO FAST,
READ IF THOV CANST, WHOM ENVIOVS DEATH HATH PLAST
WITH IN THIS MONVMENT SHAKSPEARE: WITH WHOME,

QVICK NATVRE DIDE: WHOSE NAME, DOTH DECK Y^S TOMBE,

FAR MORE, THEN COST: SIEH ALL, Y^T HE HATH WRITT,
LEAVES LIVING ART, BVT PAGE, TO SERVE HIS WITT.

A painting of the monument that completed before its 1748/49 restoration by John Hall, a limner - confusingly also bearing the same name as Shakespeare's son-in-law - was commissioned to restore the bust. The faded painting shows Shakespeare holding a small quill pen - rather than the more ostentatious pen in the current version - and no piece of paper under the left hand, so this painting seems to pre-date the restored monument and may well have been used by John Hall as a working plan. If Dugdale's sketch was accurate, changes to the statue must have been made between the errection of the bust, and the 1748-49 restoration. Perhaps it was subject to vandalism by the puritans whose iconoclastic mentality damaged so much ecclesiastic heritage.

In 1748/49, long after Shakespeare's legitimate descendants had died out, the Reverend Joseph Greene, Headmaster of Stratford Grammar School, rganised the first known performance of a Shakespeare play in Stratford to fund the restoration of the monument. It was Greene who proposed that the painter, John Hall, undertake the restoration work, stipulating

that the monument shall become as like as possible to what it was when first erected

Upon completion Greene said it had been *repaired and re-beautified*

He continued

I can assure you that the bust and cushion before it (on which as on a desk this our poet seems preparing to write) is one entire limestone . . .

adding that

.. really, except changing the substance of the Architraves from alabaster to Marble; nothing has been chang'd, nothing alter'd, except supplying with original material, (sav'd for that purpose,) whatsoever was by accident broken off; reviving the Old Colouring, and renewing the Gilding that was lost

It can be seen from the engraving of Dugdale's sketch that quite a lot has been changed from the original, so it seems that both Greene and Hall were under the misapprehension that the bust that Hall began work on in 1748 was the original.

The existing statue shows that Shakespeare's arms and hands were repositioned, the of sack of grain was removed and replaced with a tasseled cushion, a quill pen was put in the right hand and a piece of paper anchored by the left hand over the cushion. Not an obvious choice for a writing desk, but perhaps there was no alternative without replacing the *entire limestone* to which Greene referred. If the memorial had remained as it originally was - as noted by Dugdale - observers would undoubtably ask why no visual sign of the playwright's main profession, writing?

25 John Hall: Shakespeare bust

This alteration to the poet's monument made by people who never met him might be viewed as an allegory of how time can change our perception of people and events. Particularly so, when it is someone whose writing is so sublime, that his life and assumed behaviour has been made to fit his reputation as a writer to the point that he has effectively been canonised.

There are, of course the written inscriptions, but neither of them clearly reflecting Shakespeare's towering literary stature universally recognised at the time of his death. SIEH ALL, Y^T HE HATH WRITT is the only reference to his writing, The doggerel inscription on Shakespeare's grave gives a clue that Shakespeare might have dabbled in poetry.

Good friend for Jesus sake forbeare, To dig the dust enclosed here. Blessed be the man that spares these stones, And cursed be he that moves my bones my bones would lead us to conclude that Shakespeare wrote this verse, hardly his greatest poetry, unlikely to encourage the prospective reader to explore much further. The Stratford memorial certainly gives the SAQ believers a helpful start.

Perhaps in Stratford, Shakespeare's reputation as a dealer in commodities, a land owner and a usurer was greater than his reputation as a writer. None the less, the omission of any reference to him as the highly successful playwright and poet he had become, is very surprising. The statue was commissioned by Shakespeare's son-in-law, Dr John Hall, husband of Susanna.

Why would Dr Hall choose to steer away public thoughts on Shakespeare's unique writing talent towards his much less prolific, more prosaic, commercial activities? Janssens would know precisely how highly thought of Shakespeare's plays were in London and at the seats of learning, surely he would have discussed this when the memorial was commissioned.

Although Dr Hall was a puritan whose adherents disapproved of the theatre, might his decision to play down Shakespeare's literary life be motivated by concern for the sensitivities of his wife and her family. if visitors to, and the congregation of Holy Trinity, were to be tempted to explore the scurrilous revelations in the sonnets printed a decade earlier?

On one of my visits to Japan as a member of the Philharmonia Orchestra in the 1980s I had a business meeting with Joe Barnett the British Council Representative in Tokyo. During our conversation I asked him what was Britain's biggest export to Japan, expecting "Scotch Whisky" or "Land Rovers" to be the reply. His answer came as a total surprise, "Shakespeare" he said.

When there is so much controversy over Shakespeare's authorship of the plays and poems how could that most discerning of nations, the Japanese be taken in by deception? In Shakespeare's lifetime no one really questioned his authorship. Now in relatively recent years there have been eminent individuals who have proclaimed their belief that the man from Stratford didn't write the Shakespeare canon. The skeptics include Freud, Whitman, Helen Keller, Orson Welles, Charlie Chaplin and Shakespearean actors Sir John Gielgud, Sir Derek Jacobi and Sir Mark Rylance as well as the celebrated early inaugurator of the skepticism, the unfortunately named J. Thomas Looney.

However, there is an equally impressive list of individuals who think that there is no need to doubt that Shakespeare is indeed Shakespeare. These include such luminaries as Milton, Pope, Dr Johnson, Garrick and from our own time Sir Kenneth Branagh, Sir Ian McKellen and Dame Judi Dench. No one doubts that Bach composed the *St. Matthew* and *St. John Passions*, or Mozart collaborated with Lorenzo da Ponte on three great operas, or Milton wrote *Paradise Lost*, so why the question over Shakespeare's authorship in particular?

It is perhaps his rural family background, lack of university education, the many different spellings of his name including his own inconsistency in that regard, his unique ability to write from a female perspective, but not ensure his daughters were literate, the author's extensive knowledge of courtly life, the classics and Italy, paucity of documentation, no books mentioned in his will, questionable aspects of Shakespeare's personal life and business conduct, forgery and endless well-meaning speculation - in which every Shakespeare biographer is forced to indulge - which has over time given prominence to the authorship question.

It is probably the convention of Elizabethan authors to collaborate on plays that has given the authorship doubters most credence. This aspect of the Elizabethan theatre has been thoroughly explored by Gary Taylor and John Jowett, editors of the 2016 publication, the *New Oxford Shakespeare*. They have concluded that George Peele was involved with the writing of *Titus Andronicus*, Thomas Kyd with *Hamlet* and *King Lear*, Christopher Marlowe in *Henry Vl* Parts 1, 2, and 3, Thomas Nashe in *Henry Vl* Part 1, John Fletcher in *Henry Vlll*, *The Two Noble Kinsmen* and the lost play *Cardenio*, George Wilkins in *Pericles, Prince of Tyre* and that Thomas Middleton revised *Macbeth, Measure for Measure, Timon of Athens* and *Alls Well that Ends Well*.

There is no doubt that Shakespeare had plays and poems published with his name on them both in his lifetime - the two early poems dedicated to Southampton, (1593 and 1594) *The Merchant of Venice* (1600) *Henry lV* (1599) - and shortly after his death contemporary writers acknowledged his authorship in print. We have already mentioned Thomas Morley, the composer, Francis Meres, the Shakespeare fan and Robert Greene, *Shakespeare's a plagiarist* accuser, each from their individual perspective, have no doubt that Shakespeare wrote the plays that existed at the time of their comments.

Another later mention of Shakespeare as a playwright but still whilst he was alive was from the performance of play by an anonymous author at St John's College, Cambridge, *The Return from Parnassus*, from 1601-02. In it a much-quoted passage has Burbage, as a character, declare

Why here's our fellow Shakespeare puts them all down; aye and Ben Jonson, too. O that Ben Jonson is a pestilent fellow; he brought up Horace, giving the poets a pill, but our fellow Shakespeare hath given him a purge that made him bewray his credit

The mention of Shakespeare and Jonson together prompts us to consider what his younger friend, colleague and fellow playwright had to say about William. We can assume that Jonson met Shakespeare by the summer of 1589, at the very latest, when he was writing *Everyman in his Humour,* in which Shakespeare took a lead role.

In the prose introduction on the frontispiece of the First Folio, Ben Jonson not only acknowledges the greatness of his writing but also aspects of his character. He calls Shakespeare *gentle* comments that he had *wit* - this attribute coincides with the last word *witt* on the memorial epitaph - and that the contents of the first folio were *his Booke*, no one else's.

Shakespeare and Ben Jonson weren't the only outstanding writers who didn't graduate from a university. In more recent times Brendan Behan, Dylan Thomas, Charles Dickins, H.G.Wells and Mark Twain are examples of self-educated, but successful authors, who possess an individual voice. Although he won a scholarship to Westminster School, Jonson's early living was earned in his step-father's trade, brick-laying. He also served briefly as a soldier in the Netherlands.

His famous eulogy on Shakespeare is worth quoting in full, not just because it is one of the biggest obstacles that those who doubt Shakespeare's authorship have to overcome, but also because it tells us much about Shakespeare, the man, in the words of someone who knew him as a friend and colleague.

It begins by addressing the dead poet personally:-

To the memory of my beloued,
The AVTHOR
Mr. WILLIAM SHAKESPEARE:
AND
what he hath left vs.
TO draw no envy (Shakespeare) *on thy name,*
Am I thus ample to thy Book and Fame:
While I confesse thy writings to be such
As neither Man, *nor* Muse *can praise too much*
'Tis true, and all mens suffrage. But these wayes
were not the paths I meant unto thy praise:
For seeliest Ignorance on these may light,
Which, when it sounds at best, but echo's right;
Or blinde Affection, which doth ne'er advance
The truth, but gropes, and urgeth all by chance;
Or crafty Malice, might pretend this praise,
And thinke to ruin, where it seem'd to raise.
These are, as some infamous Bawd or whore,
Should praise a matron. What could hurt her more?
But thou art proofe against them, and indeed
Above th' ill fortune of them, or the need.
I therefore will begin. Soul of the age!
The applause! delight! the wonder of our stage!
My Shakespeare, *rise; I will not lodge thee by*
Chaucer, *or* Spenser, *or bid* Beaumont *lye*
A little further, to make thee a roome:
Thou art a Moniment, without a tombe,

And art alive still while thy Booke doth liue,
And we have wits to read and praise to giue.
That I not mix thee so, my braine excuses;
I meane with great, but disproportion'd Muses:
For, if I thought my iudgment were of yeeres,
I should commit thee surely with thy peeres,
And tell how farre thou didst our Lily *out-shine,*
Or sporting Kyd, *or* Marlowe's *mighty line.*
And though thou hadst small Latine, *and less* Greeke,
From thence to honour thee, I would not seeke
For names; but call forth thund'ring Æschylus,
Euripides, *and* Sophocles *to us,*
Paccuuius, Accius, *him of* Cordoua *dead,*
To life again, to heare thy Buskin tread,
And shake a Stage; Or, when thy sockes were on,
Leaue thee alone, for the comparison
Of all, that insolent Greece, *or haughtie* Rome
Sent forth, or since did from their ashes come,
Triúmph, *my* Britaine, *thou hast one to showe,*
To whom all scenes of Europe *homage owe.*
He was not of an age, but for all time!
And all the Muses *still were in their prime,*
When like Apollo *he came forth to warme*
Our ears, or like a Mercury *to charme!*
Nature her self was proud of his designes,
And ioy'd to weare the dressing of his lines!
which were so richly spun, and woven so fit,
As, since, she will vouchsafe no other Wit.
The merry Greek, *tart* Aristophanes,
Neat Terence, *witty* Plautus, *now not please;*
But antiquated, and deserted lye
As they were not of Natures family.
Yet must I not give Nature all: thy Art,
My gentle Shakespeare, *must enioy a part.*
For though the Poets *matter, Nature be,*
His Art doth giue the fashion. And, that he
Who casts to write a liuing line, must sweat,
(such as thine are) and strike the second heat
Upon the Muses *anuil: turn the same*
(And himself with it) that he thinkes to frame;
Or for the laurell, he may gaine a scorne,
For a good Poet's *made, as well as borne,*
And such wert thou. Look how the fathers face
Liues in his issue, even so, the race
Of Shakespeares *minde and manners brightly shines*

In his well-turned, and true-filed lines:
In each of which, he seemes to shake a Lance,
*   As brandish't at the eyes of Ignorance.*
Sweet Swan of Auon! *what a sight it were*
*   To see thee in our waters yet appeare,*
And make those flights upon the bankes of Thames,
*   That so did take* Eliza *and our* James!
But stay, I see thee in the Hemisphere
*   Advanc'd, and made a constellation there!*
Shine forth, thou starre of Poets, *and with rage,*
*   Or influence, chide, or cheere the drooping stage;*
Which, since thy flight from hence, hath mourn'd like night,
*   And despaires day, but for thy volumes light.*

BEN: IONSON.

The epithet *Soul of the age* and favourable critical comparisons *tell how far thou didst our Lyly outshine, Or sporting Kyd, or Marlowe's mighty line*

Would Jonson, known for his outspoken candour, really have written those words, if he knew that the works of Shakespeare were written by someone else? *Mr Shakespeare* is highly significant too, the title Mr acknowledges Shakespeare's right to be called a gentleman.

Little doubt, despite his lack of formal education - *small Latin and less Greek* - that Ben Jonson couldn't have thought more highly of Stratford's Shakespeare - the *Sweet Swan of Avon* - and his work *writings to be such as neither man nor muse can praise too much.*

The poet and translator Leonard Digges (1588–1635) wrote two verses in praise of Shakespeare, a eulogy in the first folio and a paean in the second edition of the Sonnets of 1640. Digges was personally connected to Shakespeare via his step-father, Thomas Russell, who is named as one of the overseers of Shakespeare's will, so he should have been informed on the authenticity of Shakespeare, the author.

Digges singles out particularly well-loved characters who *ravish'd* Shakespeare's audiences in the early C17. In particular, Beatrice and Benedick, the witty couple from *Much adoe about Nothing* are seen as fail-safe crowd-pleasers.

Shakespeare was a member of the *Lord Chamberlain's Men* and later the *King's Men* and might well have been an actor in the *Queen's Men* and *Derby's Men* as well. His acting career alone seems to have lasted for more than twenty years. John Heminges and Henry Condell his fellow actors collected the prompt books of the plays and edited them for publication as the First Folio. They can have had no doubt that Shakespeare, their friend and colleague, was the author of the plays they so lovingly prepared for print, declaring in their 1623 dedication to the Earls of Pembroke and Montgomery their motivation

onely to keepe the memory of so worthy a Friend, & Fellow alive, as was our
SHAKESPEARE

This rests the case for the defence.

8. *Did Shakespeare authorise publication of the Sonnets?*

more peroured eye, To swere against the truth so foule a lie

(Sonnet 152.13-14)

In Sonnet 152, most modern editors change "eye" to "I", this ambiguity is a small example of the many textual problems that wouldn't have occured if Shakespeare had overseen publication of the Sonnets.

I think Shakespeare would have been off of his head to authorise Thomas Thorpe to reveal such self-incriminating evidence of infidelity to the public at large and his family in particular. He knew it was cause colossol and unnecessary trouble.

The general view is that Anne Shakespeare never learned to read or write - although Germaine Greer questions this assumption - nor do we really know how literate, if at all, his two daughters were. However, by 1609 the year Thorpe published Shakespeare's Sonnets, Susanna, Shakespeare's eldest daughter, had been married for two years to Dr John Hall, a physician, who was highly literate and would have taken an interest in his father-in-law's latest anthology.

In 1610 a year after the publication of his Sonnets, Shakespeare returned home to Stratford-upon-Avon, he had by this time become a wealthy man having bought New Place in May 1597, renovating the neglected building to become one of the most desirable residences in the town. He was also the owner of extensive tracts of local agricultural land

Shakespeare's adultery with his mistress, and his deep troubled love for her, is candidly recorded in the Sonnets. The last two sonnets (153/4) indicated that he had contracted a sexually transmitted disease, which at the time of their writing, he remained infected.

I sick withal the helpe of bath desired. And thether hied, a sad distemperd guest. But found no cure (153.11-13)

In Elizabethan times the mineral waters of the City of Bath were long thought to be a cure for venereal disease, this belief was endorsed in William Turner's 1562 book of herbs and cures.

Not only did Shakespeare have his wife's views to consider, by 1609, Southampton had for five years been released from captivity in the Tower of London and despite the odd argument, was otherwise in favour at the court of

James I. Southampton had a wife and four children and would be unusual if he wanted earlier sexual exploits, of whatever gender orientation, to be made so openly public. Emilia was the wife of one of Southampton's serving officers, so whatever Alphonso's attitude to his wife's infidelities, revelation of the affair would have been scandalous.

Southampton was in a strong position to ban publication, but only if he had known it was about to occur. Once publication had happened, Southampton had the power to suppress both sales and further editions. It may be significant that of all the Shakespeare works published in his lifetime, it is only the Sonnets that didn't get a second edition. That had to wait until 1640 over twenty years after the poet's death and even then, John Benso, the editor reversed the pronouns from male to female, in order to dilute the impression of homoeroticism. He also published the poems in a very different numerical order.

Why, particularly when he didn't need the money, would Shakespeare wreck his retirement with a public confession of his questionable conduct and the prospect of an outraged patron and an incandescent wife?

Shakespeare's reputation was such that someone in Stratford would have obtained a copy of the 1609 Sonnets. In a small country town rumours of the salacious contents would soon spread, some meddling busy body would have informed Anne. How did he explain himself to her - *a literary flight-of-fancy*? - an explanation unlikely to convince. The authorship questioners have an even more difficult task, would Anne believe *I didn't write them, Darling, it was the Earl of Oxford*!

In *Shakespeare an Ungentle Life* Katherine Duncan-Jones concludes that the last years of the poet's life in Stratford were unhappy, with his will providing evidence that the relationship between himself and close members of his family was strained.

It is likely that a copy of Thorpe's publication had arrived in Stratford, some of its juicier contents relayed to Anne creating irresolvable domestic turbulence. Perhaps he was permanently banished by Anne to the *second best bed*, famously mentioned, as an afterthought, in his will as the only nominated inheritance to his wife.

There is also the possibility of reading a continuing homosexual relationship with his *lovely boy* into the earlier sequences. Although by the time James I had ascended the throne the extreme official disapproval view on homosexual relations had eased somewhat, the punishment for breaking the law in the 1533 Buggery Act was still death. This law that wasn't repealed until 1861. How times have changed

At least one bisexual aristocrat, Mervyn Tuchet, 2nd Earl of Castlehaven, was found guilty of sodomy and executed in 1631, only two decades after the publication of the Sonnets. Whether or not Shakespeare had indulged in sex with his *lovely boy*, public revelation of the sequence would give embarrassing evidence of illegality for any potential enemies of either of them.

If these emotive, but nonetheless forceful reasons, aren't good enough by themselves, then there is the publication itself to consider. If it was the poet who initiated publication, he would had to have either acquired the originals, probably kept in the Southampton household, or kept duplicate copies of the originals. Shakespeare had never used Thorpe as a publisher before, why should he start now when Field's publications of *Venvs* and *Lucrece* had been so commercially successful?

About half of the collections of poems, plays, instrumental and vocal music at the time of Shakespeare, contained a flowery and flattering dedication page, usually to an influential member of the aristocracy, with the express intention of seeking or continuing patronage. Shakespeare's own dedication pages to Lord Southampton in both *Venvs and Adonis* and the *Rape of Lucrece* are good examples of flattery and over modest self-denigration of the author that was typical.

TO.THE.ONLIE.BEGETTER.OF.
THESE.INSVING.SONNETS.
Mr.W.H. ALL.HAPPINESSE.
AND.THAT.ETERNITIE.
PROMISED.

BY.

OVR.EVER-LIVING.POET.

WISHETH.

THE.WELL-WISHING.
ADVENTVRER.IN.
SETTING.
FORTH.

T. T.

26 SHAKE-SPEARS Sonnets dedication page

The cryptic dedication page of Shakespeare's Sonnets stands in stark contrast to the dedications of a decade and a half earlier. The sparse text, less than thirty words, but with the poet, three protagonists. Two are only identified by their initials Mr W.H. and T.T. these few words have been the subject of endless speculation.

Shakespeare's plays were published in his life time, these are known as the 'Quarto' edition. These were printed by Thomas Creede, William Standby, James Roberts, Valentine Simmes, Simon Stafford, William Jaggard and George Eld, for a variety of publishers; Andrew Wise, Thomas Heyes, Thomas Pavier, John Smethwicke and R. Bonian but Thorpe doesn't feature.

Although we shouldn't read too much into this, since it is unlikely that Shakespeare had any influence over who published the plays because, unlike *Venvs* and *Lucrece* the play scripts were probably sold to the publishers by the acting companies who retained ownership. There was no copyright law giving intellectual property rights to the author at this time.

Richard Field, publisher of *Venvs* and *Lucrece,* was the poet's old Stratford-born childhood acquaintance. He was three years older than Shakespeare and his reputation as a publisher had burgeoned by 1609, so would have been an obvious choice if Shakespeare needed a publisher.

Field was the son of a tanner - the preservation properties of the occupation referred to in the graveyard scene in *Hamlet* - who lived in Bridge Street when John Shakespeare, a glove maker, lived in adjoining Henley Street. This shows an almost inevitable business connection between the fathers and makes an early acquaintance between the two boys, William and Richard, certain.

In 1601 Field published another Shakespeare poem, *The Phoenix and the Turtle* a contribution to an anthology by other contemporary poets. If there had been a falling-out between Field and the poet, then surely Shakespeare would have made certain that the quality of the publication was at least equal to that of Field's 1593, 1594 and 1601 publications? The Sonnets are far less well presented and very poorly proof-read, Sonnet 116 numbered 119, when the compositor slipped in the six die upside down, for example.

There were three draft applications to the College of Arms for a grant of arms by William on behalf of his father John Shakespeare. Charles Hamilton, the American handwriting expert, has convincingly argued that all three extant drafts for the application including the sketch of the coat-of-arms itself are in Shakespeare's own hand. By the time that the Sonnets were printed, the *Garter King of Arms*, the disreputable Sir William Dethick, had made the Shakespeares armigerous more than a decade before.

This gave William the right to display his coat-of-arms and call himself a *gentleman*. He certainly titled himself *gentleman* when he wrote (according to Charles Hamilton) and signed his will in March 1616. I have little doubt that if Shakespeare had authorised and assisted in Thorpe's publication, he would have insisted on *gentleman* appearing after his name.

As you can see the dedication to Mr W.H. isn't Shakespeare's dedication. The initials at the bottom of the page - T. T. - are those of the publisher, Thomas Thorpe and so Mr W.H. is Thorpe's dedicatee. Some have argued over the meaning of the word *begetter*. Does it mean *procurer*, *inspirer*, or even, as has been suggested, *autho*r?

I believe that it was the procurer of the autograph text that Thorpe was referring to. *Venvs and Adonis* and *The Rape of Lucrece*, unlike *The Passionate Pilgrime*, were authorised for publication by Shakespeare, who probably oversaw the printing, including the proof-reading and formatting.

There have been numerous suggestions about who owned the initials, William Hunnis, an obscure early poet, William Hall, a stationer's assistant, William Haughton, the dramatist, William Hathaway, Shakespeare's brother-in-law and even William Himself and an ingenious suggestion, a reversal of the initials would give us Henry Writhiosley.

In 2015 Geoffrey Caveney, an American academic published a research paper that proposed that Mr W.H. was William Holme, a contemporary of Thomas Thorpe, who bequeathed the autograph sonnets to Thorpe in 1607. Cavenney believes that the unusual layout of the dedication page is in imitation of a Roman funerary monument. This theory has found favour with many, but I remain unconvinced. I still stick with Rowse's suggestion that the *onlie begetter* of the poems, Mr W.H. was Sir William Hervey, widower of the Countess of Southampton who inherited the *Sonnets* and *A Lover's Complaint* on the death of his wife, Southampton's mother.

Thomas Thorpe, the publisher was, like Gustav Mahler, the son of an innkeeper, he was born in Barnet around 1570. At the age of fourteen he began a nine year apprenticeship to Richard Watkins who ran a London shop at Little Conduit in Cheapside. Watkins was a respected member of the Stationers' Company and had even been its Warden and Master.

On the 4th February 1594 Thorpe too became a member of the Stationers' Company which gave him the right to publish, but not to print. We don't know the whereabouts of Thorpe during the six years between the time he gained his freedom from his apprenticeship until 1600 when he published his first book, Marlowe's *The First Book of Lucan,* a translation from Latin concerning the relationship between Caesar and Pompey.

The work had originally been entered in the Stationers' Register by publisher John Wolfe in September 1593. At some later date its copyright was assigned to Edward Blount who passed in on to his young friend, Thorpe. Blount had become friendly with the publisher and remained so throughout Thorpe's career.

Blount had also been a good friend of Christopher Marlowe and of Marlowe's patron, Thomas Walsingham, cousin of Francis. We know this because when Blount published Marlowe's *Hero and Leander* posthumously in 1598 he dedicated the book to Walsingham and in the dedication referred to Marlowe as *the man that hath been dear to us*

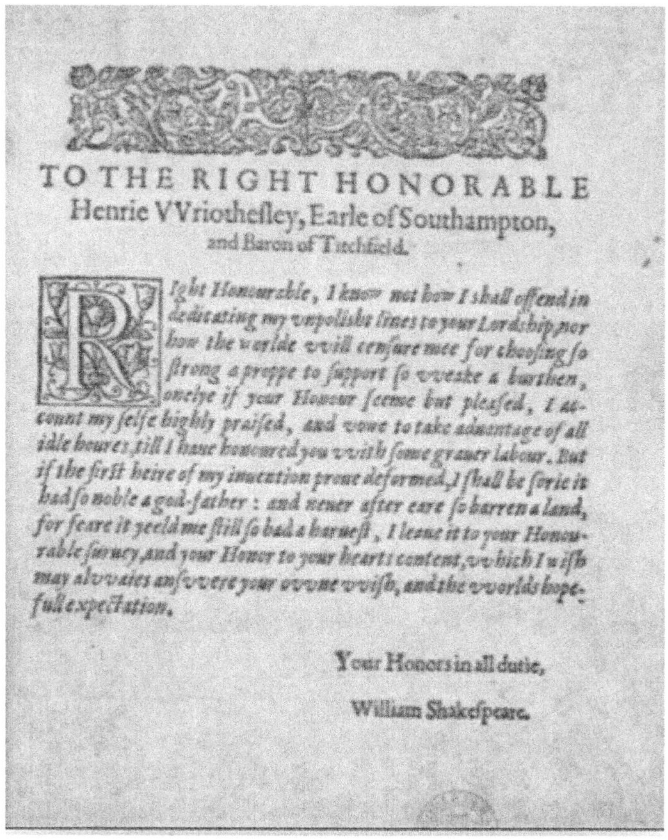

27 Venvs and Adonis dedication page

Both *Venvs and Adonis* and *Lucrece* are attractively produced, the dedication pages in particular, are presented with great care, ornately decorated capital and frieze, careful spacing and typesetting, very professionally done. Compare these with Thomas Thorpe's inferior quality page layout and typesetting.

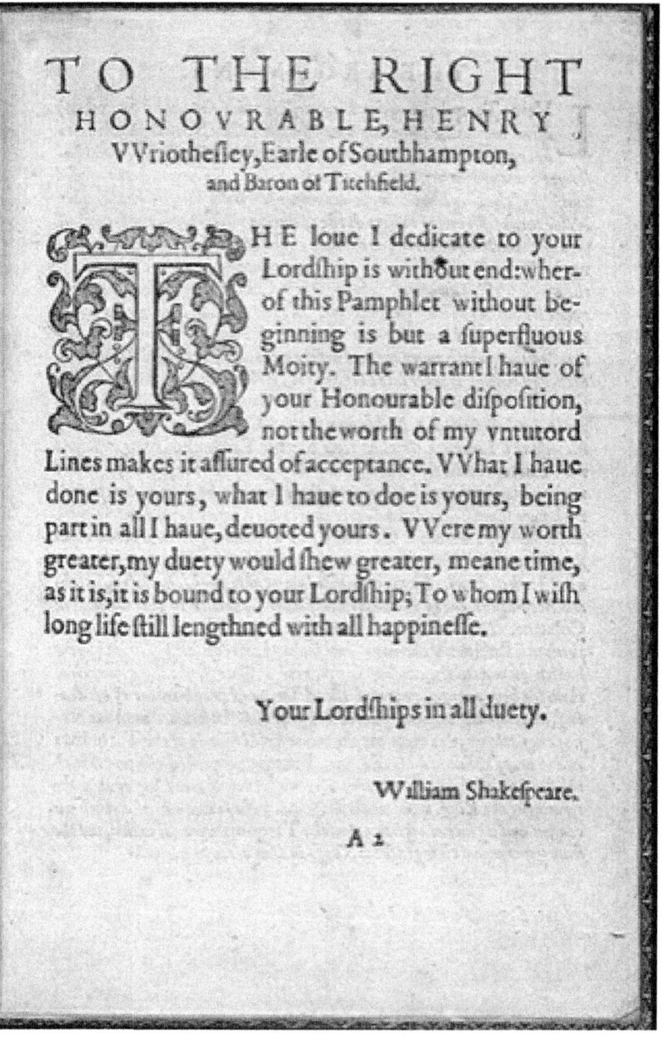

28 Rape of Lucrece dedication page

Both Field publications are unequivocally dedicated to Henry Wriothesley, Earl of Southampton, a nomination made and openly acknowledged by the poet, since his name William Shakespeare appears signature-like conventionally type-set at the bottom of the page, in contrast to Thorpe's bleak SHAKE-SPEARES.

The wording of the dedications in *Venvs* and *Lucrece* is precise, clear and to the point. We can detect an increase in familiarity and confidence publicly declared between the April 1593 dedication of *Venvs and Adonis - Right Honourable, I know not how I shall offend in dedicating my vnpolisht lines to your Lordship* - and the May 1594 dedication of *Lucrece - The loue I dedicate to your*

Lordship is without end. In the first dedication Shakespeare tentatively hopes that he won't *offend* his dedicatee, in the second his concern has been happily answered, *The warrant I haue of your Honourable disposition*

There is no question that this young lord, only nineteen, when the poet first publicly sought his patronage had responded well to the first publication. If Southampton is the *Fair Friend* of the Sonnets then there is clearly a much more formal public relationship in the printed word, as opposed to the familiar and affectionate sonnets circulating *among his private friends, &c*

In 1709 Nicholas Rowe, Shakespeare's first biographer, quoted the foremost actor and theatre manager, Thomas Betterton over Southampton's patronage of the poet. Betterton, although born nineteen years after Shakespeare's death had been apprenticed to John Holden, Sir William Davenant's publisher. Davenant was a playwright, poet, theatre manager and Poet Laureat who claimed to be Shakespeare's Godson and rumoured to be his biological son too:-

According to Rowe, Betterton said:-

There is one instance so singular in the magnificence of this patron of Shakespeare that, if I had not been assured that the story was handed down by Sir William D'Avenant, who was probably very well acquainted
with his affairs, I should not have ventured to have inserted; that my Lord South-ampton at one time gave him a thousand pounds to enable him to go through with a purchase which he heard he had a mind to

Is it possible that the phrase in the dedication to Southampton in the *Rape of Lucrece The warrant I have of your Honourable disposition,* infers that Lord Southampton has already paid the poet something for his earlier *Venvs and Adonis* dedication, or *Venvs* and Sonnets combined, as well as *A Midsommer Nights Dreame* for the dowager Countesses' marriage to Thomas Heanage in May 1594.

Even if Sir William Davenant's basic information is correct, it seems unlikely that Southampton would have parted with £1,000, a huge sum of money, particularly when in the winter of 1594 Southampton was required to pay a fine of £5,000 to Lord Burghley for rejecting the hand of his grand-daughter. Southampton's mother, though remained a wealthy woman, so it is possible that she may have paid Shakespeare.

In respect of the accuracy of the anecdote it is worth considering Davenant's claims and family background. He was probably born in the winter of 1606 in Oxford, the son of John Davenant, Mayor of Oxford and his wife Jane, proprietors of the Crown Tavern, an overnight stop on the journey from Stratford to London. William was baptised on 3 March, he claimed his godfather was Shakespeare who would have been in Oxford for the christening. John Aubrey relates a story heard from the lips of the poet and satirist, Samuel Butler.

Mr. William Shakespeare was wont to go into Warwickshire once a year, and did commonly in his journey lie at this house [the Crown] in Oxon, where he was exceedingly respected. Now Sir William [Davenant] would sometimes, when he was pleasant over a glass of wine with his most intimate friends--e.g. Sam Butler, author of Hudibras, etc., say, that it seemed to him that he writ with the very spirit that did Shakespeare, and seemed contented enough to be thought his son. He would tell them the story as above, in which way his mother had a very light report, whereby she was called a Whore.

In 1592 John Shakspeare, the poet's father was in enough financial difficulty to avoid his legal obligation to attend church, *for feare of processe of debt*. It is, of course possible that Southampton parted with enough money to bring relief to the poet's father.

Within the next few years there were other much greater expenses for Shakespeare, the first application for arms in 1595 would have required substantial fees for the herald, in spite of the poet's personally hand written applications.

Then, two years later, there was the purchase of New Place for more than £110 - even though it was likely to have been in poor repair - both of which may have been assisted with financial help from Southampton.

These two very public dedications demonstrate how Shakespeare expected his work to be presented when he was personally involved with its publication. Had he given consent to the publication of the Sonnets in 1609, he would surely have included a clearly worded dedication page, even if to a new prospective patron, certainly not the cryptic lines that were printed by Thomas Thorpe.

If Shakespeare didn't authorise publication, how then did Thomas Thorpe get hold of all 154 Sonnets and *A Lover's Complaint* too, and why was he confident enough to publish without the go-ahead from the author? The clue to answering these questions lies in Thorpe's dedication. Mr W. H. is Thorpe's nominee, not Shakespeare's, and therefore is unlikely to be the young man of the first 126 sonnets, although many researchers have worked on the assumption that Mr W.H. is the aristocratic *Fair Friend*.

So who is Mr W. H? William Hervey distinguished himself fighting against the Armada, where he was said to have personally executed the aristocrat Hugo de Montcada, Captain of the *San Lorenzo*, with an arquebus shot to the head. He became the third husband of Southampton's mother.

Since Meres had told us that the sonnets were written for reading *among his private friends* it is most likely that it was Lord Southampton who originally held the autograph sonnets including the poem *A Louer's Complaint*.

Why though would Hervey risk upsetting his step son by publishing personal revelations in the Sonnets? Hervey and Southampton had already fallen out with one another because of Southampton's strong opposition to his mother's remarriage to a younger man with a reputation as a ruthless adventurer. Hervey's date of birth is thought to be 1565, some four years younger than Mary. He continued to live for another thirty five years after Southampton's mother's death at the age of fifty five.

In 1598 Southampton married Elizabeth Vernon, the daughter of John Vernon of Hodnet by his wife Elizabeth Devereux. Elizabeth was in an advanced state of pregnancy and the marriage showed Southampton's acceptance of paternity.

By this time, Southampton, as the dedicatee of many writers - Barnes, Markham, Florio and Nashe as well as Shakespeare - had amassed a large collection of poems, both printed and in the authors' respective holographs. It is unlikely that he would want his new wife reading the highly personal secrets in Shakespeare's sonnets to say nothing of Nashe's shamelessly pornographic *The Choise of Valentines or the Merie Ballad of Nash his Dildo*.

Did he keep them at Southampton House, his London residence, or was Southampton's mother - as putative commissioner of the first seventeen procreation Sonnets - a possible choice to take care of her son's controversial papers until they could be safely returned?

Only three years after his marriage, in 1601, Lord Southampton, as a participant in the Essex plot was, like Essex, sentenced to death. This punishment was later commuted to life imprisonment in the Tower of London.

The autograph versions of the sonnets probably remained stored with the rest of Southampton's documents in his mother's house.

Southampton only served less than three years of this sentence because he was immediately pardoned by King James on his ascent to the English throne, shortly after the death of Elizabeth 1.

My assumption is that his mother retained the original hand-written sonnets after his release from captivity. Once the Southampton's mother died in 1607, her estate passed to her widower, Sir William Hervey. It took him a year or two to sort out the papers, but by the time he did Shakespeare had become a best selling author. Hervey realised that in the sonnets he had inherited something of value to a prospective publisher, as well as a method of revenge against his errant step son.

An author in Jacobean England, had no copyright over his own work, the owner of intellectual property at this time was who ever possessed the original manuscript, in this case Sir William Hervey. If Mr W. H. is Sir William Hervey, why didn't Thorpe print *Sir W. H*? The reason for this is that it was common for knights to be addressed as Mr, there are numerous cases of this Jacobean convention. The tradition exists still in modern day medicine where a surgeon, long qualified as a doctor, is referred to as Mr.

What about the rest of the dedication? A year after Lady Southampton's death, Hervey re-married a young woman, Cordell Annesley (Shakespeare appears to have borrowed her Christian name for the youngest of King Lear's daughters). In 1609 Thorpe is wishing Sir William *all happiness, and that eternity promised by our ever-living poet*, the meaning being that now he has a young wife, he can procreate as the *ever-living poet* had encouraged in the earlier sonnets.

The dowager Lady Southampton was forty six when her marriage to Sir William took place. The union was never blessed with children, one can only assume that by the time of their marriage Lady Southampton's child bearing years were over. On the other hand, the marriage between Sir William, later to be ennobled as the 1st Baron Hervey and Cordell was a fruitful one producing several children, Henry, John and William and daughters Helena and Dorothy who both died unmarried. A third daughter, Elizabeth married her cousin John Hervey of Ickworth.

As well as inheriting the sonnets, Hervey had also inherited considerable wealth from Lady Southampton. He remained a seafaring adventurer throughout his life. He was knighted after the capture of Cadiz in 1596. He was owner of the ship *Darling* docked at Portsmouth which he captained. In 1597 as Captain of the *Bonaventure*, along with Sir Walter Raleigh, he took part in Essex's ill-fated Islands Voyage, a mission whose purpose was to intercept the Spanish treasure fleet as it sailed from the Americas through the Azores. An abortive mission, its only success was the capture of *Fayal*.

In spite of the failure of the fleet, Queen Elisabeth I rewarded Hervey with a Keepership of St. Andrew's Castle in Hampshire, and subsequently, command of a Royal ship.

1609 was the year when the Second Charter to Virginia was released. This was a highly attractive investment to anyone with cash to spare and regarded as an adventure because the plan was to setup the first English colony in America. Hervey was busy with Virginia Company matters and the term *adventurer* was commonly used to mean an explorer of unknown regions. Might this then be the meaning behind *wisheth the well-wishing adventurer in setting fourth*?

9. A Louers Complaint – the Dark Lady's voice

Ere long espied a fickle maid full pale
Tearing of papers, breaking rings a twaine,
Storming her world with sorrows, wind and rain

(A Louers Complaint 5-8)

A *Louers Complaint* was printed as a postscript to the 1609 edition of the Sonnets. It is a female-voiced complaint and as such duplicates similar responses which were often added to sonnet sequences. Other examples include Samuel Daniel's *Complaint to Rosamund*, which follows *Delia* (1592), Thomas Lodge's *Complaint of Elstred*, which follows *Phillis* (1593), Michale Drayton's *Matilda the Faire*, after *Ideas Mirrour* (1594), and Richard Barnfield's *Cassandra*, following *The Affectionate Shepherd*.

A Louers Complaint relates to the section of the story retold simultaneously in Sonnets 34-42 and 133-139, the betrayal of Shakespeare by Southampton with Emilia and her other lovers. Who the real seducer was is thrown into doubt by the conflicting narrative. The voice of the *lover* in *A Louers Complaint* makes it clear she would like us to believe that it was the man that seduced her. Shakespeare, on the other hand, casts the female as the sexual predator

And when a woman woes, what womans sonne, Will sourely leave her till he haue preuuiled? (41.8-9)

As another example of editors potentially misleading readers, some modern editions change the *he* in the last phrase, to *she*.

The poem consists of forty-seven seven-line stanzas, a metre identical to that of Shakespeare's poem The Rape of Lucrece. This form is used by Emilia in two of her dedications in *Salve Devs* the first to *Princess Elizabeth*, James 1's daughter, and the second to *all vertuous Ladies*.

The four protagonists of the narrative are an observer, a fickle maid, a reverend man and the silken-tongued young seducer. As in the Sonnets the observer speaks in the first person, again it is the voice of William Shakespeare we hear. Emilia is the *fickle-maid*, Henry Carey, Lord Hunsdon, the *reverend man*, and Henry Writhiosley, Lord Southampton, the *young seducer*. Three of these identifications are consistent with the identifications in the Sonnets.

The poem begins with a description of a young woman weeping at the edge of a river, close to a hill from which resounds an echo. Distracted, she tears up papers (perhaps love letters or sonnets), breaks rings in two and generally bemoans her abandoned state. An elderly gentleman nearby approaches the woman and asks what troubles her. She immediately responds, revealing intimate details, telling him of a former lover who pursued, seduced, and finally abandoned her. She recounts in detail the attributes, appearance and persuasive speech that the young man uttered which seduced her. She concludes her sorrowful story by paradoxically conceding that she would succumb to the young man's deceptive charms again.

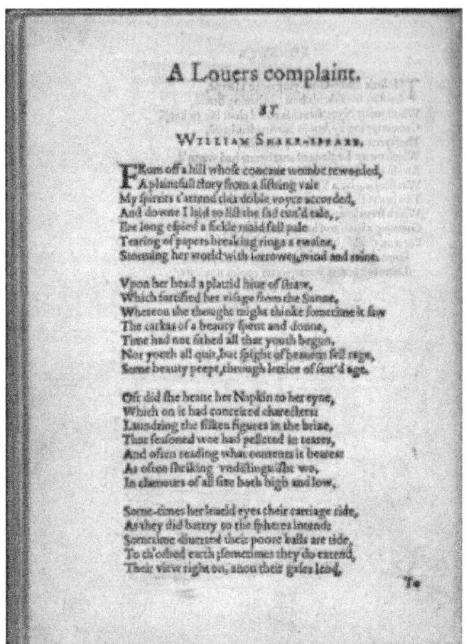

29 A Louers complaint title page

I would suggest that the venue is the Bisham Estate on the banks of the Thames near Maidenhead. Bisham Abbey was the home of Sir Edward Hoby and his mother the twice married Elisabeth Russell, Lady Russell, formerly Lady Hoby, neé Cooke. Emilia's country house poem, *The Description of Cooke-ham,* is published at the end of *Salve Devs*. Cookham is Bisham's neighbouring Thames-side village. There are some associations with *A Louers Complaint* and the *Speeches to the Queen,* a short masque commissioned by the recently widowed Lady Russell to welcome Elizabeth I to Bisham in August 1592.

I believe that it was Emilia who wrote the masque to greet and entertain the Queen, it contains a mixture of comedy, feminism, obsequiousness and flattery. The last three characteristics a consistent feature of *Salve Devs*. The full text is recorded in a later chapter.

A Louers Complaint shows that Shakespeare was aware of the *Speeches to the Queen* at Bisham and may even have acted one of the two male parts in the masque.

The phenomenon of an echo at the scene appears in three separate works - *A louers Complaint,* the *Speeches to the Queen* at Bisham and *Salve Devs* - making it a unifying factor,.

FRom off a hill whose concaue wombe reworded A plaintfull story from a sistring vale. My spirrits t'attend this doble voyce accorded (ALC.1-3)

None durst answere, or would vouchsafe, but passionate Ecchoe (Speeches to the Queen)

In Emilia's *Description of Cooke-ham* at the end of *Salve Devs* she refers to an echo, afeature of the steep opposing wooded hills on either side of the Thames.

Each brier, each bramble, when you went away, Caught fast your clothes, thinking to make you stay: Delightfull Eccho wonted to reply To our last words, did now for sorrow die (Cooke-ham 195-9)

A performance direction in the *Speeches to the Queen* notes:

At the bottome of the hill, entring into the house, Ceres with her Nymphes, in an harvest cart, meet her Majesty, having a crown of wheat-ears with a jewell:

A Louers Complaint mentions similar head gear

Vpon her head a plattid hiue of straw, Which fortified her visage from the Sun (ALC.8-9)

The woman playing Ceres, the goddess of agriculture, in *Speeches to the Queen* at Bisham was obliged to sing this song accompanying herself upon a lute

Swel Ceres now, for other Gods are schrinking,
    Pomona pineth,
    Fruitlesse her tree;
    Fair Phœbus shineth
    Only on mee.

Conceite doth make me smile whilst I am thinking,
    How every one doth read my story,
    How every bough on Ceres lowreth,
    Cause heaven's plenty on me powereth,
    And they in leaves doe onely glory,
    All other Gods of power hereven,
    Ceres only Queen of Heaven.

With robes and flowers let me be dressed,
    Cynthia than shineth
    Is not so cleare;
    Cynthia declineth
    When I appeere,
    Yet in this Ile shee raignes as blessed,
    And everyone at her doth wonder,
    And in my ears still fonde Fame whispers,
    Cynthia shalbe Ceres Mistres,
    But first my carre shall rive asunder.

Helpe, Phœbus, helpe; my fall is suddaine;
Cynthia, Cynthia, must be Sovereigne.

It isn't known who set the words of this song to music, perhaps Emilia herself, or maybe one of Emilia's composing cousins, Augustine, Ludovico or Jerome Bassano, or possibly John Dowland because Lady Russell was his patron.

After the song Ceres has the final word in a paean of homage and benign wishes for the Queen.

A *Louers Complaint* brings in another character

A reuerend man that graz'd his cattell ny
Sometime a blusterer, that the ruffle knew
Of Court of Cittie, and had let go by
The swiftest houres, observed as they flew,
Towards this afflicted fancy fastly drew:
And priuileg'd by age desires to know
In breefe the grounds and motiues of her wo. (ALC.57-63)

I believe this is a reference to Lord Hunsdon, Emilia's elderly paramour, from c.1588 until her forced marriage to Alfonso Lanier in October 1592 brought the publicly open affair to an end.

Since the love affair with Southampton was a year or more after Hunsdon, it is quite feasible that she should unburden herself to her former lover, who she may, by this time, come to regard as something of a father figure.

Hunsdon's daughter, Margaret was married to Sir Edward Hoby and so he was a frequent visitor to Bisham. Hunsdon, who by 1592 had retired from soldiering but remained active as *Lord Chamberlain* and shortly to become patron of his own acting company, the *Lord Chamberlain's Men*, was described by Sir Robert Naunton who used the same word as Shakespeare, *ruffle*, to describe Hunsdon:

As he lived in a ruffling time, so he loved sword and buckler men.

Hunsdon's life had often been at court but his longest period of active service had been in Berwick-upon-Tweed and at the time of the Spanish Armada he was put in charge of the Queen's personal bodyguard.

When *A Louers Complaint* was published, Hunsdon had been dead for twelve years, dying in 1596 at the age of seventy. But if, as I suspect, it was written in the summer of 1594, he would have been in his late sixties, in Elizabethan terms *privileged by age*

On to the young man, the Earl of Southampton.

His browny locks did hang in crooked curles (ALC 85)

Smal shew of man was yet vpon his chinne (ALC.92)

His qualities were beauteous as his forme (ALC.99)

The Cobbe and Hilliard portraits bears witness to the accuracy of these physical descriptions.

I think the following verse on the young man's skilled horsemanship refers to Southampton?

Wel could hee ride, and often men would say
That horse his mettell from his rider takes
Proud of subiection, noble by the swaie,
What rounds, what bounds, what course, what stop he makes
And controuersie hence a question takes,
Whether the horse by him became his deed,
Or he his mannad'g, by 'th wel doing Steed. (ALC 106-112)

In 1599, during the *Nine Years War* (1595–1603), Southampton accompanied Essex to Ireland, where he was made *General of the Horse*, but the Queen insisted that the appointment be cancelled. However Southampton remained on in what was described as personal attendance upon the Earl, rather than as an officer of the state.

To his credit, Southampton remained combative during the campaign and prevented a defeat at the hands of the Irish rebels when the cavalry drove off an attack at Arklow in County Wicklow.

In the two thousand lines of *Venvs and Adonis* there are ten occurrences of the word *horse*, four of *steed* and eight of *rose* showing that the poet consistently associated Southampton with his riding skills and that *the rose* was synonymous with his name.

That hee didde in the general bosome raigne
Of young, of old; and sexes both inchanted,
To dwel with him in thoughts, or to remaine
In personal duty, following where he haunted,
Consent's bewitcht, ere he desire haue granted,
And dialogu'd for him what he would say,
Askt their own wils and made their wills obey. (ALC.127-133)

The word *wills* has a treble meaning, the obvious one, a sexual one and a reference to the poet.

Southampton's effeminate looks are evidenced by his portraits and a document alleging homosexuality exists. Shortly after the Essex rebellion in February 1601, William Reynolds, a soldier who had served with Essex in Ireland in 1599, mentioned Southampton in a letter to Sir Robert Cecil. Naming some of the conspirators involved in the rebellion who had not yet been arrested,

Reynolds wrote:

I do mervell also what becam of pearse edmones, the earle of Essex man, borne in strand neare me, and which has had many rewards & preferments by the earle essex, his villany I have often complained of, he dweles in London, he was corporall generall of the horse in Ierland under the earle of Sowthamton, he eate & drank at his table and lay in his tente, the earle of Sowthamton gave him a horse, which edmones refused a 100 markes for him, the earle Sowthamton would cole and huge him in his armes and play wantonly with him

Katherine Duncan-Jones has suggested that Reynolds' letter hints that *rewards could be obtained from either or both of the two Earls in return for sexual favours*. On the other hand, she suggests that Reynolds may have been a paranoid schizophrenic, and that by his own statement he had written over 200 letters to the Queen, Privy Council, and members of the clergy wherein he had

complaynid of al the abewses and vilent oppresseones & sodometicall sines over flowing this land

The distinctiveness of Southampton's eyes were renowned.

But with the invndation of the eies: What rocky heart to water will not weare? (ALC.290-1)

O, that infected moysture of his eye (ALC.323)

Barnabe Barnes, in a sonnet extolling Southampton says:

Vouchsafe, right virtuous Lord! with gracious eyes, (Those heavenly lamps which give the Muses light) (Parthenophil and Parthenophe)

His qualities were beautious as his forme, For maiden tongu'd he was, and thereof free (ALC.100)

So on the tip of his subduing tongue (ALC.120)

Gervase Markham mentions the sweetness of his voice an *eares-inchanting man*. Southampton then is a very strong contender for the *young seducer* of *A Louers Complaint.*

The *fickle-maid*

Ere long espied a fickle maid full pale
Tearing of papers, breaking rings a twaine,
Storming her world with sorrowes, wind and raine. (ALC.5-7)

And often kist, and often gaue to teare,
Cried O false blood thou register of lies,
What vnapproved witnes doost thou beare!
Inke would haue seem'd more blacke and damned heare!'
This said in top of rage the lines she rents,

Big discontent, so breaking their contents. (ALC.51-6)

I sense Emilia's feminist temperament in these lines; the exclamation marks are Shakespeare's. In the Bisham *Speeches to the Queen* in dialogue over the stitches used in samplers, she writes

Men's tongues, wrought all with double stitch, but not one true.

In *Salve Devs* the lines most quoted by the feminist academics and writers are

evill disposed men, who forgetting they were borne of women, nourished of women, and that if it were not by the means of women, they would be quite extinguished out of the world, and a finall ende of them all, doe like Vipers deface the wombes wherein they were bred, onely to give way and utterance to their want of discretion and goodnesse (SD. to the Vertuous Reader 19-24)

30 Salve Devs title page

Undoubtable in writing her defamation in the Sonnets, no doubt Emilia thought Shakespeare lacked discretion and goodness.

As well as both being poets, I have often thought that Emilia and Beatrice from *Much adoe* share a similar mercurial Italianate temperament. When Hero is falsely denounced at the altar on her wedding day by Claudio, the bridegroom, her Sicilian cousin rails

Beatrice
uncovered slander, unmitigated rancour, - O God that I were a man! I would eat his heart in the market place (4.3.1925)

Of course I accept that Emilia doesn't possess a monopoly amongst the female sex to rant and rave, or to accuse men of deceiving, but the lines Shakespeare gives the fickle-maid in *A Louers Complaint* point us in her direction.

What about the suggestion that Shakespeare is parodying Emilia's writing style? Anaphora, the rhetorical device with the repetition of a word, in this case, at the beginning of a line is more common in speech than prose or poetry. Anaphora is used several times in *Salve Devs* but only once in *A Lover's Complaint* in the very last verse:-

O that infected moysture of his eye,
O that false fire which in his cheeke so glowd:
O that forc'd thunder from his heart did flye,
O that sad breath his spungie lungs bestowed,
O all that borrowed motion seeming owed,
Would yet againe betray the fore-betrayed,
And new peruert a reconciled maide. (ALC 324-330)

How blinde were they could not discerne the Light!
How dull! if not to vnderstand the truth,
How weake! if meekenesse overcame their might;
How stony hearted, if not mov'd to ruth:
How void of Pitie, and how full of Spight,
Gainst him that was the Lord of Light and Truth:
Here insolent Boldnesse checkt by Love and Grace. (Salve Devs .505-512)

Emilia wrote as she spoke and Shakespeare observed this. Anaphora is used six times in *Salve Devs* but only once in *A Louers Complaint*, in the very last verse, when after the reported speech of the *young seducer*, the *fickle-maid* speaks her own mind. Is this Shakespeare letting Emilia have something she was used to getting, the last word?

Even though she is distraught, there is the *fickle-maid's* personal confession of the most intimate kind to consider. One of Emilia's characteristics Forman notes is *she can hardly keep secret.*

Shakespeare's authorship of *A Louers Complaint* was first questioned in the early C19, when the English literary critic, William Hazlitt, expressed doubts about the quality of the writing, and therefore its authenticity. Later Sir Sidney Lee observed

If, as is possible, it be by Shakespeare, it must have been written in very early days

In 1917 the Scottish journalist and Liberal MP, John Robertson, suggested that the poem, and several plays, were written by George Chapman. More recently the English scholar, Sir Brian Vickers suggested that the poem was written by John Davies, an author of theological pamphlets. Edmond Malone called the poem *beautiful*, and suggested that Shakespeare may have been trying to emulate Edmund Spenser.

Even though critics have seen thematic parallels to situations in *All's Well That Ends Well* and *Measure for Measure* commentators remain uncomfortable with authenticating *A Louers Complaint* as Shakespeare's work when they regard it as inferior poetry.

What I would like to suggest is that not only was Shakespeare relating in Emilia's voice her *spun* version of her seduction, but that he was also parodying her poetic style of writing as I suggest he did in Sonnet 130, *My mistress' eyes are nothing like the sun* against her own *Of Gold all burnisht like the sun.*

10. Emilia and Hunsdon

What win I if I gaine the thing I seeke? A dreame, a breath, a froth of fleeting ioy

(*Rape of Lucrece* 211-2)

So mused Sextus Tarquinius standing at the doorway to Lucrece's bedroom, inflamed with lust at her beauty, before violently forcing himself upon her. The ignominy of the act provoking her suicide.

Like Tarquin, Henry Carey, Lord Hunsdon, was a soldier and commander of his country's army and a national hero. How exactly a sixty three year old man found himself in bed with a woman in her late teens, without coercion, is a matter of speculation. Emilia, though, unlike Lucrece, decided life must go on and continued the intimate relationship for more than three years and possibly even after her marriage.

Hunsdon was appointed as Governor of Berwick and Warden of the East Marches in 1568. Although Scotland was a foreign kingdom with its own institutions, Elizabeth could no more afford to let it come under the strong influence of a foreign power - France or Spain for example - than she could Ireland.

The six regions of the Scottish Marches were established as an attempt to control the Anglo-Scottish border by providing a buffer zone under a treaty signed by Henry III of England and Alexander III of Scotland in 1249.

From 1568 Hunsdon spent the best part of twenty years based in Berwick. Lady Hunsdon initially accompanied her husband to the North of England because in 1569 she wrote to Burghley addressed from Berwick complaining about domestic privations.

Early on Hunsdon had significant success in battle against Leonard Dacre's northern rebellion, killing or capturing hundreds of his soldiers. The State Papers contain copious correspondence from Hunsdon on Scottish affairs; raids into Scotland, disorder along the Border and the trial and execution of thieves.

In 1577 Hunsdon became a member of the Privy Council and attended meetings as much as his Berwick appointment would allow. In 1584 he became Captain of the Pensioners, the small and select bodyguard of the Queen, and finally appointed Lord Chamberlain in 1585.

1588 was the year of the Spanish armada and Walsingham's efficient spy network made the government aware that the large fleet being assembled in La Coruña posed a serious threat of invasion. The intelligence caused the Queen to relieve Hunsdon of his northern responsibilities and bring him south to be made commander of the Queen's bodyguard of 36,000 soldiers, taking responsibility for her personal safety at Tilbury Fort. After the Armada's defeat, Hunsdon, along with Sir Walter Raleigh, had become a national hero.

John Hudson suggests that Emilia joined Hunsdon in the north when she was thirteen, from 1582 until his permanent return to London, in 1585. *Salve Devs* makes reference to Emilia's early life with Susan Bertie but there is nothing in *Salve Devs* to suggest that three or four years of her teenage years were spent in the hostile environment of the far north of the country.

Hunsdon, like Forman, seems to have enjoyed a vigorous and varied sex life, fathering twelve legitimate children with his wife Anne, and at least one illegitimate one, conceived in Berwick, who took his patronymic, Valentine Carey was to become Dean of St Pauls and later Bishop of Exeter. It would appear that extra-marital affairs were commonplace for Hunsdon since Sir Robert Naunton, a spy for the Earl of Essex remarked

his custom of swearing and obscenity in speaking made him seem a worse Christian than he was, and a *better Knight of the Carpet than he should be*

Hudson assumes that the affair with Emilia began when she was just thirteen, Juliet's age, of course. I doubt that it started this early, because of evidence suggested by William Byrd's 1589 dedication to Lord Hunsdon, in *Songs of sundrie natures.* **This** collection has significant textual contributions by Emilia. In **his dedication Byrd recounts**

Having observed (Right Honorable) that since the publishing in print, of my last labors in Musicke, divers persons of great honor und worship, have more esteemed & delighted in the exercise of that Art, then before

Byrd's previous collection, *Psalmes, Sonets, & songs of sadnes and pietie* was published in 1588.

In the 1589 collection, David Mateer has identified Thomas Watson as the poet that supplied the text for many of the forty seven songs, but there are at least ten songs - a mixture of sacred and secular - in which the text was supplied by Emilia. I was first alerted to this by a number of clues showing similarities to the writing with *Salve Devs*, one of them, a translation of the Psalm *Domine ne*, possesses two of Emilia's hall-marks, feminism and anaphora. It uses the phrase

give teares, give grace, give penitence, unto my sinfull sex (SSN.III.2)

in Elizabethan times, only a woman would write the phrase *my sinful sex.*

In *Salve Devs* Emilia extolls the virtues of a number of biblical women including the apocryphal Susanna - whos is like Lucrece, a potential rape victim -

Susanna appears in both *Salve Devs* and the Byrd collection.

Byrd's thoughtful wording in the 1589 dedication shows that something has happened in Hunsdon's life that has recently increased his interest in things musical. He had acquired a profoundly musical mistress, this is the most likely reason why Hunsdon should become more interested in music.

No doubt Emilia beguiled the great man with songs by Dowland and Byrd, accompanying herself on the lute, and impressed him with her technical prowess on the keyboard with virtuoso pieces by Byrd, Bull and Tallis.

At the time of its 1589 publication Byrd had been excluded from the court musicians because of his Catholic belief and suspected sympathy with the ambitions of Catholic plotters. His exclusion from court meant his professional attendance at church ceased but his conscience wouldn't permit him to voluntarily attend a Protestant service, and so he was classified as a recusant.

In the five years that Byrd found himself excluded from court duties more Catholic plots were uncovered. Nonetheless Byrd had sufficient confidence to advertise himself as *one of the Gentlemen of the Queens Maiesties honorable Chappell* long before he returned to professional court duties.

To the right honorable my very good Lord, Sir Henry Carye, Baron of Hunfdon, knight of the moft noble order of the Garter, Lord Chamberlen to the Queenes moft excelent Maieftie, Lord Warden of the Eaft Marches towards Scotland, gouernor of Barwycke and the Caftle of Nerham, Captaine of the Gentlemen Pencioners, Iuftice in Oyer, ouer all her Maiefties Forrefts and Chafes, on this fide the Riuer of Trent, & one of her Maiefties moft honorable priuie councell. William Byrd wifheth increafe of honor, with all true felicitie.

Auing obferued (Right Honorable) that fince the publifhing in print, of my laft labors in Muficke, diuers perfons of great honor and worship, haue more efteemed & delighted in the exercife of that Art, then before. And being perfwaded, that the fame hath the rather encreafed, through their good acceptation of my former endeuors : it hath efpecially moued and encouraged me to take further paines to gratifie theyr curteous difpofitions therevnto, knowing that the varietie and choyfe of fongs, is both a prayfe of the Art, and a pleafure to the delighted therein. And finding no perfon to whome the dedication thereof fo fitly and properly belonged, as vnto your Lordship, by whome (through the honorable office which you exercife about her Maiefties perfon) both my felfe (for my place of feruice,) & all other her highneffe Muficions are to be commanded, and vnder your high aucthoritie to be protected. And for many fauors to me shewed, being moft deepely bound vnto your Honor, hauing not in me any other powre of feruifeable thanckfulneffe then in notes & tunes of Muficke. I moft humbly befeech your Lordship to take into your Honorable protection, thefe my poore trauells in that Art, accepting them as feruants redy to giue your L. delight, after you haue bene forewearied in affayres of great importance. Befeeching almightie God to giue you a long, healthie, and happie lyfe, with a bleffed end. I humbly take my leaue.

Your Lordfhips moft bounden,

William Byrd.

31 Songs of sundrie natures dedication page

There is little doubt that Hunsdon, who controlled the court musical appointments, was pivotal in having Byrd restored to his former life at court.

The composer Byrd, was just as careful in his choice of aristocrat to praise, as any Elizabethan poet and made sure that the contents of the publication contained items that were of interest to its dedicatee. Two songs - *From Citheron the warlike boy* and *Wounded I am* - were chosen to appeal to the soldier in Hunsdon. Another two - *The greedy hawk* and *Compel the Hawk to sit* - are personally appropriate because of Hunsdon's role as *Master of the Queen's Hawks*, a position he had held since 1560.

The full title of the collection is

Songs of sundrie natures, some of grauitie, and other of myrth, fit for all companies and voyces

which shows the choice of songs as an eclectic mix of Psalm settings in English, biblical subjects and secular madrigals, including love songs. Some of the latter I think designed to turn Hunsdon's thoughts to his new young lover, in particular *See those sweet eyes.*

There is connection between Byrd and Susan Bertie's brother, Peregrine, Baron Willoughby. In 1590 Willoughby returned home from assisting the Protestant Henri de Navarre, heir presumptive to the French throne, where he was victorious at the Battles of Arques and Ivry, but failed to take Paris after laying siege to the city. Byrd wrote a set of Variations on the popular jig from the play *Rowland and the Sexton* to celebrate Willoughby's safe return home.

The year in which Willoughby returned home was also the year in which Emilia inherited three or four London properties and £100 in cash under the conditions of her father's will. £100 was equivalent to some £18,000 in modern values. Not exactly an heiress, but not destitute either.

Byrd's dedication and the date of publication 1589 would appear to show that Emilia became Hunsdon's mistress at the age of eighteen or nineteen, a year, or so after the death of her mother in 1587. My feeling is that she returned to her family home supporting her mother, the solitary and ageing Margaret, either shortly after Susan Bertie's marriage, or after the trip to Elsinore.

As Lord Chamberlain, Hunsdon was responsible for the appointment and supervision of the Queen's musicians, since Emilia's uncles and cousins occupied so many of the places in the court music establishment, he would have been more than aware of a girl who bore the name Bassano. She will no doubt have become known to Hunsdon from an earlier age whilst she was at court accompanying Susan Bertie and the Duchess of Suffolk and it is likely that the errant *Knight of the Carpet* had an eye on her for his future attention.

If my assumption about the very public reference to Emilia in Byrd's dedication is correct, once Emilia did become Hunsdon's mistress she appears not to have been concealed from court or hidden away from public life. Forman says she was *maintained in great pride,* as befits the treasured mistress of a great statesman and close relative of the Queen. I wonder how the Queen viewed Hunsdon's relationship with Emilia?

It is of course possible, that after the Armada was defeated that the relief from the life-threatening invasion meant the Queen was briefly less concerned with sexual peccadilloes at court. The assumption is that despite the forty three year age difference that Emilia's life with Hunsdon was a mutually happy one.

By the time their affair started Hunsdon and his wife, Anne were effectively separated, she living away from their London residence, Somerset House. Emilia, meanwhile, moved into the luxurious accommodation of Hunsdon's London home and, if Forman is correct, appears to have accompanied him on social occasions as if she were his wife.

In 1591 Hunsdon commissioned Markus Gheeraerts the younger to paint his portrait. As you can see it is a portrait that emphasises the importance of his office. Hunsdon is depicted holding the Lord Chamberlain's rod of office and wearing the official chain, the fingers of his left hand caressing the badge of office.

The wording on the left hand side states:

Henry Carey
Lord Hunsdon
BY MARK GEHARDS
The top right
ATATIS SUA 66
AN' 1591

Hunsdon must have been happy with his portrait because the following year Gheeraerts was commissioned to paint Hunsdon's granddaughter, Elizabeth Carey.

By 1591, the time of the Gheeraerts Hunsdon portrait, Emilia had been Hunsdon's live-in mistress for two or more years, knowingher *high minded* character

from Forman's writings, it is hardly

32 Marcus Gheeraerts: Lord Chamberlain Hunsdon

surprising, even if he didn't offer, that she cajoled him into having Gheeraerts paint her too. Unlike the Hunsdon portrait, the Lady in Black portrait has no date, no identification of the painter nor the name of the sitter.

The painting is held in the Bowes Museum at Castle Barnard under the cata-

33 Gheeraerts Lady in Black, Emilia?

logue no. B.M. 1014 and is thought to be a late acquisition by John Bowes the C19 art collector. It was attributed to Markus Gheeraerts the younger by Sir Roy Strong in the 1970s.

I suppose that the fact that this portrait is of an unidentified sitter, is not especially remarkable. The sitter was expected to be identified by their contemporaries particularly if the portraits were hung in a family home. Even for a grandee like Hunsdon, having his young mistress painted and then her identity shown on the front or back of the portrait was inviting unnecessary trouble. As you can see although the hair line and style and shape in the Hilliard painting is similar, there is a difference in colouring, fairer in the Gheeraerts painting probably dates from 1591.

This would have been a time in which Emilia was in frequent attendance at court and dying her hair a lighter colour, in imitation of the Queen, would have been tempting. Shakespeare refers to this change of hair colouring in the first three lines of the very first Dark Lady Sonnet

IN the ould age blacke was not counted faire,
Or if it weare it bore not beauties name:
But now is blacke beauties successiue heire (127.1-3)

there is a pun here hair/heir

The same sonnet goes on to talk about the use of cosmetics

For since each hand hath put on Natures power,
Fairing the foule with Arts faulse borrow'd face, (127.5-6)

Berowne (AKA Shakespeare) talking about Rosaline's (AKA Emilia) hair colouring in *Loues Labour's lost* says

O if in blacke my Ladies browes be deckt,
It mournes, that painting vsurping haire
Should rauish doters with a false aspect:
And therfore is she borne to make blacke, faire (4.3.1499-1502)

Earlier on in the play Rosaline is described as

A whitly wanton, with a veluet brow. With two pitch bals stucke in her face for eyes (3.1.934-5)

A whitely wanton is unkind, but the two lines seem to be an accurate description of the sitter in Hilliard's miniature

It is very likely that it was whilst she was living with Hunsdon that Emilia's interest in the theatre, plays, actors and playwrights was aroused. Since the 1560s Hunsdon was patron of his own company of players, performing in London and around the country under his badge and protection. The actors' touring schedule which ran the length and breadth of England, included Leicester, Norwich, Malden, Canterbury, Plymouth, Gloucester, Bristol, Bath and Exeter.

At Christmas 1582 Hunsdon's Men played at court where they enacted the anonymous play *Beauty and Housewifery*. It has been assumed by many that Shakespeare joined one of the touring companies of actors before settling in London, the *Queen's Men, Strange' s Men* or *Leicester's Men* have been suggested, but this doesn't rule out *Hunsdon's Men*. It is just one of the many possibility of how Emilia and Shakespeare came to know one another, before Shakespeare joined Hunsdon's new company, the *Lord Chamberlain's Men*, founded in 1594.

A powerful patron provided much needed protection for actors. Hunsdon sided with James Burbage, **actor, impressario, joiner and theatre builder,** when the Lord Mayor moved to have *The Theatre* and *The Curtain,* two of Burbage's play houses, demolished. The action was thwarted because of Hunsdon's influence.

Although in 1597 *The Theatre* was moved apocryphally *overnight*, this was at Burbage's instigation after a difference of opinion between him and the land owner. Once *The Theatre* was demolished, the sections were moved to a location south of the Thames at Southwark, where it was reconstructed and re-named *The Globe*.

Audiences at *The Theatre* saw many of the Shakespeare plays performed; *Henry Vl* Parts 2 & 3 and *Richard lll* given by *Pembroke's Men* in 1592/3 and *Loue's Labours lost, Two Gentlemen of Verona* and *Romeo and Juliet* given by Hunsdon's newly formed *Lord Chamberlain's Men.* **This was** a year after Emilia's marriage, so if she attended, it wouldn't have been on Hunsdon's arm.

In 1587 *Hunsdon's Men* played an early version of *Hamlet* at Newington Butts (south of the river near the Elephant and Castle) whether this play was by Kyd, Shakespeare or an unidentified author is uncertain. In 1588 the anonymous highly popular comedy *Mucedorus* was produced at *The Theatre*, it is probable that Emilia, perhaps masked as was the custom for ladies, accompanied Hunsdon to see his actors perform it. It is also likely that she went to one or other of the London theatres accompanying Hunsdon throughout their co-habitation, from say 1589 until the closure of the theatres in June 1592.

She could have seen as many as thirty plays, including *Rowland and the Sexton* - the popular tune from the concluding *jig* set for keyboard by Byrd - Marlowe's *Jew of Malta*, Kyd's *The Spanish Tragedy*, Greene's *Friar Bacon & Friar Bungay, Orlando Furioso, Scottish History of James the Fourth and Edward I*, Shakespeare's *Henry VI, Parts 1 and 2 and Edward 111*, all of which would have been of great influence on Emilia's development as a writer. There were at least two occasions when Emilia might have seen John Lyly's *Midas.* It was played at Pauls in 1589 and at court in January 1590.

I propose that around the beginning of 1592 Emilia, whose reputation as a poet was well known because of her collaboration with Byrd, was commissioned by Elizabeth Cooke, Lady Russell to write an entertainment, *Speeches to the Queen*, to welcome the Queen for her three day visit to Lady Russell's home, Bisham Abbey, in August of that year. Lady Russell had two daughters who it seems were to take part in the *Speeches to the Queen* which was written in the form of a masque. Lady Russell's daughters, Anne and Elizabeth, played the *two Virgins keeping sheep, and sowing in their samplers* and I believe Emilia played *Ceres*, the goddess of agriculture.

There are a number of significant concordances in *Midas* and the *Speeches to the Queen*. Mutual characters: Pan, Apollo, nymphs and shepherds and mutual words: *conceit, hill, pipe, sheep, virgin, men, women, mistress, bodies, lute* (inevitably!), *savage, sex, shrink, utter, music, God, envy, fearful, years, courting.*

These relatively common Elizabethan words may not be thought significant except because the *Speeches to the Queen* runs to less than two thousand words the concordances are unlikely to be coincidence. Stylistically too, there is much in common with *Midas* and the *Speeches to the Queen*, witty brief exchanges and a feminist edge. It is these concordances and other similarities, plus the timing of the performances of *Midas* which indicate that Lyly's English version of Ovid's *Midas* provided the inspiration for Emilia's writing.

Around the time that Emilia took part in the *Speeches to the Queen* to welcome the Queen to Bisham she became pregnant. I would suggest that after the successful performance the actors and musicians celebrated, probably drank too much - as is still common at the end of a stressful performance on tour - and amorous liaisons resulted.

Because of the reference in Sonnet 127 to the name Henry, when the child was born, *Slandring Creation with a false esteeme*, the most likely candidate for the father of her unborn child is William Shakespeare, which shows that he was present at Bisham and took part in the Speeches to the Queen too. There are two male roles, A Wild Man and Pan. Perhaps because of Emilia's experience of the theatre she recommended the professioonal actors who she wanted to play these parts.

Hunsdon was absent from Bisham, he didn't attend the Privy Counsel meeting held there, in fact he missed the next two meetings held in Reading and Aldermaston rejoining the court in Newbury on 26th August.

Whether or not Emilia tried to conceal her pregnancy, it would only have been a matter of weeks, because of obvious anatomical changes, that Hunsdon realised that he had a pregnant mistress on his hands. He had a quick decision to make, something that as a soldier and Lord Chamberlain he was used to. A special licence was obtain by Jhon Jvoot (this curious name may just be a whimsical spelling of something less unusual by the scrivener) in order to hasten Emilia's marriage to Alphonso by 18 October.

It is likely that Alphonso was present at Bisham, making him to all intents and purposes - as Forman put it *for colour* - a potential father.

One can only speculate as to why Hunsdon chose to absent himself from Bisham Abbey, which was his daughter's home. Perhaps, Margaret, Lady Hoby had invited her mother already and Emilia's acceptance of Lady Russell's invitation to write the *Speeches to the Queen* made her role too prominent for Hunsdon to feel comfortable.

Not surprisingly the marriage of Alphonso and Emilia was a desperately unhappy one.

Although Hunsdon appears to have settled jewellery and £40 a year for Emilia, substantially more that the annual pay for court musicians. Alphonso's name first appears in the Calendar of State Papers four months after his wedding, on 19 February 1592/3, when he is listed last in the court recorder ensemble as one of a much larger number of musicians excused payment of subsidies granted:

Augustino Bassano	£9. 12s.	
Ludovico Bassano		£9. 12s.
Arthur Bassano		£9. 12s.
Edward Bassano		£9. 12s.
Jeronimo Bassano		£9. 12s.
Alphonso Lanier		£9. 12s.

As you can see at the time of the Lady Russell commission, five of the six members of the court recorder consort were cousins of Emilia and the sixth was to become her husband in a forced, unwelcome and unanticipated marriage.

If, as I suspect Alphonso was one of the cornett (not to be confused with the C.19 brass band cornet) players demanded in stage directions for the *Speeches to the Queen - At the top of the Hill going to Bissam, the Cornetts sounding in the Woods* - then Hunsdon's choice of Alphonso makes very good sense.

The cornetto was an instrument virtually unknown in England until the arrival of the Bassano family, who made and played the instrument. As the name suggests the instrument is horn shaped, constructed from wood, bound in leather with finger holes very similar to a recorder, but with a small trumpet-like acorn sized mouthpiece buzzed into by the player.

Alphonso was "bought" by being given a life-long court appointment, he was present at the exact time of Emilia's child's conception, even if Hunsdon suspected that he himself wasn't the father, it was in the interests of saving face to allow Emilia to let the world at large think the child was his. Hence his generous financial settlement to Emilia and better terms and conditions for Alphonso - freedom for release from official duties - than any other member of the court musical establishment.

Alphonso's official life-time appointment didn't take place until 23 March 1593 and is documented in the Calendar of State Papers as

Patent for Alphonso Lanyer, musician in place of William Damano, deceased; 20d. a day and a yearly livery of £16. 2s. 6d., from the Exchequer, for life, from the death of William Damano

Curiously there appear to be three St Botolph-without-Aldgate parish records for Emilia and Alphonso's marriage all with different wordings in three different sets of handwriting

1) under the side entry *October*
Alfonsall Lanier and Emilia Bassanoe the Eightentye

2) under the heading *October, m, Anno 1592*
Alfonso Lanyer one of the Queens musicians & Emilia Bassano by James Davies Maryed the 18 Day off october in Anno Domino

3) *Alfonso Lanier one of her Majesty's musicians dwelling in the minories and Emilia Bassano dwelling also in the minories solemnised the xviii day of october anno 1592 by vertue of a lycence procured by Jhon Jvoot*

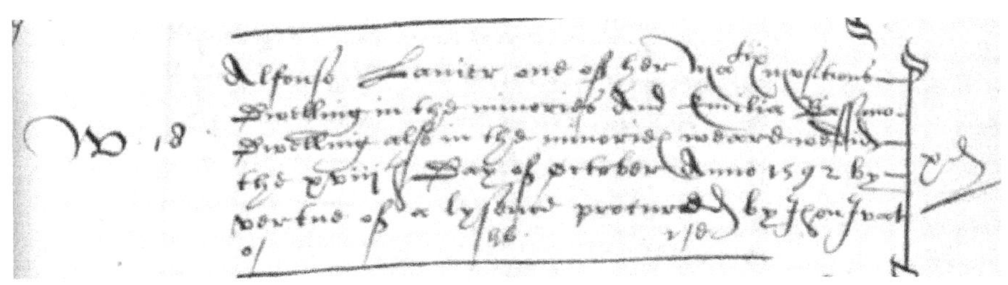

34 St. Botolph-without-Aldgate parish register

Presumably Jhon Jvoot, whoever he may have been, was ordered by Hunsdon to obtain the licence which meant the wedding ceremony could be speedily arranged before Emilia's pregnancy became obvious.

At the time of their marriage Alphonso wasn't one of the Queen's musicians, he wasn't appointed intil five months later, the fact that he had the scrivenor write that he already was *one of her Majesties musicians* shows that Hunsdon had, as with Byrd, promised him a court place.

The name Minories, derives from the Abbey of the Minoresses of St. Clare without Aldgate, the Poor Clares were the female branch of the Franiscan order of monks, Emilia's great grandfather's employers in Crespano.

The area was in the ancient parish of St. Botolph without Aldgate, in 1557 it became extra-parochial. Historically the location was a papal peculiar outside of the jurisdiction of the English bishops. The abbey was dissolved in 1539 when the property passed to the Crown. St Botolph Aldgate and Holy Trinity Minories were clandestine places of marriage in early modern London. The chapel of the former abbey became the Church of Holy Trinity, Minories, and other buildings were used as an armoury and later as a workhouse.

The Minories area historically hosted a large Jewish community. Since Emilia's address is also given as the Minories, it would appear that Hunsdon had moved her out of Somerset House to live with Alphonso, or a member of his family, before the wedding. It is likely that the residence in the Minories was owned by the Lanier family since around this time John and Frances Lanier had their children baptised at Holy Trinity.

Emilia inherited three properties from her father, after her mother's death, in the parish of St. Botolph Bishopsgate and another in the parish of St Christopher le Stocks on the south side of Threadneedle Street but they were possibly rented out at this time.

Notwithstanding that Emilia was a property and jewellery owner with an income of £40 a year, the exponential social descent from the grandeur of Somerset House to the humility of a small house in the Minories must have hit her very hard.

The opportunity for love affairs - particularly one with the attractive young Earl of Southampton - as a reprieve from the total disinterest of her husband might have felt like something of her former life had been restored.

11. Life After Marriage

....those lips of thine,
That haue prophan'd their scarlet ornaments,
And seald false bonds of loue as oft as mine,
Robd others beds reuenues of their rents.
(Sonnet 142,5-8)

It anybody's bed was robbed of its rent, it was Alphonso Lanier's, but I don't think he cared.

Given the early numbering of the *bastard* Dark Lady sonnet (127 of 154) must mean that Sonnet 127 dates to after the birth of Emilia's son Henry in May 1593. Unfortunately no record of Henry's christening has been discovered to give us an exact date of birth.

The betrayal of Shakespeare with Southampton is referred to in sonnets 34-42 in the *Fair Friend* sequence and 133-140 in the *Dark Lady* sequence showing that the affair between Emilia and Southampton was far more than just a one night stand.

My assumption is that the affair first took place in the winter of 1593/94, beginning whilst Shakespeare was away from London. Southampton's line in eloquent seduction is reported by Emilia in her guise as the *fickle maid* in *A Louers Complaint.*

So on the tip of his subduing tongue
All kinde of arguments and question deepe,
Al replication prompt, and reason strong
For his aduantage still did wake and sleep,
To make the weeper laugh, the laugher weepe:
He had the dialect and different skil,
Catching al passions in his craft of will. (ALC 120-126)

In order to persuade Southampton to release his heterosexual persona from captivity, Shakespeare was foolhardily enough to suggest to him, and perhaps Emilia too, to explore a new erotic path.

All men make faults, and euen I in this,
Authorizing thy trespas with compare,
My selfe corrupting saluing thy amisse,
Excusing their sins more than their sins are (35.5/8)

A licentious suggestion, that his sixteen sonnets on the subject, show he bitterly regretted. Perhaps because she was married to a homosexual herself, Shakespeare thought that Emilia would know better than anyone how to en-snare a reluctant male partner.

In 1594 Nicholas Hilliard completed a miniature of Southampton. Early on in the year Southampton's mother, the Dowager Countess must have felt optimistic about life, because in May she was to marry the courtier, Sir Thomas Heanage. Perhaps she commissioned the painting as a twenty first birthday present for her son's autumn celebration.

Like many miniatures it is painted in watercolour on vellum on a playing card, a three of hearts. Hilliard kept a collection of prepared cards with differing background colour which could then be matched to the sitter's skin colour.

Symbolism and fortune telling for Elizabethans were a part of everyday life. We still see symbolic importance to our ancestors on coats-of-arms, and other heraldic devises in churches and other historic buildings. Forman's busy consultation room shows just how common it was for people to consult fortune tellers, as did the Queen with Dr Dee.

The decision to use the three of hearts card wasn't a whimsical one, it would have been seriously considered. I would suggest its choice denotes the tri-angular relationship that existed between Southampton, Shakespeare and Emilia at the time of the painting.

On the front of the miniature and to the left in gold is the year *Ano Dm 1594* and on the right, also in gold, the Latin words *Etatis suae* followed by the figure '*20*' which shows at the time of the miniature's completion he was still twenty and wasn't due to be twenty one until October.

It is of significance that the Hilliard portrait of Emilia should be painted on the back of a five of spades playing card - very much a black suit - and the colour of the subject's hair. One interpretation of the five of spades in cards is the foretelling of the end of a romantic relationship between two people.

The relationship between a married commoner and an aristocrat five years younger was inevitablly bound to end at some stage, both parties must have realised that. Perhaps, as Tony Haygarth suggested, Southampton paid Hilliard to paint Emilia as a parting gift for her.

In 1597 Alphonso was serving in the Azores campaign with the Earl of Essex, and he was again with the Earls of Essex and Southampton in 1599, this time in Ireland, leaving in March 1599 returning six months later at the same time as Essex, unwashed and unchanged from travel, surprised the Queen in her bed chamber. A *faux pas* from which his favour with the Queen never recovered.

Emilia's daughter Odillia, was christened on 2nd December 1598 at St Margaret's Westminster the parish church of Longditch, but buried nine months later at St Botolph's Bishopsgate, indicating a change of address. Perhaps returning to one of the less fashionable properties in Bishopsgate inherited from her parents.

Although Alphonso's return from the Azores was in time for his wife to conceive, I doubt that he was the father. Who was, Shakespeare, Forman, or perhaps someone else? Was Emilia's allegation to Forman that he was the father of Odillia that had him noting in his diary *whether she intendeth any more villainy*?

It would seem that there was a move of residence, never a straight-forward exercise, whilst Alphonso was away serving in Ireland with Essex and Southampton. No doubt this was another bone of contention between the couple.

There are a large number of receipts in 1599 and 1600 for sums of money paid by Sir Gilly Meyrick, on behalf of Essex, to nineteen men including Thomas Lee, Henry Cuffe, P. Edmondes (the officer accused of cavorting with Southampton in Ireland) and Capt. Alphonso Lanier.

This is the first documented occurrence of a title for Alphonso, indicating that Essex had promoted him as an officer, but disappointed him, by not bestowing the knighthood he had hoped for. During the Ireland campaign Essex, earned the Queen's further disfavour by knighting over eighty new gentlemen, some recipients it seemed didn't merit the distinction, so it would appear that Alphonso narrowly avoided the preferment the couple had hoped for.

Lee, Cuffe and Meyrick were to meet their end at Tyburn in March 1600, the death sentences pronounced after the guilty verdicts at trial accusing them of treason because of their involvement with the Essex plot. Alphonso appears to have been lucky to have escaped prosecution, as was Shakespeare and his company of actors, after Meyrick paid them forty shillings on condition that they performed *Richard ll* on Saturday, 6 February, the day before that fixed for the rebellion.

Emilia revealed to Forman that

her husband hath delte hardly with her and spent and consumed her goods and she is nowe…in debt

Some detail is known about how it was that Alphonso wasted Emilia's capital and income. He appears to have been as adventurous with Emilia's money as he was with his own person.

Around 1594 he was given a royal grant, supported by Sir Robert Cecil, for the grant of goods and chattels of certain fugitives. Sir Robert was Burghley's son and a first cousin of Lady Russell, who was very likely at Bisham two years earlier, where he could have met both Alphonso and Emilia.

The financial success of the enterprise wasn't without its difficulties . On the 14th October 1601 Alphonso wrote to Sir Robert bemoaning the problems he experienced collecting £100 per annum he felt was due to him. Nonetheless this frustrating experience of taking possession of fugitives' property didn't deter him from entering into a similar business arrangement six years later.

Another huge drain on the household budget would have been Alphonso's military service. It was well known that enlisting to fight in foreign campaigns, even when the commander, in this case Essex, was paying something towards expenses, was a potentially ruinous commitment.

Whilst Alphonso was away in the Azores and Ireland he wasn't being paid as a court musician. With the death of Hunsdon in the summer of 1596 it is most likely that Emilia's £40 per annum income had ceased, so the household budget which included at least two servants, would have been in crisis. After his return from service abroad, Alphonso embarked upon another risky business enterprise.

On the 31st July 1601 he used his court connections to gain a grant to himself and his brother, Jerome and one William Ballard *the possession of goods and lands of diverse persons seized by customs*. One assumes that these *diverse persons* were recusant Catholics who had hurriedly fled the country.

The court documents show a distinction for the reasons for the bestowal of the Queen's grant between the Laniers and Ballard. The Laniers were rewarded for *the good and lawful service heretofore done unto us* and Ballard was given the task of an agent in locating the *goods and chattels of the fugitives*.

A year later a letter from Richard Percival, secretary to Sir Robert Cecil, to his master refers to Lanier buying the lease of a property valued at £50 per annum, or less, for an asking price of £300 from Sir Thomas Knollys. Knollys was a courtier and MP and the father of Katherine Howard, Countess of Suffolk, one of the dedicatees of Emilia's *Salve Devs,* so it seems possible that she was known to the Laniers.

Only £160 of this sum was paid before Alphonso sold it on to one Dallender - probably Richard Dallender - a buyer and seller of land and property, for £500. It would appear that Dallender in turn only paid £300 of the agreed price and Alphonso tried to gain Percival's assistance in getting Dallender to pay up the remainder of the purchase price.

In April 1602 Alphonso had returned to court for long enough to pick up his annual salary of £24 with 64s for his livery.

Jeronymo Bassano	£24	64s.
Augustino Bassano, alien	£24	68s.
Arthur Bassano	£24	64s.
Edward Bassano	£24	64s.

| Robert Baker | £24 | 64s. |
| Alphonso Lanyer | £24 | 64s. |

In ten years the recorder consort had changed little, with Robert Baker, the first English member of the recorder consort since its founding in 1540, replacing Ludovico, Augustine's younger brother who had died in 1593.

A few days after Christmas 1602 Alphonso and John Wenham of Sussex received £140 from Peter Bradshaw of London, merchant tailor. Around the same time Alphonso borrowed £30 from Robert Stybbing.

At the end of April 1603 Alphonso made his swan song as an instrumentalist playing at the funeral of Elizabeth 1st. Before playing a note in the ceremony, he first joined the stately procession of more than a thousand mourners in the cortege's short journey from Whitehall to Westminster Abbey, witnessed by a huge crowd.

As well as being a momentous occasion for the nation as a whole, it was of great significance personally to the second generation of Bassanos, all of whom had served at court under the watchful eye of the greatest monarch in the country's history. Unlike the celebrated music composed for the funeral of Queen Mary by Purcell at the end of the century in 1695, no one knows what music was played at Elizabeth's laying to rest but no doubt it would have been impressive and memorable.

In 1575 Elizabeth I granted Thomas Tallis and William Byrd - the two best English composers of the era - sole rights to the printing of music and the staved manuscript paper. Tallis had died before the Queen but very likely anthems or psalm settings in English by William Byrd were sung - despite his well known Catholic faith - he remained the Queen's favourite composer throughout her life.

When Alphonso should have appeared on the list of musicians sworn in to serve the new King, James I, his name is missing and the vacant position filled by yet another of Emilia's cousins, Andrea Bassano.

Alphonso's social standing would appear to be higher than that expected of one of the royal musicians. One indication of this preferment is information in a letter written on behalf of Alphonso by his *old fellow and loving friend* the Bishop of London, the sixty year old bachelor, Richard Bancroft shortly to become Archbishop of Canterbury. Bancroft's 14th August 1604 letter is addressed to Sir Robert Cecil who as James 1st's chief minister had recently been ennobled to Viscount Cranborne

Captain Alphonso Lanier, the late Queen's and now his Majesty's servant, mine old fellow and loving friend, has obtained a suit of his Highness for the weighing of hay and straw about London. I have seen a letter of Mr Solicitor's, whereby I perceived that both he and my Lord Chief Justice do not think it inconvenient. Besides, he was put in hope of your favour by the Earl of Southampton, when his bill

*should come into your hands. I therefore very heartily entreat you on his behalf…
We served both together the Lord Chancellor, which makes me the bolder to crave
your acceptance of my desire of good success to his said bill, remaining now and
stayed by your Lordship. I the rather presume this for upon your favour because, if
any incon venience might in time ensue of his Majesty's grant, the same is referred
in the grant to be referred by and two of his Majesty's Privy Council and the Lord
Chief Justice for the time being.*

The mention of the assurance of Southampton's support, only a year after
his release from captivity, shows that Alphonso must have retained a personal connection with him from the days of their military service together.
Whether he knew of the affair between Soputhampton and his wife is unknown.

Although Cecil had argued for commutation of Southampton's death sentence to imprisonment for his part in the Essex plot, he still didn't fully trust
him. It could be that mention of Southampton's advocacy was a disadvantage
to Bancroft's suit on behalf of Alphonso. Whatever the reason for the long
delay the grant wasn't finally approved until May 1612.

The terms of the grant gave Alphonso a twenty one year entitlement to

*have for weighing of hay and straw to the cities of London and Westminster and
the suburbs thereof to be sold, for reforming of abuses and deceits in not making
a true and just weight of their loads of trusses according to the ancient Assize of
this realm, and for his charges on providing of scales and weights and many dep-
uties in and about the execution of the same, his Majesty's grant unto him to take
indifferently as well of the buyer as of the seller an indifferent and reasonable
allowance of 6d. the load of hay and 3d. the load of straw or a 1/4d. the truss of
hay and a 1/4d. for every two trusses of straw.*

Some three years before, in March 1609 Alphonso got himself into a spot of
bother in the village of Hackney some three miles north east of Bishopsgate.
He and Henry Popwell, who appears to have been employed as a server of
writs or other legal papers, were both bound over to keep the peace *for that
they abused the headborough* [a parish officer similar to a constable, probably
rather like Dogberry in *Much adoe*] *and kicked him and pulled him by the nose
when he was executing his office.*

It isn't clear if the Laniers were living in Hackney at this time or whether Alphonso and Emilia had separated, or if Alphonso had just accompanied Popwell for some unknown reason.

Although collecting revenue from hay and straw dealers involved creating a
labour intensive organisation, the income should have been substantial for
Alphonso and his wife. Problems associated with entitlement as well as collecting revenue from the grant were to bug Emilia for years after Alphonso's
death which occurred only a year after the grant was finally approved.

The 1612 grant was the last court entry relating to Alphonso. Although there is an online record of his burial dated 20th September 1613 the source of this information is yet to be found. There is no doubt that at Alphonso's death Emilia was left in great financial difficulty.

A decade earlier, around the time of the Queen's death, Emilia went to live with Margaret Clifford, Countess of Cumberland (1560-1616), and her daughter, Lady Anne Clifford (1590-1676) in Cookham. Both of these ladies were two of the ten named dedicatees chosen by Emilia in *Salve Devs.* How long she remained there with the Cliffords is uncertain, but months rather than weeks, and possibly as long as two years.

Margaret Clifford was Lady Russell's sister-in-law and since Cookham was geographically close to Bisham they were neighbours of Lady Russell, and her son and daughter-in-law, Sir Thomas Hoby and Lady Margaret Hoby (neé Carey). The Hobys were London neighbours of Emilia and Alphonso in Westminster a few years earlier. Margaret and Anne visited Cookham twice in late 1603, and her mother dated five letters *from Cookham in Berkshire* between September and November 1604, during those years Anne's mother was separated from her father. They must have been in residence months before, or months before because of summer references in Emilia's *Cooke-ham.*

The Walkes put on their summer Liueries,
And all things else did hold like similies:
The Trees with leaues, with fruits, with flowers clad,
Embrac'd each other, seeming to be glad

The Description of Cooke-ham (21-4)

The marriage arranged in childhood between Margaret and George Clifford, 3rd Earl of Cumberland was not a happy one. Margaret's permanent separation from her husband was caused by the revelation of an intrigue between her husband and an unidentified lady at court, which wasn't the first occasion either. Notwithstanding a reputation as a philanderer, the Earl remained a favourite with the Queen, renowned for his prowess in the tilts, his Hilliard portrait ostentatiously sports his jousting lance.

It seems that mother and daughter were the central core of a group of early feminists, kindred spirits because of their mutual personal experience at the hands of male chauvinists. Margaret and Anne bore a deep perception of grievous injustice caused by the unfairness of male primogeniture tradition, as well as apparent male preferment over females under the law.

The house at Cookham in which they lived was most likely one that was kept vacant for guests, *Dyers* at Cookham Dean, on the Bisham Abbey estate owned by the Hobys. Whether, as relatives of the Hobys and Lady Russell, their tenancy was a *grace and favour* one, or whether they paid rent is unknown. Emilia's spelling and use of hyphen in *Cooke-ham* is another indication that the house was owned by the family of Lady Elizabeth Russell, because her maiden name was Cooke.

Lady Anne Clifford's education had been overseen by Samuel Daniel - later to become *Poet Laureate* - dedicated poems to her and was held in the highest esteme by Lady Anne until the end of his life. She paid for his memorial bust at the site of his grave in Beckington, Somerset. This was the second benevolence shown by Lady Anne to the memory of a poet. The earlier instance was payment for a mural to commemorate the life of Edmund Spenser in Westminster Abbey.

By listing her as a dedicatee in *Salve Devs*, **Emilia** hoped for the largesse bestowed on Daniel and Spencer to come in her direction too, preferably whilst she was still alive. In that, she was disappointed. Perhaps the revelations in the 1609 Sonnets had made both Shakespeare and Emilia *persona non grata* in the eyes of the aristocracy.

The Great Picture, originally hung in Appleby Castle but now owned by Abbot Hall Art Gallery in Kendal, is attributed to Jan van Belcamp, a Dutch artist working in England.

Anne commissioned the painting in 1646 with the intention of showing the Clifford family's immediate aristocratic history, highlighting her personal artistic accomplishments and literary interests, employing a combination of portraiture, text and symbolism.

35 Jan van Belcamp: The Great Picture

The left side panel of the triptych depicts Anne in 1605 at the age of fifteen, the year her father died. Portraits of Anne Taylor and Samuel Daniel, are placed above the shelves of books, which include books by Ovid, Chaucer and Cervantes' *Don Quixote*. Mrs Anne Taylor, was Anne's governess who was in charge of her pastoral care.

The choice of books and portraits point to Anne's highly literate classical education and refined upbringing. The most prominent feature of this panel is a lute in the lower right hand side of the painting and Anne's left hand resting on a music part book. I imagine that it was as a musician - a lute and voice specialist - that Emilia was brought into the household. We can recall the actions of Greene's Lamilia

taking a lute in her hand..... shee sung this sonnet with a delicious voyce

It is possible that the Queen, a close friend of Margaret Clifford, one of her *ladies in waiting*, had earlier suggested Emilia as a lute teacher. The Queen probably harboured fond memories of Emilia's father, Baptista, coaching her in lute technique as a nineteen year old at Hatfield. The Queen would have heard Emilia sing and play the lute at Bisham in 1592, recognising an inherited musical talent when she heard it.

At the time of Emilia's stay in Cookham, her son, Henry would have been nine or ten, a few years younger than Anne. Henry was probably apart from his mother at the time because he would have started his musical apprenticeship.

It would appear from *Cooke-ham* **towards the end of** *Salve Devs* that in the winter of 1604, after the departure of Margaret and Anne, Emilia was put in charge of closing up the house.

The house cast off each garment that might grace it,
Putting on Dust and Cobwebs to deface it.
All desolation then there did appeare,
When you were going whom they held so deare.

Description of Cooke-ham (201-205)

With the death of Anne's father in 1605 unwelcome and unanticipated stipulations in his will propelled Anne and Margaret into a state of indignation that was to occupy their combined adversorial efforts until the end of Margaret's life and Anne's sole effort almost until the end of her life too.

Anne's lawful legacy was the total inheritance of her father's property and assets but this was side-stepped by the Earl's will - which entailed settling substantial debts - bequeathing his complete estate to his brother, Francis Clifford, albeit leaving the substantial sum of £15,000 in compensation to Anne.

The diversion of the legacy was a direct breach of an entail dating back to the time of King Edward II, which stated that the Clifford estates - which included the spectacular northern castles of Skipton, Brougham, Brough and Appleby - should descend lineally to the eldest heir, whether male or female.

From the time of her disinheritance until the end of her life Anne struggled for justice. It is indicative of her concern for the welfare of women, that in her sixties, she paid for the erection of almshouses for the poor widows of Appleby. An example of philanthropy specifically for women which was preceded by an endowment for an identical cause by her mother.

Anne finally achieved her rightful inheritance in 1643 when all of the extensive Clifford estates reverted to her at the death of her cousin. The experience of injustice at the hands of men encouraged mother and daughter to found, at Cookham, an enclave of artistic, musical and devout protestant women who found solace in their mutual interests and one another's company.

Perhaps it was some of the *Psalms of David* translated from Latin into English by Emilia that Byrd had set to music in three parts - easily managed by female voices - that the ladies sang together, throughout the day, if Emilia's narative is to be believed.

With louely Dauid you did often sing,
His holy Hymnes to Heauens Eternall King.
And in sweet musicke did your soule delight,
To sound his prayses, morning, noone, and night.

Description of Cooke-ham (87-90)

The right side panel of the Great Picture shows Lady Anne in late middle age, when she finally regained the Clifford estates. Portraits of Lady Anne's two husbands hang behind her. The first, Richard Sackville, third Earl of Dorset, who died in 1624, and the second, Philip Herbert, fourth Earl of Pembroke and first Earl of Montgomery, who died in 1650. It seems that Anne, like her mother was to endure unhappy marriages.

A further misfortune occurred when she was thirty four, shortly after the death of her first husband, a bout of smallpox caused her face to be disfigured. The depiction of Lady Anne at fifty-six, shows no sign of the *disease* [that] *did so martyr my face* as she put it, and was used as the model for many subsequent portraits and is probably the only likeness in *The Great Picture* to have been painted from life. It appears the artist had been instructed to ignore the pox-marks.

The central panel depicts Lady Anne's parents, Margaret Russell and George Clifford, third Earl of Cumberland, with her older brothers who did not survive to their teens; Francis (1584-1589) and Robert (1585-1591), tragic early childhood deaths which inflicted a heavy life-long burden on Margaret, their mother. Anne noted

The death of her two sonnes did so much afflict her as that ever after the booke of Jobe was her dayly companion

The death of a child - the greatest tragedy that can befall anyone - was another mutual experience shared with Emilia.

On the walls behind the family group hang portraits of four of Lady Anne's aunts; Lady Frances Clifford, Baroness Wharton, Lady Margaret Clifford, Countess of Derby, Lady Anne Russell, Countess of Warwick and Lady Elizabeth Russell, Countess of Bath.

As Anne was not born until 1590, she does not appear in the central panel as such, but the positioning of Lady Margaret's left hand symbolically hints that the daughter who would ultimately become the Clifford heir, had already been conceived.

The triptych is a composite work by a skilled copyist working from miniatures, portraits and whatever gowns and armour were still in Lady Anne's possession. The inscriptions identifying the sitters and the identities of the portraits on the walls were added by a different hand, possibly by the same scribe who copied out Lady Anne's *Great Bookes of Record,* which were begun by Lady Anne's mother in an attempt to gather evidence to support her daughter's claim to her inheritance.

It isn't clear whether Daniel accompanied Margaret and Anne south to Cookham and Emilia was appointed as temporary tutor - more likely specialist music tutor - and perhaps companion to Anne.

It is likely that Anne shared Emilia's interest in acting. In 2015 Yasmin Arshad proposed that a portrait of a woman in a masque costume, formerly known as Lady Raleigh, was in fact Anne Clifford. The whereabouts of the portrait itself is unknown after its private sale some seventy years ago, but the National Portrait Gallery owns a black and white photograph of the painting.

Anne played the role of Berenice in Ben Jonson's *Masque of Queens,* in 1609, shortly before her marriage to Richard Sackville. Arshad thinks that Clifford reused the costume of Berenice as another Egyptian Queen, Cleopatra, when the protrait was made. This is because the painting has a page showing the heroine's final lines from the 1607 edition of Daniel's *Cleopatra,* a commission from Mary Sidney.

Arshad suggests that Anne Clifford played the role of *Cleopatra* after her marriage in a private performance The female characters in masques were often non-speaking roles but performances at court and in private houses allowed ladies to speak, something that was not permitted in public

The title page of the 1611 *Salve Devs* advises

Written by Mistris Æmilia Lanyer, Wife to Captaine Alfonso Lanyer, Seruant to the Kings Majestie

My assumption is that Emilia returned to Alphonso in the winter of 1604, after closing up the house at Cookham. The publication of Shakespeare's Sonnets in 1609 with its unkind revelations about Emilia, and hideous personal comments - *the bay where all men ride* (137.6) and *Who art as black as hell, as darke as night* (147.13-14) - even though she was unnamed, must have been shattering for her. The equivalent of modern revenge porn, gentle Shakespeare at his most un-gentle.

Even though I think Shakespeare didn't personally authorise publication of the sonnets, he wrote them and Emilia would realise that the views revealed were his honest opinion of her. If Emilia and Shakespeare ever met after the publication of the Sonnets I imagine he would have been the recpient of an unforgetable tongue lashing.

It could be argued the publication of *Salve Devs,* only two years after the defamatory sonnets appeared was written in response. The title page proclaims the contents are *not vnfit to be read* unlike Emilia's view of the sonnets.

This publication also connects Emilia to Shakespeare, because Valentine Simmes, her printer also printed the second edition of *Richard II* in 1598. The whole anthology could have been written by Emilia in order to initiate a damage limitation exercise to save her reputation.

Of the existing copies two were presented as gifts from the Laniers. The first to King James's son, Prince Henry, and the second to Thomas Jones, Archbishop of Dublin and Lord Chancellor of Ireland who Alphonso knew from his service in Ireland. The subject matter includes *the passion of Christ* and *Eves apology in defence of women,* her close connection to the late Queen, residence with the Cliffords at Cookham.

The flowery dedications to numerous well known pious lady aristocrats most of whom were known to her personally. The use of her husband's title, Captain Alphonso Lanyer, hoping to lend her writing masculine authority,. Changing the spelling of her name to the Roman version, Æmelia, all seemed designed to help her regain an air of respectability. Unfortunately it didn't work.

After the death of her husband, probably in 1613, Emilia's life was a downward economic and social slide until her death. She spent a great deal of her energy in litigation, in a period when, unlike now, it wasn't exclusively for the wealthy. None-the-less some of the legal action she was obliged to conduct *in forma pauperis,* the law allowing the poor to litigate without incurring costs.

Now a widow with no obvious source of substantial income Emilia was forced to provide for herself. Her son Henry was twenty but didn't get his court appointment, paid at a modest 20d per day, until 1629.

In order to alieviate her economic difficulties in August 1617, Emilia rented a house in the rural parish of St Giles-in-the-Fields, where she established a school to teach the children of the well to do. She rented the building from Edward Smith to house her students but, due to disputes over the correct rent price and rent arrears, she was arrested on two different occasions between 1617 and 1619. On the second occasion, at the age of fifty, she suffered an ignominious eviction.

A lawsuit of 1620 relating to the school Emilia testified that

he [Alphonso] *having spent a great part of her estate in the service of the late Queen in her wars of Ireland and other places..... she was obliged to support herself for her maintenance and relief was compelled to teach and educate the children of diverse persons of worth and understanding*

After Alphonso's death the grant for the weighing of hay and straw brought into London passed to his brothers, firstly Innocent, later to Clement. Emilia was in dispute with her brothers-in-law over their inheritance of the grant. She claimed that it was she who had been left the grant by Alphonso but she agreed to allow Innocent to take over her right if he allowed her half of the profits, which he failed to do. Presumably she had no means of employing the workers needed to supervise the weighing.

Emilia's son, Henry Lanier, married Joyce Mansfield on 18 August 1623 in St Andrew by the Wardrobe. He was appointed as a court flautist in September 1627. By November 1632 Henry had run up a substantial debt because John

Ady (probably the composer, John Adson) petitioned against him for a the sum of £37.8s.

Less than a year later in October 1633, at the age of forty, Henry Lanier, putative illegitimate son of William Shakespeare, was buried in St James, Clerkenwell. One can only imagine the distress that his passing - the second of her only two children - would have caused Emilia and perhaps Shakespeare too.

Shortly after her husband's death Joyce, Henry Lanier's widow petitioned the Lord Chamberlain that her son be trained in music. This was agreed and it was ordered that

Andrea Lanier to take this Child into his care & to instruct him in Musique as soone as hee shall be capable therof

The Lord Chamberlain in 1633 was Philip Herbert, 4th Earl of Pembroke, husband of Anne Clifford and along with his brother, a dedicatee of the 1623 Shakespeare first folio. I imagine Pembroke knew that Henry Lanier's grandmother had taught his wife to play the lute, but did he suspect that the boy was Shakespeare's grandchild?

Henry (2) was just four when his mother's request for an apprentiship was granted, so he probably wouldn't have started his training for some three or four years. His mother didn't live long enough to see her son begin his musical training.

In 1634 Emilia complained against Innocent Lanier, alleging she had only received £8 from him, less than half of the profits due to her. This legal document showed that she had inherited further responsibilities *being in great misery and have two grandchildren to provide for*. The grand-children were seven and four at the time, Mary born in 1627 and Henry in 1630.

When Nicholas Lanier was appointed the first ever *Master of the Kings Musick* in 1625 by Charles 1, his annual pay was £200 and with daily access to the ear of the King was in a position of great influence. He was a composer with a unique voice, albeit one influenced by Monteverdi, he sang and played the lute, and like Monteverdi, was a bass gamba player too.

A truly renaissance man he was also an accomplished painter and expert on art. He was sent by Charles 1 to the court at Mantua negotiate for the Gonzaga Family's renowned collection of paintings. His mission was successfully achieved and a great number of the art works held in Britain's national collections - including paintings by Correggio, Fetti and Tintoretto - are from the Mantuan purchase. In April 1626 Lanier was paid £2,000 for buying and transporting the paintings back from Italy.

The court musical establishment under Charles I had increased exponetially, with it, the cost of providing music. The Privy Purse was paying £36 per annum each for six drummers who doubled on fife, £48 for seventeen trumpet players, between £48 and £60 for twenty wind players, £48 for twelve string players, £40 for nine lute players, £22 for thirty two choiristers. In addition Andrea Lanier, Alphonso's youngest brother, was given a patent for £60 a year to teach two boys on the flute and cornett, for life.

As if this wasn't enough money spent on musicians, in 1625 until 1642, when she left for Holland, Queen Henrietta Marie had her own substantial musical establishment. This was a colossol drain on the court's finances and was indicative of the difficulties brewing between court and parliament.

When Emilia was complaining of being in great misery in 1634 at least twelve members of the court musical establishment were related to her, by blood, or marriage. If only Emilia had managed to stay on good terms with her relatives her final years could have been so different.

She might have provided text - poetry and prose, perhaps still under the cloak of anonymity - for Lanier's songs and masques like *Lovers made Men,* the 1617 collaboration with Ben Jonson, in which he created both the music and the scenery. Nicholas Lanier's grandmother was Lucretia Bassano, he was Alphonso's nephew, therefore first cousin once removed to Emilia's grandchildren and up until the Civil War, was in a position to be financially and socially supportive, if he'd wanted to be.

Perhaps the disputes and subsequent litigation that Emilia conducted against his uncles, Clement and Innocent, made Nicholas reluctant to get involved. Emilia's propensity for entering arenas of conflict had finally proven insurmountably disadvantageous to her.

Emilia lived through the the reigns of three monarchs; the last thirty three years of Elizabeth I, all of James I's twenty two years, and the first twenty years of Charles I. She died in the middle of the Civil War after the court had moved to Oxford but when the services of the majority of court musicians had been dispensed with, their pay left owing, and London's theatres closed by Parliament.

If, by January 1645 she had been fit enough to leave her home, she could have witnessed the pikeman of Sir Thomas Fairfax's *New Model Army* exercising. The innovation of soldiers singing psalms as they marched into battle, is something that she would have approved of, by this time in her life.

Emilia was seventy-six when she died, a great age for her time. She was buried at St James's Church, Clerkenwell, on 3 April 1645. She shares her final resting place with two other Elizabethan writers and fellow parishioners, Thomas Heywood and Thomas Decker. The church was rebuilt in the late C18, no gravestone has been found for her.

12. William Shakespeare an appraisal of the Evidence

To seeke the light of truth, while truth the while
Doth falsely blinde the eye-sight of his looke:

(Loues Labour's lost 1.1.75)

Historic documents, monuments and inscriptions are generally regarded as reliable information on the life, assets and relationships of individuals, but, as we have seen in the portraiture, not universally accepted to be so in the case of our elusive poet.

So much of the documentary evidence has been questioned and inevitably speculation arrises to complete the detail of the brevity of the text revealed in legal documents. This includes questions over what was Shakespeare's wife's real name, was the first record of Shakespeare acting a forgery, to the notion that the name William Shakespeare printed on the frontispiece of *Venvs and Adonis* and the *Rape of Lucre*ce were the first uses of a *nom di plume* for some literary aristocrat or female writer who didn't want to be publicly identified?

There are several pieces of historic evidence, recorded in one source, the parish records of Holy Trinity Church, Stratford-upon-Avon, that it is difficult to dismiss as unreliable. The romantic notion that William was born and died on 23rd April, St George's day isn't entirely a flight of fancy, but remains unprovable.

What cannot be denied is that his arrival in our world was one, two, three or a few days before 26 April 1564 when his baptism was recorded in Latin, *Gulielmus filius Johannes Shakspere* (William son of John Shakespeare) and his departure, shortly before April 25 1616, when his burial was inscribed in English, *Will Shakspere gent*. This seemingly trivial linguistic point demonstrates the historically turbulently times into which the poet was born and through which his parents had lived.

Just over a decade before Shakespeare's birth, Queen Mary returned the country to Catholicism. During her five year reign (1553-1558) around three hundred protestants were executed for their faith, earning the her the epithet *Bloody Mary*, now transmogrified into a homeopathic hang-over cure.

During Mary's reign a Christian subject could be convicted of heresy if he professed disbelief in transubstantiation and only a few years later - when Elizabeth became Queen - the opposite belief could bring analternative heretical charge. If religious fanaticism didn't shorten one's life under the Tudors then there was a far greater threat, starkly recorded in the Stratford Parish Register, when William was just three months old, *Hic incipit pestis, here begins the plague.*

In 2020 the world was subjected to Coronavirus, COVID 19, a deadly plague the like of which was unknown to us since 1918. The modern precaution - *social distancing* - is the same as it was four centuries ago. After 1564, in order to avoid contagion, Stratford's residents eschewed public gatherings as much as possible, including Council meetings. John Shakespeare was one of the few members of the Council, brave enough, or foolhardy enough, to attend.

The baptisms of William's brother Gilbert in 1566 and his sister Joan in 1569 suggest welcome additions to the family that any toddler would enjoy. Court documents are another reliable source of evidence. In October 1568 John Shakespeare was accused of usury when he lent John Mussum the large sum of £100 at an illegal interest rate. This could have resulted in imprisonment for John, but it appears to have been settled with his accuser, Anthony Harrison, out-of-court.

In February 1570 John Shakespeare appeared in court after he was again accused of illegal money lending by James Langrake when he was fined forty shillings. It seems that whistle-blowing on usury was a common method of extracting money from those indulging in money lending and trade under the complex Elizabethan laws, with one hundred and eighty one accusations of illegality in a single year.

If, as seems likely that William attended the King's Free Grammar School, a place made eligible by John Shakespeares's position as town alderman. This would have been in 1571 when the boy was seven, the same year that William's sister Anne was born. Another brother, Richard was born three years later.

At the end of 1571 and later in February 1572 Langrake again informed against John, accusing that he had illegally bought 100 tods (2,800 pounds) of wool from local sellers in Snitterfield, and 200 tods of wool in another transaction in Westminster a year earlier. In 1573 John Shakespeare and John Mussum, an apparent business associate were both sued in the Court of Common Pleas by Henry Higford of Solihull who claimed they each owed him £30. This action appears to have been renewed by Higford in 1578.

In another legal case John sued John Walford a clothier of Marlborough for failing to pay £21 for twenty one tods of wool. These brushes with the law were to continue with both John and William involved in litigation.

From 1574 John Shakespeare began to suffer financial hardship, losing or re-mortgaging property, information difficult to keep secret from a ten year old.

Tragedy for the family in 1579, when William's sister Anne died at the age of eight, a cruel turn of fate for everyone, maybe particularly so for a sensitive adolescent brother. Next year, another child arrived in the household. Edmund was destined to follow his older brother into the acting profession in London where he died at the age of twenty seven, having reputedly fathered an illegitimate child.

His burial was noted in the records of St Saviour's Church, now known as Southwark Cathedral, a stone's throw from the site of the Globe Theatre. Edmund shares his resting place with other notable men associated with his profession, Gower, Fletcher, Henslowe, Kempe and Massinger. It seems most likely that it was his older brother, William, who by 1607 was wealthy, paid the twenty shillings for the funeral expenses which included the tolling of a passing-bell poetically recorded as *a forenoone knell of the great bell.*

In 1575 the Earl of Leicester entertained the Queen and her court for three weeks at Kenilworth, twelve miles from Stratford. It is likely that the eleven year old William was taken by his father to see the famous entertainment.

This extravagant performance has some parallels with Emilia's more modest entertainment to greet the Queen at Bisham twenty three years later. A savage man and an echo for example, although these ingredients were common to the genre. It is the report of the sequence listed as the *Station of the song of Protheus* that provides a strong literary link to Shakespeare. After the Queen freed the Lady of the Lake, a water pageant began with Protheus appearing on a dolphin float with a musical consort inside.

the Dolphyn was conueied vpon the boate, so that the Owners seen to bee his Fynnes. With in the which Dolphyn a Consort of Musicke was secretly placed, the which sounded, and Protheus clearing his voyce, sang his song of congratulation

Was it Shakespeares's reminiscence of the Kenilworth pageant and the knowledge that it would revive in the Queen fond memories when she saw a *Midsommer nights Dreame,* that encouraged him to write Oberon's lines?

Since once I sat vpon a promontory, And heard a Meare-maide on a Dolphins backe, Vttering such dulcet and harmonious breath, That the rude sea grew ciuill at her song, And certaine starres shot madly from their Spheares, To heare the Sea-maids musicke (2.1.508)

I doubt an eleven year old boy predicted that, within a decade, he would not only be obliged to marry a woman eight years his senior but would have baptised three children; Susanna on 26th May 1583, the twins Hamnet and Judith on 2nd February 1585. Nor at the age of thirty three suffer that unthinkable family tragedy, the burial of a son, Hamnet on 11th August 1596 at the age of eleven, the same age that William was when he visited Kenilworth.

Events registered a day or two after births and death, can be regarded as authentic milestones in Shakespeare's life, all tersely noted in the Stratford Parish Register.

No such incontrovertible documentation exists to prove that Shakespeare attended the local grammar school, or the date and venue of the marriage between William and Anne, the bearer of his dead sister's name. Anne's pregnancy called for special measures designed to avoid scandal. The process was sped up, as in the case of Emilia and Alphonso, by special licence.

The document that proves that the marriage did in fact take place is the marriage bond, signed by two Stratford farmers, Fulk Sandells and John Richardson. This document, dated November 28 1582 states that there was nothing to prevent the marriage of William Shagspere, eighteen, and Annc Hathaway, twenty six, from taking place, and that the bishop of Worcester, who in 1582 happened to be John Whitgift - elevated to Archbishop of Canterbury a few years later - issued the marriage licence would be indemnified from any future possible objections.

It is one of two documents recording the marriage, but the evidence isn't without intriguing ambiguity. An entry, dated the day before this bond, in the bishop of Worcester's register, records that a licence was granted to William Shakespeare for his marriage to Anne Whateley of Temple Grafton.

This difference has led to the Irish/American author Frank Harris in *The Man Shakespeare* proposing that these two documents are evidence that Shakespeare was involved with two women. He had chosen to marry one, Anne Whateley of Temple Grafton five and a half miles from Stratford, rather than the other one from Shottery, only one mile away from Stratford. When this became known he was immediately forced to marry the pregnant Anne Hathaway. The general consensus now is that these recorded inconsistencies are simply clerical spelling errors.

The marriage bond is only one of three documents which might have been produced to procure the licence (now lost) and, of the three, is unfortunately, the least informative. It is though, an original document and thus more likely to be more accurate than the register entry which is a later copy.

In the Worcester diocese, a bond required that two relations, guardians or friends of the couple, acting as sureties, bound themselves for £40 - a large amount of money - that certain conditions are met.

The conditions were that there was no impediment to the marriage, that there was no legal process pending concerning it, that the groom should not proceed with the marriage without the consent of the bride's friends or relations and that the groom should indemnify the bishop from any challenges to the marriage which might arise. All of these conditions were met in the Shakespeare/Hathaway bond.

This licence also authorised the marriage to take place outside the parish of normal residence, allowing William and Anne to be married outside of Stratford-upon-Avon avoiding local gossip. The parishes of Luddington, Bishopton, Billesley, and Temple Grafton have all been suggested as possible venues for the wedding, with Temple Grafton the most popular speculation amongst scholars, unfortunately the records for the parish church of St Andrew have been lost.

Unusually in these circumstances, the sureties were not relatives of William or Anne, but Fulk Sandells and John Richardson, each described as an *agricola*, that is farmer, of Stratford. Normally the groom would stand as one of the sureties, but because legally William was still a minor, that was not possible. The other surety was often the father of the bride, or another close relative, but Anne's father had recently died. It is surprising that John Shakespeare didn't act as surety on behalf of his son. Perhaps shortage of money meant he couldn't, or disapproval of the marriage, meant he wouldn't. Sandells and Richardson were chosen because of their connections to the Hathaways rather than the Shakespeares.

Both men are mentioned in Richard Hathaway's will dated June 1582, in which they are described as *my trustie frende and neighbours*, when he appointed them supervisors of his will. Richard died in September 1581, a month after Anne became pregnant so missed the marriage of his daughter by two months.

Richard left *Agnes* an alternative name for *Anne* the sum of ten marks or £6 13s 4d to be paid *at the day of her marriage*. This modest dowry probably came at a welcome moment for the finances of the Shakespeare family.

I suppose it might have been the emotional state of a woman whose father was dying - the writing of a will was often made at a time when death was anticipated - that predisposed her to agreeing to sex, or perhaps even initiating sex, with a young man, eight years her junior.

When the twins were born Shakespeare was still just twenty one, it is here that the documentary evidence for Shakespeare's life ceases for seven years until Greene's reference to him in London in 1592. Because there are no documents we cannot prove when or why Shakespeare left Stratford-upon-Avon, or what he was doing before becoming a professional actor, dramatist and poet, in London. There are many theories, everyone who speculates about it, is likely to have their own favourite version of what might have caused Shakespeare to leave his wife and young family behind.

One popular story revolves around Shakespeare's difficult relationship with Sir Thomas Lucy, a local Stratford-upon-Avon landowner, magistrate and persecutor of catholics. It was suggested that Shakespeare wrote a lampooning verse about Lucy, it was additionally reported that he poached from Lucy's estate, the nearby Charlecote Park. Richard Davies, an Oxford man who, in 1688, inherited papers belonging to a Gloucestershire clergyman, William Fulman, including notes on Shakespeare. Rev Fulman wrote:-

Shakespeare was much given to all unluckiness in stealing venison and rabbits, particularly from Sir -----Lucy who oft had him whipped and sometimes imprisoned and at last mad[e] him fly his native country to his great advancement.

It has been pointed out at the time that there were no deer at Charlecote, but that could just be an error of detail.

Another story was related by John Aubrey, who in 1681 wrote that Shakespeare *had been in his younger years a schoolmaster in the country.*

Others speculate that because of his apparent preoccupation with Italy, he must have visited that country. Or that because of his knowledge of the law and legal terms, he was employed as a lawyer's clerk. His knowledge of fighting techniques in battle lead some to think he became a soldier. It isn't also beyond the realms of possibility that he stayed living in Stratford, and helped out with the family business.

It is probable that he joined one of the companies of players which visited Stratford in the late 1580s, a theory in combination with the difficulties encountered with Sir Thomas Lucy that I warm to as reasons for a young man, who means to be of note, to abandon his only known home, wife and young family.

No one knows where William and Anne were living with their three children, it might have been at either family home, the Shakespeare's in Henley Street, or more likely, the Hathaway's farm in Shottery. Generally speaking, poets begin writing at an early age. In order to succeed they need free time accompanied by peace and quiet. William was hardly likely to get tranquility in either family home. Perhaps this was another reason for him leaving when the opportunity arose.

An opportunity arose in 1587 because of an incident which took place some some fifty miles away from Stratford in the Oxfordshire market town of Thame. William Knell, one of the leading actors for the *Queen Elizabeth's Men*, was killed in a brawl with another actor, John Towne. Samuel Schoenbaum was one scholar to suggest that the sudden gap created in the company, gave Shakespeare the chance he was looking for, when shortly afterwards the company - a crucial man short - visited Stratford, and was desperate to fill the vacancy.

There are a number of things that give this suggestion credence. The repertory of *the Queen's Men*, until the company's demise in at the beginning of the 1590s, included plays that were either early versions of plays written by Shakespeare, or other writers, but later re-written and developed by Shakespeare. These include *The Famous Victories of Henry V, King Leir, The Troublesome Reign of King John* and *The True Tragedy of Richard lll.*

Two other plays in the Queen's Men's repertoire were Robert Greene's *A Look-*

ing Glass for London and England and *Friar Bacon and Friar Bungay* which may have been seen by Lord Hunsdon and Emilia. This may have been when both of them first became aware of Shakespeare the actor.

It is possible that Shakespeare's knowledge of Greene's plays - and there may have been more than two in the Queen's Men's repertory - which led him to freely use text and ideas which prompted Greene to accuse the *upstart crow* of unfairly benefittting from other playwright's writing. A modern critic would accuse him of plagiarism.

Knell joined the *Queen Elizabeth's Men* at its formation in 1583. Elizabeth I expressly established the company to thwart the ambitions of the exist-ing acting companies under the patronage of rival aristocrats by poaching their best actors. The Queen, under advice from her spy-master Walsingham, recognised the usefulness of touring actors in collecting information from around the country.

Knell must have been a talented actor because he quickly rose to play leading parts and there are several testimonials to his prowess on stage. He is known to have played the role of the King Henry V in the play of that name, opposite Richard Tarlton, who played Dericke the clown. A record of the event says that

Knel, then playing Henry the fift, hit Tarlton a sound boxe indeed, which made the people laugh the more.

On 30 January 1586, Knell married the 15-year-old Rebecca Edwards. Rebecca was widowed the following year on 13 June. Knell drew his sword and at-tacked Towne, who retreated to a small ridge in a place called White Hound Close, near the toll gate. As Knell approached, Towne drew his own sword in self-defence, stabbing Knell in the neck who died within half an hour. Towne was cleared of murder at a subsequent inquest. The report states that

William Knell continuing his attack as before, so maliciously and furiously, and Towne... to save his life drew his sword of iron (price five shillings) and held it in his right hand and thrust it into the neck of William Knell and made a mortal wound three inches deep and one inch wide.

In December 1587, Rebecca Knell, although only seventeen, became admin-istratrix of her late husband's estate. On 10 March 1588 Rebecca remarried another actor, the twenty two year old John Heminges. Heminges was later to become one of Shakespeare's closest colleagues in the *Lord Chamberlain's Men*, a trustee in Shakespeare's purchase of the Blackfriar's gatehouse, beneficiary under Shakespeare's will of 26 shillings and 8 pence to buy a mourning ring and, most significantly, joint editor of the First Folio.

Embarking on editing the complete Shakespeare plays, from a variety of sources, was a colossal task. Might it be that Heminges was was encouraged to get on with it, by Rebecca, who felt a strong personal interest? The very start of Shakespeare's theatrical career was when he replaced her dead husband in the *Queen's Men*. Did she feel that printing Shakespeare's works for posterity - with his all-encompassing philosophical wisdom - might be the most suitable memorial to commemorate William Knell, her short-lived husband?

In 1591 *Queen Elizabeth's Men* made their final appearance at court. At the company's demise Shakespeare could have joined *Lord Strange's Men.* When Ferdinando Stanley, Lord Strange inherited the title. Earl of Derby, the company's name was changed to the *Earl of Derby's Men.* Between February and June 1592 the *Earl of Derby's Men* played at Henslowe's Rose Theatre, where they performed twenty three plays that included one or more of Shakespeare's *Henry Vl* trilogy.

During that season, Shakespeare, may have had a hand in one of their plays, *A Knacke to knowe a Knaue.* Hanspeter Born has published research pointing out that the text makes reference to the works of Greene, Marlowe, Lodge and Peele. That there are verbal similarities between the text of *Knave* and that of *The Taming of the Shrew* one of Shakespeare's earliest plays.

There are also remarks in the *Groatsworth of Wit* pamphlet satirising his fellow playwrights, which have been argued provide evidence of Greene's annoyance that the up-and-coming Shakespeare had re-written some of *A Knacke to knowe a Knaue* text. The first mention of this play is in the diary of Philip Henslowe listing the play as performed by the *Earl of Derby's Men* on10 June 1592. The diary shows that the play went on to be performed several times at the Rose in 1592 and 1593.

The title page of its published form describes it as *a most pleasant and merry new comedy* and highlights the inclusion of *Kemp's applauded Merrimentes of the Men of Gotham*, who are introduced by the stage direction *Enter mad men of Goteham, to wit, a Miller, a Cobler and a Smith.* This, of course, has resonances with *A Midsommer nights Dreame* when the *rude mechanicals* - a carpenter, a joiner, a weaver, a bellows-mender, a tinker and a tailor - act the play within a play, *Pyramus and Thisbe.*

Derby's Men gave three more court performances in the winter of 1592-3. A long period of plague broke out from August 1592 until May 1594 which kept the theatres closed. A combination of Strange's and Admiral's actors, led by Edward Alleyn, toured the countryside in 1593-4, but I don't think Shakespeare was with them, because there is evidence to suggest that in the autumn of 1593 he left the country for some three months on a journey the final destination of which was North Italy and the Veneto.

That I haue hoysted saile to al the windes Which should transport me farthest from your sight. (117.7/8)

When he returned he wrote *Romeo and Juliet,* written at the time of his affair with Emilia and set in Verona, *en route,* by land, to Venice. The play is the earliest known example of the use of a balcony as a theatrical devise. Balconies are a common feature of the Venetian *piano nobile* architecture.

In her *tour da force* book *Women of Will,* with deep feminine insight, Tina Packer comments

Something happened to change Shakespeare's understanding of the world..... it is [in] Romeo and Juliet that Shakespeare wrote about a sexual passion which was so consuming and so enlightening that it created an energy between the two lovers which in turn led them to understand the very source of spirituality itself. I don't think Shakespeare could have found this visceral knowledge simply through reading or studying.

In *Romeo and Juliet*, there is more than a hint that Shakesperare has recently been spending time amongst musicians. Exchanges between three of them and the illiterate servant, Peter - who has a reputation as a bad singer - demonstrate. Like the Bassano's former name *Piva* meaning *bagpipe*, Shakespeare names his musicians after words associated with instruments.

When the band is dismissed from its celebratory duties after Juliet, the putative bride, has been pronounced dead, there is a tension breaker in the light-hearted dialogue:-

Peter
Musitions, oh Musitions,
Hearts ease, hearts ease,
O, and you will haue me liue, play hearts ease.

Hearts Ease is a light-hearted song, a totally unsuitable suggestion for such a tragic moment, the Elizabethan audience would know that. *Hearts Ease* is also the name of a flower, a viola (a musical pun too) mentioned in the Bisham *Speeches to the Queen*

Musician 1
Why hearts ease;
Peter
O Musitions,
Because my heart it selfe plaies, my heart is full.
Musician 1
Not a dump we, 'tis no time to play now.

A "*dump*" is a lament

Peter
You will not then?

Musician 1

No

Peter

I will then giue it you soundly.

Musician 1

What will you giue vs?

Peter

No money on my faith, but the gleeke. [gleeke = insult] *I will giue you the Minstrell.*

Musician 1

Then will I giue you the Seruing creature.

Peter

Then will I lay the seruing Creatures Dagger on your pate. I will carie no Crochets, Ile Re you, Ile Fa you, do you note me?

a reference here to note lengths and pitches in this exchange

Musician 1

And you Re vs, and Fa vs, you Note vs.

Musician 2

Pray you put vp your Dagger, And put out your wit. Then haue at you with my wit.

Peter

I will drie-beate you with an yron wit, [drie-beate = equals three beats] *And put vp my yron Dagger. Answere me like men: When griping griefes the heart doth wound, then Musicke with her siluer sound. Why siluer sound? why Musicke with her siluer sound? what say you Simon Catling?*

Catling is a cat-gut string

Musician 1

Mary sir, because siluer hath a sweet sound.

Peter

Pratest, what say you Hugh Rebicke?

Rebeck is a small string instrument, forerunner of the violin

Musician 2

I say siluer sound, because Musitions sound for siluer

The author has learnt that professional musicians only play for money

Peter

Pratest to, what say you Iames Sound-Post?

The sound-post is a part of a string instrument, in this particular case, probably a lute

Musician 3

Faith I know not what to say.

Peter

O I cry you mercy, you are the Singer.

(*Romeo and Juliet* 4.5.2589-626)

In April 1594, close to the time that *Romeo and Juliet* was being written, Derby
died, whilst his company was on tour in East Anglia and Hampshire. The
actors returned to London in June, after the plague had abated. The company
endured a radical re-organisation at this time many members, probably including Shakespeare left to join a new version of another company, under the
patronage of Lord Hunsdon, the *Lord Chamberlain's Men*

If the first seventeen sonnets were written as a seventeenth birthday present
for Southampton on 6th October 1590, it is at this celebration that is the
most likely time for Shakespeare to first meet the young earl. Their friendship
began then and developed over time, the progress of the relationship tracked
with the sycophantic but appropriately distant dedication of *Venvs* of 1593 to
the much closer, friendlier, dedication of *Lucrece* in 1594.

The importance of Robert Greene's reference in *Groatsworth* to the *upstart
crow* and the *Shake-scene* as the first document that identifies Shakespeare
in London has long been recognised. What hasn't been recognised, is that
Groatsworth is the first document that in its characters, *Shake-scene* and *Lamilia*, puts the names of Shakespeare and Emilia together.

Peter Levi writes about Emilia

*if her name had been recorded in some scrap of contemporary gossip about Shake-
speare no one would have doubted the identification for a moment*

might Greene's *Groatsworth* be that scrap of gossip?

In September 1592 in the same month that Greene's *Groatsworth* was published, back at home in Stratford, John Shakespeare's name appeared in a list
of Warwickshire recusants - that is parishoners who failed to attend church -
which was a legal requirement.

Some have seen this as a sign of John Shakespeare's retention of a Catholic faith but it is far more likely that John wished to avoid the service of prosecution papers pursuing him for debt as he arived or left church, where he should have been found on a Sunday, to say nothing of the ignominy of having legal papers served in so public a place.

By this time Shakespeare had written at least five plays: *The Comedy of Errors, Titus Andronicus* and *Henry VI, Parts 1, 2,* and *3.* Earlier than these, Shakespeare had a hand in writing the plays *A Knacke to knowe a Knaue* and *Sir Thomas More.* The authors of *More* are considered to be Anthony Munday and Henry Chettle but revised by several writers. The manuscript is particu larly notable for a three-page handwritten revision now widely attributed to Shakespeare (Hand D). It was paleographer, Sir Edward Maunde Thompson who in 1916 first published an analysis of the handwriting of the addition and judged it to be Shakespeare's. The case was strengthened with the publication seven years later, by five noted scholars of *Shakespeare's Hand in the Play of Sir Thomas More* who looked into all aspects of the play.

More recently hand-writing expert, Charles Hamilton believes that Hand D is in the same hand writing as in Shakespeare's will and the applications to the heralds for the family coat-of-arms.

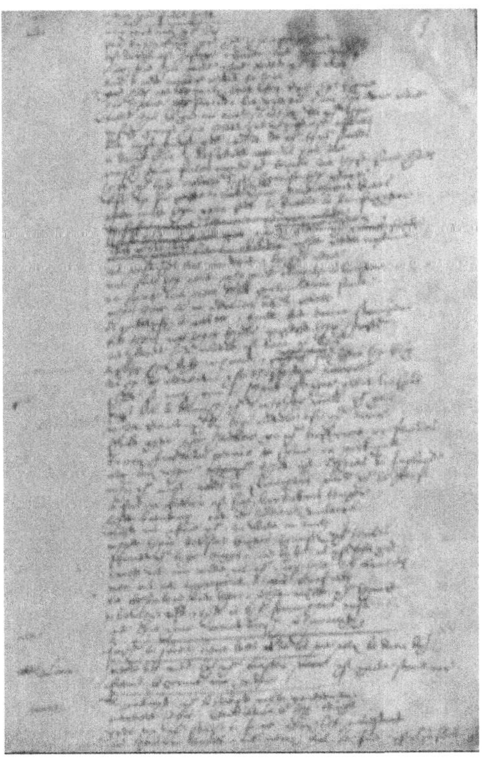

36 Sir Thomas More, Hand D

Sir Thomas More was most likely written to be acted by *Lord Strange's Men,* the only company of the time that could have mounted such a large and demanding production. Philip Henslowe's *Rose Theatre,* was the only London theatre which possessed the special staging requirements - large-capacity second-level stage and special enclosure - called for by the play.

The demanding role of Sir Thomas More, had some eight hundred lines, a huge test of memory, was probably written with Edward Alleyn in mind, the only actor known to have played such large-scale roles.

A few days before Shakespeare's twenty ninth birthday, on 18 April 1593, *Venvs and Adonis* was registered at the Stationer's Company. On 2 May 1594, *The Taming of a Shrew* which bears many similarities to *The Taming of the Shrew* was registered and the *Rape of Lucrece* was entered a week later on May 9, 1594, its title in the register, *the Ravyshement of Lucrece.*

This was entered by the bookseller John Harrison, also a printer and publisher. The first edition was printed later that same year by Richard Field - whose family were Stratford residents and knew the Shakespeares - and sold by Harrison. The poem, dedicated to the Earl of Southampton, like *Venvs* before it, was highly popular and went through eight quarto editions before 1641.

In 1594, there is evidence to suggest that *Edward lll*, one of a number of plays not included in the First Folio, but attributed to Shakespeare by some scholars, was given a private performance by the newly formed *Lord Chamberlain's Men* to their Patron, Lord Hunsdon and his family.

It would appear that the playwright used the annotations made by Hunsdon in his personal copy of Froissarts' *Chronicles* kept at Somerset House because *verbatim* bits of text were included in the play as a compliment to Hunsdon. Edward lll Act 1 Scene 2 quotes the last line of Sonnet 94 *Lillies that fester smell far worse then weeds.* Does this make the two works contemporaneous to the year 1594? I think it does.

Shakespeare is first named as a member of a theatrical company in a set of accounts with a payment made to him dated 17 October 1595. The accounts were submitted to court by someone who knew Shakespeare herself, Southampton's mother. After the death of Sir Thomas Heneage, who was Treasurer of the Royal Household from 1579 to 1596, his widow, submitted his accounts. These included payments for royal entertainments during the 1594–5 Christmas season. Payments to William Kempe, William Shakespeare, and Richard Burbage, servants to the *Lord Chamberlain*

for twoe seuerall Comedies or Enterludes shewed by them before her maiestie in Christmas tyme laste paste viz vpon St Stephens daye & Innocents daye.

The two *Lord Chamberlain* plays were paid at £20, from payments to another company it is clear that the plays were reimbursed at a flat rate of £10 each. The *Lord Chamberlain's* company performed on December 26 and 28. The date of payment was March 15, 1595. From independent evidence we know that the court over Christmas 1594 was situated at Greenwich, we can conclude that Shakespeare didn't spend Christmas with his family.

Nearly a year later the performance of another Shakespeare play was mentioned in a letter. On 7 December 1595 Sir Edward Hoby, a London neighbour of Alphonso and Emilia, wrote to his cousin Robert Cecil, Lord Burghley's son, the letter included a reference to the play *Richard ll.* Sir Edward, the son of Lady Russell and her late husband Thomas Hoby was resident at his country home and birthplace Bisham Abbey, when Emilia's *Speeches to the Queen* was presented there to welcome the Queen on her arrival.

A very important event in the family was Shakespeare's success in securing a grant of arms for his father from William Dethick, Garter King at Arms. From the 20th October 1596 John Shakespeare and his descendants were armegirous and the male descendants permitted to style themselves *gentleman*. William Shakespeare, was the first actor ever to become a *gentleman*, this was the beginning of achieving respectability for a profession that was at the time held in low esteem. In our time many successful actors are awarded high honours, in the case of Laurence Olivier, the highest, a life peerage and the Order of Merit.

It would appear that William wasn't above telling the odd whopper to achieve his aim. He claims John Shakespeare's *antecessors* gave *valieant & faithfull service* to King Henry VII - historians question this suggestion, and so far, no evidence has emerged to support the claim. He claims that Robert Cooke, *Clarenceux King of Arms* had drawn up a *pattern* for a coat-of-arms for his father twenty years earlier, but that document wasn't available then, and hasn't emerged since.

37 Shakespeare's application for a coat-of-arms

Cooke had died a few years before, so he wasn't able to corroborate William's claim. At a time when his father was being pursued for debt, he created for his father a ficticious fortune of £500 with *lands and tenements in Stratford*. One honest and accurate claim was that in John's marriage to Mary Arden he had wed into an armigerous family.

It isn't known precisely what fee Dethick charged Shakespeare for his grant of arms, but presumably a substantial amount. In 1602 Ralph Brooke, *York Herald*, questioned the validity of the grant of arms to twenty three people, including Shakespeare, who Brooke said had obtained their grant of arms by less than honest means. Unusually for the time Brooke, used precisely that spelling of the poet's name, "Shakespeare".

Charles Hamilton claims to have identified nine documents that are in Shakespeare's own hand-writing. I will concentrate on the three most important ones. Hamilton argues that Hand D in *Sir Thomas More*, Shakespeare's two draft applications to the College of Arms for a grant of arms - including the sketch of the arms - and Shakespeare's will are all in the same hand. It is clear that the autograph applications to the College of Arms, are all in the same hand, and it definitely isn't the handwriting of William Dethick.

38 Sir William Dethick's Handwriting

The late Charles Hamilton enjoyed a reputation as an esteemed paleographer, I am therefore surprised that his identification of the handwriting in these three important documements, hasn't received wider recognition.

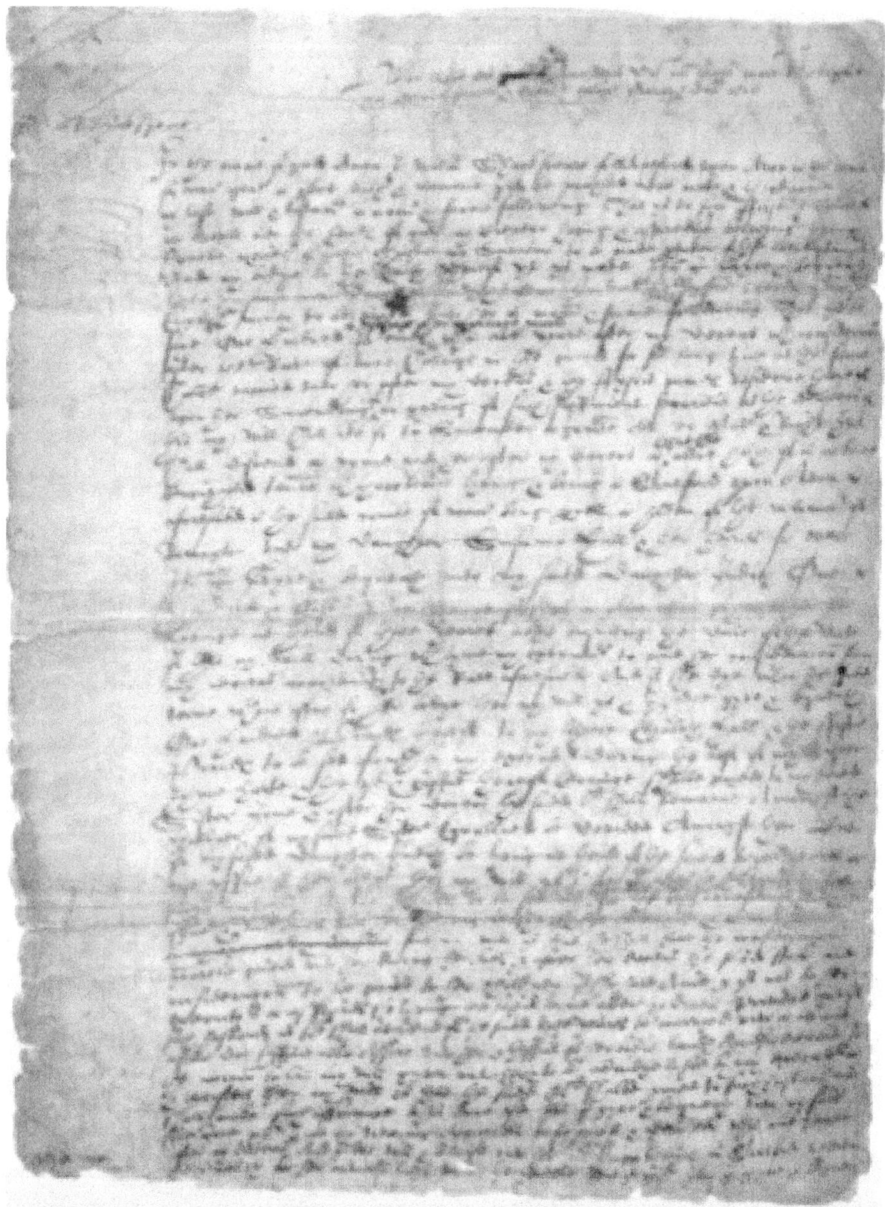

39 Page 1 Shakespeare's Will

Hamilton's book *In Search of Shakespeare* with his revelations about Shakespeare's handwriting was published in 1986. One chapter of his book dwells on the suggestion that the deterioration in handwriting in Shakespeare's will was symptomatic of arsenic poisoning. He suggests that both Shakespeare and Margaret Wheeler, the woman impregnated by Thomas Quiney, Shakespeare's future son-in-law were murdered by arsonic poisoning at Quiney's hand. It could be that this sensational suggestion has been disadvantageous to the wider acceptance of Hamilton's revelations over Shakespeare's hand writing.

A threat to murder is a very serious offence. An entry in the King's Bench Controlment Roll for Michaelmas term 1596 would lead one to believe that Shakespeare was somehow involved in a threat to kill William Wayte. On 29 November a writ of attachment was issued to four people resident in Southwark. It's in Latin, the translation reads

Be it known that William Wayte craves sureties of the peace against William Shakspere, Francis Langley, Dorothy Soer wife of John Soer, and Anne Lee, for fear of death, and so forth. Writ of attachment issued by the sheriff of Surrey, returnable on the eighteenth of St Martin.

Writs of attachment were a way of keeping the peace. As Schoenbaum reports in his *Documentary Life*

the complainant swore before the Judge of Queen's Bench that he stood in danger of death, or bodily hurt, from a certain party. The magistrate then commanded the sheriff of the appropriate county to produce the accused person or persons, who had to post bond to keep the peace

Francis Langley was an unscrupulous goldsmith, a money broker and owner of the Swan playhouse and was in later life a multi-litigant. Nothing is known about Dorothy Soer and Anne Lee, speculation has them identified as prostitutes, but no-one knows. The writ was issued to the sheriff of Surrey, indicating that the parties resided in that county, probably Southwark, and was returnable 29 November 1596, the last day of Michaelmas term.

The notice was preceded by a writ returnable on 3 November 1596 sworn by Francis Langley against William Gardiner and his stepson, William Wayte.

Be it known that Francis Langley craves sureties of the peace against William Gardiner and William Wayte for fear of death etc. Writ of attachment to the sheriff of Surrey, returnable on the morrow of All Souls, 3 November 1596.

Leslie Hotson exonerates Shakespeare from threatening violent behaviour by showing that the real quarrel was not between Francis Langley, William Shakespeare and William Wayte, as the later writ suggests, but between Langley and William Wayte's stepfather, William Gardiner.

A couple of years after Shakespeare's brush with the law there is evidence of more plays appearing in performance. In the *Comparative Discourse* section of *Palladis Tamia*, Francis Meres lists a dozen Shakespearean plays, identified by him as six comedies and six tragedies.

(Comedy: *Two Gentlemen of Verona, Comedy of Errors, Loues Labour's Lost,*

Loue Labours Won, A Midsommer nights Dreame, and *Merchant of Venice*; "Tragedy": *Richard II, Richard III, Henry the IV, King John, Titus Andronicus*, and *Romeo and Juliet*)

establishing these plays composition to before 1598.

There is no way of knowing how complete Meres' knowledge of the published plays was, or whether he even intended to produce a comprehensive list of all the plays. At the very least, it is generally agreed that Meres neglects *The Taming of the Shrew*, and all three parts of the *Henry VI* trilogy which were probably written by 1591. In the same year, 1598, four quarto editions of plays are identified with Shakespeare as author on the title page: the second and third editions of *Richard II*, the first edition of *Loues Labour's lost*, and the second edition of *Richard III*.

Prior to the printing of these specific editions, Shakespeare's printed plays did not bear his name. The printing of his name on subsequent title pages may suggest a development in his reputation as an author, with the inclusion of his name, becoming an advantageous form of advertisement.

Fourteen copies of the first edition of *Loues Labour's lost* are known to survive, they are sub-titled, *Newly corrected and augmented By W. Shakespere*, which has led to speculation that there was an earlier edition of the play that has not survived. The first reference of a performance of *Loues Labour's lost* appears in a sonnet sequence by Robert Tofte also printed in 1598. The collection is entitled *ALBA The Month's Minde of a Melancholy Lover*. The sonnet begins

Labour Lost, I once did see a Play, Ycleped [named] *so*

it seems he was taken to see the play by his *froward Dame* against his will.

While the play was 'Comicall' to everyone (saue me) Whilst it was *Tragick'for him*

He notes that each

Actor plaid in cunning wise his part, But chiefly Those enrapt in Cupids snare; Yet All was fained, twas not from the hart compared to his own suffering in love.

This leads to speculation if the history of William's affair with Emilia and her betrayal with Southampton and others was in the public domain.

Richard II was printed in a second quarto edition in 1598, a year after its first printing. It was again published by the London bookseller Andrew Wise and printed by Valentine Simmes. Wise was an active publisher of Shakespeare's plays, publishing not only the first three editions of *Richard II*, but also the earliest quarto editions of *Richard III, Henry IV Part 1* and *Part 2* and *Much adoe about Nothing.*

The second edition of *Richard II* is a shorter version of the play; the version we are more familiar with today would not be printed until 1608. A peerformance of the longer version was paid for by Essex's supporters, shortly before his abortive coup attempt. It is this version which features the on-stage deposition of King Richard, a potentially controversial scene. The absence of the deposition scene in the first three quarto editions has led critics to debate the possible censorship and revision of Shakespeare's plays by Edmund Tylney, *Master of the Revels.*

In 1599 Sir George Buc, designated to become Tylney's successor, purchased a copy of the anonymous play *George a Greene, Pinner of Wakefield.* Seeking to establish the identity of the playwright, Buc, approached two actors who had taken part in performances of the play and asked, who wrote this play? The replies were recorded in autograph notes to the title page as follows

Written by .... a minister, who ac<ted>
the pinners part in it himself. Teste W. Shakespea<re>

Ed. Iuby saith that this play was made by Ro. Gree<ne>

Edward Juby, a member of the *Admiral's Men,* said the play was by Robert Greene.

When in 2020 the Globe Theatre revived the play, it was advertised "by Robert Greene".

Buc noted that Shakespeare said it was by "......." - which means either Shakespeare, or Buc couldn't remember - but Shakespeare, continues Buc, had been written by .....a minister who had acted the lead part himself. Odd, to say the least. Both Juby and Shakespeare were actors, with actor's memories. Could Shakespeare really not remember the name of a lead actor that he'd worked with or the writer of a play he'd performed in? Both actors were involved in *George a Greene,* when performances were recorded in Philip Henslowe's diary in December 1593 and January 1594.

After its performances in 1593-4, *George a Greene* was entered into the Stationers Register in 1595, and published in 1599.

As *Master of the Revels*, Buc would licence plays for the press beginning in 1607, and for the stage beginning in 1610. But he had the *reversion* of the office much earlier, meaning that he had received a positive guarantee that he would become Master upon the death or resignation of Tylney. It was going to be professionally important for him to know which playwrights had written which plays.

A performance of *George a Greene* on January 21, 1594, was followed a day later by the first known performance of *Titus Andronicus* by. *Titus* was published anonymously the same year.

Shakespeare must have been involved with *George a Greene* as an actor, and with *Titus Andronicus* as both actor and playwright. It's hard to believe that when questioned by Buc, that Shakespeare didn't remember that *George a*

Greene was written by Robert Greene. Perhaps he didn't want to give any artistic support to the reputation of his, and Emilia's, detractor of two years earlier. There is no known playwright of the time who was also a minister, Greene's debauched life was very different from any clergyman's

It seems that Shakespeare had a selective memory when it suited him.

13. William Shakespeare, the actor

(*Hamlet* 3.2.1800)

All actors, musicians and dancers work tirelessly on performing technique. In our time most ambitious students have assistance in consolidating their abilities from teachers who have experience as performers themselves. In *Hamlet*, Shakespeare is passing on good advice to the players who have arrived at Elsinore to *catch the conscience of the King*. The words tell us much about Shakespeare's own approach to acting, and particularly what he dislikes; exaggerated gestures and overblown rhetoric of some of his acting colleagues.

Composers will consider individual performers' specific attributes when writing operas, concertos or other solo works. Mozart wrote the fiendishly difficult stratospheric Queen of the Night arias, from *Die Zauberflaute*, for his sister-in-law, the soprano, Josepha Hofer. Beethoven had Anne Milder's voice in mind when he wrote the title role of *Leonore.* Wagner chose the heldentenor Hermann Winkelmann to create the title role of *Parsifal* at the Bayreuth Festspielhaus in 1882. Walton's Violin Concerto was written for the very special talents of Jascha Heifetz and Britten's *Peter Grimes* was written for the particular vocal sound of his partner, Peter Pears. *Grimes* is set in their home town of Aldeburgh. These are all examples of composers' music tailor-made to exploit the unique qualities of their nominated soloists.

Similarly in the theatre and film world, often casting directors aim to fit an actor's character and temperament to the part he or she is to play on stage or screen. Actors whose career I would say fit this typecasting pattern are Oliver Reed, Katharine Hepburn, Daniel Craig, Charles Laughton, Christopher Lee, Judi Dench and Maggie Smith.

Shakespeare, the actor, played many roles, some of them by other authors, were they written speficially with his acting talents in mind? If we can name the roles that Shakespeare, the actor, played might that shed further light on Shakespeare the man?

In *The Scourge of Folly* (1610), John Davies of Hereford - Shakespeare scholar Brian Vicker's nominee for the author of *A Louer's Complaint* - addressed an epigram to *Mr Will. Shake-speare, our English Terence* and suggested Shakespeare that as an actor played *kingly parts in sport*

Some say good Will (which I, in sport, do sing)
Had'st thou not plaid some Kingly parts in sport,
Thou hadst bin a companion for a King;
And, been a King among the meaner sort.

Tradition has it that the parts he played were the vengeful ghost of Hamlet's father, the patriotic John of Gaunt in *Richard II*, and the all-powerful, all knowing, but merciful Prospero, seen by earlier critics as an auto-biographical character sketch when he gave his valedictory performance in the London theatre in *The Tempest*. These are all *kingly* parts. A less royal role assigned by posterity is that of the loyal and generous old servant, Adam in *As You Like It*.

Donald Foster, a New York professor of English, suggests that Shakespeare played relatively minor parts in his own plays, and mainly the parts of older men. Professor Foster arrived at his conclusion by employing computer analysis of the language in the plays. Might he have played older roles be because he was less mobile than other actors? Shakespeare twice makes reference to his lameness in the Sonnets.

So I, made lame by Fortunes dearest spight (37.3)

and

Speak of my lamenesse, and I straight will halt: (89.3)

This notion brought back memories of Robert Stephens - post hip-replacement operation - playing Falstaff in Stratford in 1993.

Here is a list of the parts that Professor Foster proposes Shakespeare played in assumed chronological order, you will see that Prospero isn't amongst them.

1591 *Henry Sixth Part One*: Duke of Bedford, a medieval English prince
1591 *Henry the Sixth Part Two* minor parts
1590/2 *The Taming of the Shrew*: The Lord (induction)

1594 *The Comedy of Errors*: Egeon, A merchant of Syracuse
1594/5 *The Merchant of Venice*: Prince of Morocco and Messenger
1595 *Richard the Second*: Gaunt and the Gardener
1595/6 *A Midsummer night's Dream*: Theseus Duke of Athens
1596/7 *King John*: King Philip
1597 *Henry Fourth Part One*; King Henry
1596/9 *Henry the Fourth, Part two* King Henry and Rumour
1598/9 *Much ado about Nothing.*: Messenger and Friar
1599 *Henry Fifth:* The Chorus and Mountjoy
1599 *As you Like it:* Adam and Corin.
1599 *Julius Caesar:* Falvius
1599-1602 Hamlet: the Ghost
1598-1608 *Alls well That Ends Well:* The King (of France)
1605/8 *Coriolanus:* Menenius, senator of Rome
1607/8 *Pericles:* Gower (chorus)
1603 *Othello:* Brabantio, Venetian senator and Desdemona's father
1605/6 *Timon of Athens:* The Poet

Twelve of these characters are of royal blood or high flying political leaders, which coincides with John Davies's identification of *Kingly parts*. The less aristocratic roles of messenger, gardener, herald, servant, shepherd, chorus and poet are also the more minor roles.

Pursuing the details of each and every character that Shakespeare may have played could be the subject of a complete book in itself. There are though one or two characters that I think worthwhile exploring here.

One play written whilst Shakespeare's affair with Emilia was still active, *The Comedie of Errors*. This was based on William Warner's translation of *Menaehmi* by Plautus completed before June 1594 but not published until 1595. Professor Foster's identification of Egeon as a role played by Shakespeare himself is of significance. The dedication of the printed version of Warner's translation was to Lord Hunsdon, who had been patron of Shakespeare's company the *Lord Chamberlain's Men* founded shortly after the death of Ferdinando Stanley, Lord Derby in April 1594.

As with *Edward III*, it is highly likely that Shaespeare read a copy belonging to Hunsdon. Emilia's long open affair with Hunsdon had come to an end shortly after the start of her pregnancy in August 1593 and before her hasty marriage to Alphonso two month's later. Shakespeare's choice of the name Aemilia - a name which doesn't appear in Plautus - for the long-lost wife, of the husband he anticipated playing on stage, appears to be wishful thinking on the playwright's part.

In Chapter fifteen I will propose that Shakespeare's affair with Emilia, strarted in an abbey, Bisham Abbey. The Aemilia of *The Comedie of Errors* is an abbess of Ephesus, highly respected by all. When Aemilia appears, she was shipwrecked years ago and lost contact with her husband and her twin sons in the aftermath. Early after her first entrance on stage Aemilia asks about the sexual conduct of the distracted Antipholus, suspecting madness caused by untreated syphilis

hath not else his eye Stray'd his affection in vnlawfull loue, A sinne preuailing much in youthfull men (5.1.1393)

Both Emilia and William at this date had been indulging in unlawful love that heightened the awareness that they were both permanently shackled to spouses neither of them wanted. Was Shakespeare, knowing that Hunsdon would be in the audience, playing with fire, so publicly naming the recently discarded mistress of his company's patron? Or was it a double bluff putting him off the scent, that he had now taken up where his company's patron had left off?

There is another character in *The Comedie of Errors*, an unnamed courtesan. Emilia's association with Hunsdon, particularly the big age difference, is precisely what society would assume that Emilia was. This perception is further prompted by the behaviour of Greene's Lamilia.

In Act 4 Shakespeare gives her some significant lines:

I see sir you haue found the Goldsmith now: Is that the chaine you promis'd me to day? (4.1.1140)

and

He rush'd into my house, and tooke perforce My Ring away. This course I fittest choose, For fortie Duckets is too much to loose (4:1.1184)

A few years later Simon Forman noted

She [Emilia] *hath £40 a year and was wealthy to him that married her, in money and jewels, she can hardly keep secret*

This information about the precise figure for her income and her possession of jewels was revealed to Shakespeare by Emilia who then publicly disclosed it in the *Comedie of Errors*.

Rings, jewels and ducats play an important symbolic role in *The Merchant* too. Shylock's gift from Leah, a ring exchanged for a monkey. Salanio reports Shylock's public despair

A sealed bag, two sealed bags of ducats,
Of double ducats, stolne from me by my daughter,
And iewels, two stones, two rich and precious stones,
Stolne by my daughter: iustice, finde the girle,
She hath the stones vpon her, and the ducats (2.8.1032)

Another character on Professor Foster's list of roles acted by William is the

Moor in *The Merchant of Venice*, which I date to being written shortly after the Lopez affair. In *the Merchant* a cornett flourish twice heralds the entrance of the moor, the Prince of Morocco, and accompanies his exit after choosing the wrong casket. I wonder if Shakespeare had himself in mind when he wrote the lines for the moor.

I have already mentioned the use of Emilia's Venetian maiden name for the character of Bassan(i)o. Cornetts were wind instruments, almost exclusively associated with the Bassano family in England but more widely played in Venice. Emilia specifies the use of cornetts in *Speeches to the Queen at Bisham*. Shakespeare only uses the instrument in four plays in the complete First Folio collection.

Unusually, the First Folio has Shakespeare describing the Moor and his dress *Enter Morochus a tawnie Moore all in white, and three or foure followers accordingly, with Portia, Nerrissa, and their traine.* On their first meeting he immediately addresses Portia on the colour of his skin

Mislike me not for my complexion, The shadowed liuerie of the burnisht sunne, To whom I am a neighbour, and neere bred. (*Merchant*. 2.1.1499)

Is *burnisht sunne* inspired by Emilia's Byrd text *Of gold all burnisht, and brighter then sunne beames*? (*Sundrie songs.XXXVI.1*)

Is the Prince of Morocco's view on possessing a dark complexion something that Emila, who Shakespeare describes her as *a moor* in the sonnets, may have identified with?

Actors in the late C16 were a quarrelsome lot, taking their fencing skills learnt for the stage into a more public arena with murderous results. We already know of Kit Marlowe's fatal stabbing in Deptford in 1593 and the death of William Knell in Thame before that.

In 1598 when Ben Jonson had so recently attended the first performance of *Everyman in his Humour*, by the *Lord Chamberlain's Men* at the Curtain, he too became involved in a fatal skirmish which saw him briefly imprisoned. He escaped the death sentence by pleading benefit of clergy but was branded with the letter T for Tyburn on his thumb. In a letter to the actor Edward Alleyn, from Philip Henlowe, dated September 26, Henslowe wrote

I have lost one of my company that hurteth me greatly; that is Gabriel [Spencer], for he is slain in Hogsden fields by the hands of Benjamin Jonson, bricklayer

Spencer - who may have played a minor role in *Henry Vl part 3* - appears to have got his comeuppance, since less than two years earlier he too had killed a man. His victim was James Feake, the son of a goldsmith, on that occasion, the violence erupted after a quarrel at the house of a barber in the theatre district of Shoreditch. The duel between Spencer and Jonson was fought on Hoxden Fields. Henslowe knew that Jonson was writing by the time of Gabriel

Spencer's death, because he'd paid him an advance, so the reference to Jonson's old trade was made perjoratively.

By 1599 the *Lord Chamberlain's Men* had moved to the newly built Globe Theatre and took their repertory, including *Everyman*, with them. Like many Elizabethan playwrights Jonson was known to have created stage characters from the circumstances and attributes of people from life. In Shakespeare's case the late Sir John Oldcastle for Falstaff and the very much alive Cordell Annesley for Lear's daughter, Cordelia, are two examples.

Several of Jonson's characters have been identified as men living at the time that Jonson regarded as suitable targets for lampooning. In *The Case is Altered*, Anthony Munday, pageant-poet of the city, translator of romances and playwright, is ridiculed in the character of Antonio Balladino.

In *Every Man in His Humour* there is a caricature of Samuel Daniel, court poet, sonneteer, tutor to Lady Anne Clifford and companion of men of fashion. Jonson was jealous of both of these men because they held positions to which he felt he was more entitled.

It seems almost certain that he attacked both of them through satirical means in *Every Man Out of His Humour*, and *Cynthia's Revels*, Daniel under the character Fastidious Brisk, and Hedon and Munday as Puntarvolo and Amorphus.

By 1610 Forman's reputation, both professional and as a philanderer saw Ben Jonson lampooning him in the title role of his comedy *The Alchemist* premiered at the Blackfriar's Theatre.

It has been suggested Shakespeare's recent acquisition of a coat-of-arms was alluded to in the character of Sogliardo, a country bumpkin, who in *Everyman*, had also recently been made armigerous.

Shakespeare wrote various roles with a specific actor in mind to play them; Richard Burbage for the serious roles of Richard lll, Hamlet, Othello and Lear and Will Kemp and later Robert Armin for comic roles. Ben Jonson wrote two plays knowing that Shakespeare, the actor would be playing a role. In *Sejanus His Fall* Shakespeare is listed as a player but it isn't clear which role he played. *Every Man in his Humour* was first performed at The Curtain in 1598 by the *Lord Chamberlain's Men* and in 1604 at Court by the *King's Men*. Shakespeare was fifty when he played the aptly named Kno'well, a pun on his immense knowledge.

There is much in *Every Man* that mirrors the factual narrative and biographical characters of the *Sonnets* and *A Lover's Complaint*. I think that his friend Ben Jonson knew something of Shakespeare's upbringing and his later life secrets and mischievously alluded to them in this play.

Actors love acting and Shakespeare, the actor, would have been no different, he would have enjoyed getting inside the character written for him by Jonson. Old Kno'well is an elderly gentleman, worried about his adolescent son, Edward. By 1598 Shakespeare was officially a gentleman - Jonson's often quoted parody of the motto attached to his grant of arms *Non sanz droict* or *Not without Right* and Sogliardo's motto in the play *Not without Mustard* shows Jonson poking good natured fun at his friend.

Is it possible that Old Kno'well represents John Shakespeare and and his son, Edward, Young Kno'well, the teenage William? After all, William's application for a grant of arms was made on behalf of his father. John was first member of the Shakespeare family legally entitled to use a coat-of-arms - an honour much protected from abuse by the heralds in their countrywide visitations - and the first entitled to call himself *gentleman*.

Jonson dedicated *Everyman* to William Camden, his old headmaster at Westminster School. As fellow members of the Society of Antiquaries, Camden was an associate of Emilia's brother-in-law, Joseph Holland. In 1597, Camden was appointed *Clarenceux King at Arms*, another strong connection between thoughts in Jonson's mind and heraldry. There is a family connection between Camden and the Bassanos. Philip Holland, Emilia's nephew - her late sister Angela's son - was an assistant to Camden at the College of Arms.

By the time *Everyman* first appeared on the stage, John Shakespeare was probably in his late sixties, old for an Elizabethan, when average life expectancy was about forty years. Edward is a well educated young man but, to his father's disapproval, has a penchant for *idle poetry*. Is this how, John Shakespeare, Alderman and Bailiff of Stratford regarded his son's obsession with the Latin verse of Ovid learnt at the Grammar School?

The 1598 version of the play was set in Florence, the 1616 version, set in London. The plot tells how an intercepted letter enabled Old Kno'well to follow his supposedly studious son to London, and observe his life with the gallants of the time. The only indication to show that John might have been in London are some instances of litigation beginning from a time before William was born. Hearings at the Queen's Bench indicate that John could have been obliged to visit London to attend.

Edward is rather impressionable, albeit street-wise, but easily led in the wrong direction. Edward is sent a letter from Wellbred who is a roguish young gallant with a taste for mischief. Might Jonson have had Southampton in mind? Wellbred deliberately causes much of the confusion that runs throughout the play, for example he sews seeds of doubt in both Kitely and his wife, that the other is being unfaithful.

Kitely is a cloth merchant, married to Dame Kitely, and brother of Mistress Bridget. He is also Wellbred's landlord, who becomes increasingly upset by Wellbred's behaviour and the company he keeps. During the progress of the play, Kitely grows more and more paranoid that he is being cuckolded and that his wife is having an affair. This provokes increasingly desperate behaviour, as Kitely tries to guard his house using his assistant, Cash, and runs across town trying to catch his wife in *flagrente delicto*.

There are parallels with Alphonso and Emilia here. The play was written at the same time that Emilia was consulting with Simon Forman, allowing him to share her bed and noting in his case books *She hath been favoured much.......of many noblemen*. Even though my suspicion is that because of Alphonso's sexual orientation, he is unlikely to get quite so animated about his wife's infidelity as Kitely does.

Wellbred's letter to Edward, intercepted by his father, invites the boy to meet him at the Old Jewry puts the play in motion, it begins

Why, Ned, I beseech thee, hast thou forsworn all thy friends in the Old Jewry? or dost thou think us all Jews that inhabit there?

semitic words that immediately associate it with the Bassano family.

Wellbred enjoys exposing and mocking the foolishness of others, such as Matthew's awful poetry.

As the dedicatee of many volumes of poetry, Southampton would recognise an inferior poet when he read one. Wellbred also orchestrates Edward's marriage to Mistress Bridget, Kitely's attractive young sister. Wellbred's invitation to Edward is to spend time at the Old Jewry, where Wellbred promises him much amusement. Much of *Everyman* is set in Moorfields, another venue associated with Emilia since it was where her family home was.

Old **Kno'well**'s most important contribution comes in Act 2, Scene 3, in which he delivers a long speech on the nature of parenthood. Part of this script would indicate that Ben Jonson knew about Shakespeare visit to Venice. The last four lines suggest references to Emilia's sexual attributes, John Shakespeare's reputation for usury and his son's preoccupation with making money

Well, I thank heaven, I never yet was he
That travell'd with my son, before sixteen,
*   To shew him the Venetian courtezans;*
*   Nor read the grammar of cheating I had made,*
*   To my sharp boy, at twelve; repeating still*
*   The rule, Get money; still, get money, boy;*

At the time Shakespeare was playing Old Kno'well on stage he had managed to get quite a lot of money - enough to buy New Place for example - but some of its acquisition was by questionable means.

Whenever Jonson and Shakespeare became friends, it was a friendship that lasted until the very end of Shakespeare's life. When the Reverend John Ward became Rector of Holy Trinity Stratford in 1662 he would have passed Shakespeare's tomb and the memorial bust every day on his way to and from the altar. It was perhaps this constant reminder that encouraged him to keep a note book which included entries on Shakespeare, the last of the five entries refers to the poet's death.

Shakespear Drayton and Ben Jhonson had a merry meeting and it seems drank too hard for Shakespeare died of a feavour there contracted

Unfortunately Ward doesn't mention his informant, but being a man of the cloth it is unlikely that he invented the anecdote. Since there would have been older Stratford residents who would have grown up with Shakespeare's daughters, it is likely that this is a true account of Drayton and Jonson visiting their old friend in his home town.

Straford is a three day ride from London, perhaps they had been invited to Judith's wedding, often an encouragement for drinking too much. If the trio had drunk as much as they did in their earlier days in London, when daily consumption made alcohol tollerance higher, then it could have left Shakespeare feeling very much the worse for wear.

Judith's difficulty with her finance's dubious conduct must have caused her father a great deal of anxiety, this too could have been a contributory factor in raising the poet's bl;ood pressure ehich provoked the stroke that seems to have been the cause of making the hand writing on the later parts of Shakespeare's will so shaky.

14. Shakespeare, the Business Man

Lear
There's money for thee.
Gloucester
O let me kisse that hand.

(*King Lear* 4.5.2472)

On 4 May 1597 Shakespeare bought New Place, the second-largest house in Stratford-upon-Avon, in a somewhat dilapidated condition, from William Underhill. New Place had been built by Sir Hugh Clopton in 1483.

Shortly after the sale in 1597, Underhill died, apparently poisoned by his eldest son, Fulke, who presumably wanted to get his hands on the cash from the property sale. A charge of murder was brought against Fulke and he was executed in 1599. Fulke's other estates reverted to the crown until his younger brother, Hercules, came of legal age in 1602. In that year, Hercules confirmed the sale of New Place to Shakespeare.

By the time Shakespeare acquired New Place, built of brick and timber, it had three storeys, five gables, two orchards and two small gardens. The £60 shown in the exchange documents as the price paid by Shakespeare is unlikely to represent the actual sum he paid. In many cases, the true purchase price is frequently twice the sum named in the documents. Much more likely that Shakespeare paid close on £120 for New Place.

We have already seen that in 1597 Shakespeare along with his London neighbour, Thomas Morley, was avoiding paying taxes in the Parish of St Helen's Bishopsgate. A year later the Lay Subsidy Roll lists him as a householder in Bishopsgate, and yet the Langley writ has him in registered in Sourthwark. Perhaps he maintained two places of residence in London.

He would seem to have earned a reputation for a man of means by this time, because in October 1598 Stratford Alderman Richard Quiney penned a letter to William seeking his assistance in raising a loan of £30. Later the Quineys were to become Shakespeare in-laws, when Richard's third son, the ne'r do well, Thomas, married William's younger daughter, Judith.

Quiney had probably been encouraged to write to Shakepeare seeking a loan because of information he'd received a year before. Quiney had been in London since late October 1597, seeking advice on renewing and extending the town's charter.

On January 24, 1598, Abraham Sturley, fellow Stratford resident, wrote to Quiney on a number of issues, one of which throws significant light on William Shakespeare's affairs. Sturley informed his friend that he had picked up from Quiney's father Adrian that

our countriman Mr Shakspere is willinge to disburse some monei vpon some od yarde land [ca. 30 acres] *or other att Shottri or neare about vs*

However, Adrian had expressed the view that it would be better if Shakespeare could be persuaded instead to *deale in the matter of our Tithes*. Sturley charged Richard Quiney, *bi the instruccions u can geve him theareof, and bi the frendes he can make* to persuade Shakespeare to invest in these tithes instead of the land purchase he was thought to have in mind.

Sturley assumed that the two men would then meet in London, and the letter further reflects a belief that Shakespeare, by now the owner of New Place, was intending to invest sums in the purchase of land close to Stratford.

A survey dated 4 February 1598, shows Shakespeare indulging in unethical conduct, the consequences of which would be detrimental to the poor. Storage of foodstuffs in a time of poor harvests, in order to sell at inflated prices, was something frowned upon. Of those storing grain in Stratford-upon-Avon, *W*[illia]*m Shackesp*[ear]*e* is listed as holding 10 quarters of malt. The survey was held because of a series of poor harvests, beginning in 1595, which had led to an increase in the price of wheat to a record 50 shillings a quarter by late 1596, a three-fold increase since 1592. Outbreaks of violence were an ever-present threat and the death rate soared as diseases associated with malnutrition took their toll. Sturley's January 24, 1598 letter refers to events in Stratford typical of this nationwide simmering of discontent.

In early 1595, the Privy Council required local justices of the peace to carry out surveys to identify those who, by storing quantities of corn and malt in their barns, were suspected of taking advantage of the shortages by releasing limited supplies at inflated prices.

The death of a father is a colossal moment in anyone's life, William was no exception. John Shakespeare was buried on September 8, 1601, according to the Holy Trinity Church parish register. The entry in the parish records is distinguished by the prefix *Mr.*, showing an elevated standing in the town, but it surprising that it doesn't say *gentlemen* an epithet that John's acquisition of armigerous status five years before qualified him.

John Shakespeare was a unique tradesmen in Stratford, the only one authorised to display a coat-of-arms and I wonder if he didn't do this somewhere inside, or outside, of his glove-merchant's premises.

Sturley's letter to Quiney also shows that Shakespeare was looking for land to purchase close to Stratford. It took four years for him to do so. In 1602 he negotiated with John Combe for the purchase of 107 acres for £320, a considerable sum to find. The conveyancing document styles both Shakespeare and Combes as gentlemen. John Combe was a wealthy member of a family that had settled in Stratford in the 1530s. In 1593 he had acquired these 107 acres of land from Rice Griffin, with his equally wealthy uncle and lawyer, William Combe of Warwick, who appears to have acted as a trustee.Deeds of conveyance were copied out twice. Shakespeare was not present when the deed was signed because it was endorsed with a note that it was handed to his brother Gilbert Shakespeare *to the use of the within-named William Shakespeare* in the presence of five witnesses, who signed their names, Anthony Nash and his brother John, William Sheldon, Humphrey Mainwaring and Richard Mason.

Although there is some evidence that Gilbert had been living in London, pursuing the trade of haberdasher in 1597, his presence in Stratford on this occasion suggests that he had returned to Stratford by 1602 and that he lived in the town until his death in 1612.

Shakespeare's purchase was not a complete block of land but a collection of strips, or *lands*, scattered across one or two of the open fields in the north-east part of Old Stratford. These fields were divided into furlongs, each furlong made up of a bundle of strips. We can therefore identify the area as roughly bounded today by Guild Street and its extension (Birmingham Road) to the south-west, Warwick Road to the south-east, and the former Clopton Park to the north. Common grazing rights were linked to this land, probably on the grass between the Warwick Road and the river.

The purchase price of land was generally calculated on its rental value multiplied by the number of years required to generate a return of 5%, namely twenty years. In the case of this purchase – 107 acres for £320 – the annual return may have been in the region of £16 to £20.

The following year, 1603, was a momentous one for the country. The anxiety over predictions of distaster which might befall the country on the death of a childless queen proved unfounded. Elizabeth's death smoothed the way for a relatively stable transition for a new monarch, King James VI of Scotland who was to become King James I of England. Once informed of his accession to the throne, James started the journey from Edinburgh to London. By the time he arrived, the ever threatening plague had struck again and so his coronation was delayed for almost a year.

As that day approached, more than a thousand royal servants were issued red or scarlet cloth, to be tailored into livery. On May 15 1604, in the accounts of the Master of the Great Wardrobe, William Shakespeare is listed as receiving 4

1/2 yards of scarlet cloth in anticipation of King James's coronation progress. This cloth was issued to all the King's servants including four of Emilia's Bassano cousins, the musicians, Jerome, Arthur, Edward and Andrew.

There are three lists of *players* (actors) in the state papers occuring separately under three headings; the servants of the King, the Queen, and the Prince, in that hierarchy. Together the lists appear to be a complete roll call of the twenty-eight adult actors who made up the three leading playing companies in the country in 1604. The individual known to have been the leading player in each company is listed first. William Shakespeare leads the *King's Men*, Christopher Beeston the *Queen's Men* and Edward Alleyn the *Prince's Men*. Incontrovertible proof that Shakespeare was highly regarded in the acting profession at this time.

Another document associated with Shakespeare is the register of Stratford's court of record, which would have begun in 1601, but not survived, the only knowledge we have of its proceedings are to be found in loose case papers. One of these papers is an undated declaration made by William Shakespeare's lawyer, William Tetherton.

The declaration concerns money owed by Philip Rogers for Shakespeare's sale to him of 20 bushels of malt for the sum of 39s. 10d, in a series of six transactions, between March and June 1604. After borrowing two more shillings from Shakespeare, Rogers repaid six shillings, ending up with a debt of 35s 10d. to which Shakespeare's lawyer added 10 shillings in damages. As this is the only paper to have survived, the outcome of the case is unknown. Given that Shakespeare had not brought the case until several unsuccessful appeals to Rogers had been made, it is likely to have been heard at some time in 1605.

Rogers has been traditionally identified simply as an apothecary, and this was indeed one of the ways he made a living. However, he was also a tavern keeper, and it was in this capacity that, after 1602, he frequently appears in the Stratford records. This means that Shakespeare's sale of malt to him. at regular intervals in the first half of 1604, was to supply Rogers's main business as a brewer and seller of beer.

The simarly dated *Revels Book* of 1604–5 reveals Shakespeare at the zenith of his success as a playwright, with seven plays and eight performances at court. The *Merchant of Venice,* written a decade before, was so admired by the King that he commanded a repeat performance. This was also a financially successful year for Shakespeare's company, which would have reaped £100 for its ten performances at £10 per play.

In the closing months of 1605 Edmund Tylney, *Master of the Revels* since 1579, submitted his accounts for the 1604–5 financial year. While most Revels accounts survive only as summaries reported in annual Exchequer rolls, original books survive for 1604–5, in addition to two others. This 1604–5 book is in the hand of William Honnyng, clerk of the Revels. Two pages of the ten page book contain a table in three columns. The first column records playing companies, the second records the play titles, dates, and venues, and the third records *The poets which mayd the plaies.*

Tylney reported a total of fifteen court performances, including two masques with music. The thirteen remaining performances were all plays, one attributed to Heywood, one to Chapman, and four to *Shaxberd.* In the first column are noted ten performances by Shakespeares's company, *the Kings Maiesties plaiers* or *his Maiesties plaiers,* and one performance each by the *Queen's players* and the *Boyes of the Chapell.*

The busiest time for the actors at court was around Christmas, in 1604, yet again, Shakespeare wasn't at home with his family. The plays expressly attributed to Shakespeare are *Mesur for Mesur, The Plaie of Errors,* and the two performances of *The Marchant of Venis.* Further plays by Shakespeare, but without acknowledgement of his authorship, are *the Moor of Venis [Othello], the Merry wiues of Winsor, Loues Labours Lost* and *Henry the fift.*

Two more plays performed by *his Maiesties plaiers,* are by Ben Jonson, although unattributed in the third column. They are *Euery one out of his Vmor* and *Euery one In his Vmor* in which Shakespeare probably acted the role of Kno'well.

In the summer of 1605, Shakespeare was able to raise the considerable sum of £440 to purchase a half-share in a lease of a portion of the Stratford tithes from Ralph Hubaud of Ipsley. As a form of property, this differed from his purchase of land three years earlier but the purpose was the same; to provide Shakespeare, and his family, with a further reliable source of investment income.

Tithes, in the sense used here, originated in early medieval England as the parishioners' payment of a tenth part of their total agricultural produce to the parish priest. Although those purchasing a right to parish tithes were often required to make some provision for maintaining the vicar and the church, the right to collect such tithes, in effect, passed out of the control of the church into lay hands.

However, tithe owners, especially by the mid-sixteenth century, did not necessarily collect the tithes. Instead, owners often rented this right to tenants for a fixed sum, leaving the tenants free to make what profit they could beyond their annual rent.

A few years later Shakespeare's portion of the tithes was said to be worth £60 a year, which after deductions to the Corporation and the Barkers, the original tithe grantees, would have left him with an annual surplus in the region of £40. In about ten years Shakespeare would thus have made back the £440 he paid Hubaud. For the remaining twenty-one years of the 1544 lease the £40 surplus would have been clear profit.

On 17 August 1608, Shakespeare began an action in the Stratford court of record to recover a debt of £6 from John Addenbrooke. A month after the action was started Mary Shakespeare died. One wonders why Shakespeare should have bothered to continue litigation for such a relatively modest sum at a time of family mourning. The case dragged on until at least June 7, 1609. The register recording the court's proceedings during this period is lost, but many cases which came before it, generated a sequence of writs and other loose papers. Fortunately, seven such items survive for the case between Shakespeare and Addenbrooke, allowing us to track the progress of this particular claim in reasonable, though not complete, detail.

These surviving documents are in Latin and all have small central holes or tears along one edge indicating they were once held together by a tie or pin to form a bundle. Two of the items, the order to produce Addenbrooke and writ to bring Addenbrooke's surety, Thomas Hornby to court subsequently became part of his papers. The writs all bear the name *Greene* in the bottom right corner, indicating that they had been issued with the authority of Thomas Greene, the Corporation's steward, who acted as the court's legal officer.

Addenbrooke, described early in his career as a yeoman. but later as a gentleman, was married at Tanworth-in-Arden in 1574. He was buried there on June 19 1609, probably before any outcome of the litigation was known. His place of residence gave rise to another problem. As Stratford's court of record had no jurisdiction outside the borough boundary, its officers were not able to carry out its instructions in cases where the defendant lived elsewhere.

None of the papers explains how Addenbrooke contracted the debt but they do provide evidence of Shakespeare's local dealings with a man of some substance not obviously linked to a routine business transaction. The relativerly small amount Shakespeare was seeking probably shows that he felt Addenbrooke had, in some way, behavioured dishonourably.

The emotional bond between a mother and son is arguably the strongest of human attachments. With the death of his mother Mary, William lost not only his sole surviving parent, but the mother that provided the safety and nurturing from a time before memory could record anything. The entry on September 9, 1608 in the Holy Trinity Church parish register reads *Mayry Shaxspere, wydowe* and is written in the hand of the curate, William Gilbert, alias Higges who may have taught Shakespeare at school.

Mary's husband, John, had died almost exactly seven years earlier. Mary's date of birth is unknown, but given that she was still unmarried in November 1556 and bore children until 1580, she was probably aged about 70 at the time of her death. As a mother she had suffered the dreadful loss of four of her eight children, two as infants, Anne as an eight year old and the twenty seven year old Edmund, a year before her own death. Her last year can't have been a very happy one.

There appears to be little or no personal connection to Shakespeare's parents in the work that was thrust into the public arena a year later, on May 20, 1609. Thomas Thorpe entered the book entitled *Shakespeare's sonnettes* into Liber C of the *Stationers' Company*. He published the first quarto edition of the poems, printed by George Eld, later in 1609.

This is one of the five times Shakespeare's name appears in the Stationers' Register. It is one of the few times that Shakespeare's name is spelt as we spell it now. The Sonnets can be interpreted as largely auto-biographical, in a candid and reveltory manner that it is unlikely the author would have wanted made public, particularly in his home town.

Perhaps it was the publication of the Sonnets had made Shakesperare *persona non grata* in Stratford when on September 11, 1611, the Corporation initially omitted his name from a list of seventy-two residents who might be successfully approached to subscribe

towardes the Charge of prosecutyng the Bill in the parliament for the better Repayre of the highe Waies and amendinge divers defectes in the Statutes alredy made

While seventy-one of the names are listed in a single column down the left-hand side of the page, and then continued on the back of the sheet, William Shakespeare's name stands completely alone in an otherwise blank space to the right, either added as an afterthought, or after pressure was brought to bear.

The Highways Act of 1555 made road maintenance the responsibility of the parishes through which roads passed, mainly through the provision of labourers. This proved totally inadequate and, following numerous complaints, there were efforts to improve the situation by means of new legislation.

Three attempts were made to introduce bills in parliament, in 1606, 1607 and 1610, all of which failed. In February 1611 the government sent letters to local justices about highway repairs and by autumn further proposals were clearly under consideration.

In response the Stratford Town Council provided a list of potential subscribers, Shakespeare's name standing in isolation might have been symbolic of his current standing amongst his fellow citizens. With many journeys to and from Stratford to London and a considerable property owner in and around the town, Shakespeare, as someone who would benefit from the upkeep of the road should have immediately sprung to mind as a likely benfactor. The absence of his name listed along with the other seventy one Strafordians is odd.

On 3 February 1612 there is a curious burial reference in the records of Holy Trinity Church *Gilbert Shakspeare, adolescens* this is generally accepted as being William's younger brother Gilbert. This was the second occasion on which William was to suffer that tragic loss, the death of a younger brother. Edmund having died five years earlier. It is the use of the word *adolescens* that raises a question. A forty six year old can hardly be described as an *adolescent*.

The three Shakespeare brothers were all living in London at the end of the C16, one imagines that they met up from time to time, perhaps at the Mermaid Tavern, since the landlord seems to have been a friend of William. Gilbert's death must have revived memories of the Shakespeare brothers happy times together in London and perhaps childhood days in Stratford too.

Gilbert was a haberdasher, a seller of needlework supplies such as thread, needles, and ribbons, living in the parish of St. Bride's, Fleet Street. In 1597, he and a shoemaker, stood surety for £19 bail for William Sampson, a Stratford clockmaker, in the Court of the Queen's Bench.

Because of his signature in place of William's on the Combe land conveyancing document, Gilbert Shakespeare seems to have moved back to Stratford by 1602, very likely to continue the family glove-making business after the death of his father.

Charlotte Stopes investigated every useage of the term *adolescens, adolocentulus* and *adolocentula* and their variants in the Stratford parish register and came to the conclusion that *adolescens* meant only that Gilbert Shakespeare died unmarried. In the absence of any records of his marriage, the baptism of any children, any other record of his death, and the fact that he is not mentioned in William's will would indicate that Stopes' conclusion is correct.

As well as being mentioned in the *Parnassus* play Shakespeare's name was included by John Webster in a list of dramatists he admired in his preface to *The White Devil*, printed in 1612 by Nicholas Okes for Thomas Archer.

Detraction is the sworne friend to ignorance: For mine owne part I haue euer trule cherisht my good opinion of other mens worthy Labours, especially of that full and haightned stile of Maister Champman. *The labor'd and vnderstanding workes of Maister* Iohnson. *The no less worthy composures of the both worthily excellent Maister* Beamont, *& Maister* Fletcher: *And lastly (without wrong last to be named) the right happy and copious industry of M.* Shake-speare, M. Decker, *& M.* Heywood, *wishing what I write may be read by their light: Protesting, that, in the strength of mine owne iudgement, I know them so worthy, that though I rest silent in my owne worke, yet to most of their I daire (without faltter) fix that of* Martiall.

It is notable that Webster's praise for Shakespeare's reputation as a playwright among his peers was written during his lifetime. As Shakespeare biographer Lois Potter notes

Shakespeare is keeping company here with two very prolific dramatists who wrote both alone and, like Webster, in collaboration

Another important document associated with Shakespeare came to light just over a century ago. In 1612 Stephen Bellott, a Huguenot, sued his tight-fisted father-in-law Christopher Mountjoy for the non-payment of his wife's marriage settlement. Mountjoy was a tyrer by profession (a manufacturer of ladies' ornamental headpieces and wigs) so very likely a supplier to the theatrical companies.

The suit was over the financial settlement that had been promised at the time of Bellot's marriage to Mary Mountjoy in 1604, a dowry of £50, which had been promised but never paid, and an additional £200, to be bestowed upon Bellott in Mountjoy's will.

The records of the case were discovered in the National Archives in 1909 by the Shakespeare scholar, Charles Wallace. The papers show that in 1604, Shakespeare was a lodger at a house on the corner of Silver and Monkwell Streets in Cripplegate owned by Mountjoy. It is the only evidence yet found of a particular London address at which Shakespeare lived and this at a time of plague too.

The importance of this litigation is that along with Bellott's step-father the trumpeter, Humphrey Fludd, Shakespeare was a material witness in the case. It might be assumed that Fludd and Shakespeare as perceived *entertainers* had much in common. That isn't the case.

Until the invention of the valves in the early C19, the trumpet wasn't the melodic instrument that it has become today. It was an instrument that could only play the natural harmonic series of notes, so at the time, it could never be heard playing dance or song tunes. It functioned as a signalling instrument, loud, so that it could be heard from a distance, relaying officer's orders to the ranks within the various army corps, on naval ships trumpeters signalled directions for raising and lowering sails and at assize courts the arrival of the judge and the start of the session was announced by two trumpeters. All the London and provincial theatres, playhouses and fairs employed trumpet players.

Shakespeare mentions the trumpet, either in the text or as stage directions, in twenty eight of his plays - often to herald the arrival of some royal personage - so it is very likely that Fludd knew some of his fellow witness's writing from his playing career, of necessity, memorising the cues that immediately preceded the trumpet entries in many of the plays. In London, control of trumpet playing standards was exercised by the Sergeant Trumpeter who made a levy upon each player and performance, so the trumpeter was regarded more of a military man than as a musician.

Shakespeare's signed deposition of evidence throws little light on Shakespeare's involvement in the case or his activities at the time, but several of the other witnesses referred to Shakespeare's role in arranging the betrothal and in the negotiations about the dowry. He had been requested to take on the duties by Mountjoy's wife, Marie. Marie was a former client of Simon Forman visiting him in the same period as Emilia. The papers supply a list of people with whom Shakespeare was personally acquainted, the Mountjoys and their household and neighbours, including George Wilkins, the playwright, Innkeeper and putative brothel owner, who may have been Shakespeare's insalubrious collaborator on *Pericles, Prince of Tyre.* It has been suggested that Montjoy, the French Herald in Henry V - although written before he became his lodger - was named after his Landlord.

In his deposition dated 11 May 1612, Shakespeare admitted that he had acted as go-between in the courtship of Stephen Bellott and Mary Mountjoy that other witnesses described. However, he said that he could not remember the crucial financial arrangements of the couple's marriage settlement. Is this another example of Shakespeare's selective memory? Without his key testimony, the Court of Requests remanded the case to the overseers of the London Huguenot Church, which awarded Bellott 20 nobles (£6 13*s.* 4*d.*). A year later, Mountjoy still hadn't paid.

There are six documents associated with Shakespeare's last property acquisition, the purchase of the Blackfriar's Gatehouse in March 1613. The vendor was Henry Walker a member of the Musicians Company, shop keeper and citizen of London, for the sum of £140. The Gatehouse was part of the former Dominican priory in London known as *Blackfriars* because of the Domincan order's black habit. It is just a minor monastic coincidence, but an interesting one, that for the first decade of their residency in London the musicians of the Bassano family lived at the Charterhouse, also a former London priory and Southampton's home, Titchfield Abbey, was a former monastery.

The purchasers of the Blackfriars' property were William Shakespeare, William Johnson, citizen and vintner of London, John Jackson, gentleman and John Heminges, gentleman. Shakespeare was the true purchaser, while Johnson, Jackson, and Heminges served as his trustees. Johnson was landlord of the Mermaid Tavern - a known drinking house for actors - Jackson was possibly a shipping magnate from Yorkshire, Heminges we know about.

It would seem that the complicated conveyancing arrangements were designed to stop Shakespeare's wife automatically inheriting the property after his death. Perhaps another indication that the relationship between William and Anne had broken down after she had learnt of the Sonnet's revelations of her husband's marital treachery in London.

The intention to exclude Anne from directly inheriting the Blackfriar's Gatehouse is proven by a document dated February 10, 1618, two years after William's death but whilst Anne was still alive. The three trustees Johnson, Jackson, and Heminges "sold" the Gatehouse to two new trustees, John Greene of Clement's Inn, London, brother of Thomas Greene, the Stratford town clerk, and Matthew Morrys of Stratford-upon-Avon.

The stipulated price of 5 shillings, compared to the £140 price in 1613, indicates that this was not a true sale, but rather a simple a transfer of title. The explicit purpose of the 1618 transfer was to secure the property for Shakespeare's daughter Susanna, wife of Dr. John Hall. In the case of Susanna's demise the property would go to any of her male heirs; then to male heirs of her sister Judith and in the case of Judith's demise, to any male heir of William Shakespeare whatsoever.

The Gatehouse was adjacent to the King's Wardrobe on the east side and to a plot of ground belonging to a widow, Anne Bacon, on the west. The third side of the property was a brick wall that faced a street leading down to Puddle Wharf on the Thames. Purchase of the property included free entry through the gate and the yard, and access to

all and singular cellars, sollars [attics], rooms, lights, easements, profits, commodities, and hereditaments whatsoever to the said dwelling house or tenement belonging, or in any wise appertaining

It is possible that Shakespeare reserved some odd corner of the property as an apartment, for anticipated occasional visits to London for easy access to his company's Blackfriars playhouse. A more reasonable supposition, given that the property was traditionally occupied by tenants, is that the Gatehouse was a financial investment rather than a residence for its owner.

William Shakespeare's last will and testament is dated 26 March 1616 and is one of the most important documents for understanding his family relationships and professional circle. The will names many of the significant people in his life, family, friends, colleagues, and neighbours, as well as describing specific items of personal property.

The Folger Library Document Exhibition says

The handwriting does not match that of Shakespeare's lawyer, Francis Collins, suggesting that the will was drawn up by a clerk

The document is written on three sheets of paper, with William Shakespeare's signature appended to each sheet, as prescribed in contemporary manuals. Charles Hamilton, the palaeographer, believes that it was Shakespeare who drafted his own will and not a clerk or scrivener.

In *In Search of Shakespeare* he writes:-

Probably in early January the poet obtained three large sheets of foreign-made foolscap, not quite matching in size but doubtless the best available in Stratford. He wrote a complete draft of his will on three pages but did not immediately sign it. Some time later, most likely two months, on March 25 1616 (the first day of the legal year), he rewrote the first page, or the first two-thirds of the first page, to include a marriage arrangement for his daughter Judith, who had been hastily wed under mysterious circumstances on February 10, 1616. Shakespeare put down January instead of March, but corrected the error. In rewriting the relevant section of the page, he crowded the lines together at the bottom and ran two lines over to the top of page 2, thus avoiding a rewrite of pages 2 and 3 already finished.......The writing on the lower third of the first page of the will and in the first two lines of page 2 strikes me as very much deteriorated from the original script on pages 2 and 3 of the will and the script at the beginning of the first page of the will. It is the penmanship of an enfeebled man. And the crowding of words and lines at the bottom of page 1 produces an even less ebullient and more cramped script. The interlinear additions and corrections show a progressive disintegration of the handwriting. By the time Shakespeare makes the last interlinear correction, leaving his second-best bed to his wife (page 3), his hand trembles violently, resulting in a script so migratory that the words are almost impossible to decipher. The poet may have penned this final addition to his will only a few minutes before his death.

It is extremely odd that the only mention of his wife - not even the conventional *beloved wife* - is to bequeth her the second-best bed. I suspect that even at death's door, William kept a sense of irony. Had he been banished to the *second-best bed*-room once his wife had discovered he'd returned home from London with an incurable dose of the pox? To say nothing of the revelation of how he caught it, so publicly disclosed in the Sonnets?

After leaving Stratford in the 1580s, Shakespeare was rarely at home, even at Christmas. Although he had made his fortune away from hom, the lack of his presence at Stratford bore heavily on Anne. Shakespeare's absence meant that she was obliged to take on all the houschold duties and children's upbringing. Particularly having shouldered all these responsibilities, I doubt any wife reading, or having read to her from the sonnets, the evidence of sexual betrayal but also declared profound love for another woman, could ever bring herself to forgive and forget.

The preamble of the will and bequests are very formulaic. Shakespeare left the bulk of his property to his two daughters Susanna and Judith, the surviving twin. He left money and clothes to his sister Joan Hart and her three sons, although he couldn't remember the name of Thomas, the third son (perhaps an indication of memory loss caused by a stroke) and plate to his granddaughter Elizabeth Hall.

The will also makes bequests of his various properties; New Place, the house on Henley Street inherited from his parents, the tithes purchased in 1605, the Combe property, the cottage near New Place, and the Blackfriars Gatehouse in London to Susanna. His monetary bequests add up to roughly £350. The only specific objects he bequeaths are a large silver gilt bowl to Judith; a sword to

Thomas Combe, the nephew of his friend John; his clothing to his sister Joan; and his second best bed to his wife.

Shakespeare left a gift of £10 to the poor of Stratford, as well as bequests to his overseer, Thomas Russell, and his lawyer, Francis Collins. He left 26 shillings and 8 pence each to his theatrical fellows Richard Burbage, John Heminges, and Henry Condell, as well as to Hamnet Sadler, William Reynolds, and Anthony and John Nash, to buy mourning rings.

All of the interlinear insertions, seem to be second thoughts, one of them, his bequests to Richard Burbage, John Heminges, and Henry Condell, three of the *King's Men*, confirming his association with members of his playing company to the last days of his life. The fact that he calls them *my ffellowes* may suggest that he still considered himself one of *the King's Men*.

Thomas Quiney was 27 when he married Judith on 10 February 1616. Judith was following in the marital footsteps of her parents in two respects, the marriage was by special licence and as with William and Anne, the bride was older than the bridegroom, in the Quiney's case only four years rather than the eight years difference in her parents' ages.

No one knows whether William was well enough to give his daughter away at the wedding ceremony. One thing is for sure the marriage didn't get off to the best of starts. Quiney had been having sexual relations with a women named Margaret Wheeler who at the time of his marriage to Judith was heavily pregnant. Whether the Shakespeares were aware of this or not, before the wedding ceremony, they certainly were soon after. Less than five weeks later, on March 15 Quiney was charged with incontinence (fornication) with Margaret, brought against him in the Stratford Peculiar Court, the ecclesiastic court. The case was of particular notoriety as Margaret Wheeler *& her Child* had been buried together eleven days earlier. It is thought that Margaret died in childbirth.

When Quiney appeared in court on March 26 and admitted the charge of carnal copulation and was sentenced to public penance dressed in white, however this was commuted, a fine of 5 shillings imposed instead. Whatever remorse Quiney may have felt by the tragic death of Margaret, it suited him. It meant he didn't have a constant local reminder of his misdemeanour by bumping into mother and child in the street, or paying maintenance, either.

It would seem that this scandal encouraged Shakespeare to revise his will. The rewording of his bequest to Judith is thought to have been designed to protect her from potential financial exploitation by her new husband. However, Shakespeare also provides his new son-in-law with an incentive, if Quiney accumulated property, Shakespeare would match it.

It is because the date of the proposed wedding fell within Lent, when weddings were suspended, why a special licence was needed, but why the hurry?

Perhaps Quiney wanted to be safely wed to Judith before Margaret gave birth to his child and he was put under pressure to do the honourable thing and marry her instead.

Whatever the reason for the special licence, pregnancy can't have been it, because the Quiney's son was baptised on 23 November 1616 over nine months after the wedding. The child, named Shakespeare Quiney, presumably in honour of Judith's father, died six months later. All in all, not the happiest of years for the surviving family.

After an incredible career in the theatre, William retired from acting in 1611, at the age of forty seven, returning permanently to Stratford. Did he enjoy his retirement? I doubt it. Most successful performers regard their active careers as the best part of their lives. Stratford would feel like a backwater after the hustle and bustle of London life.

It isn't unusual for performers at the end of their active careers to reminisce about incidents during performances and rehearsals - amusing and serious - that they have experienced, there were few in Stratford who would understand the camaraderie, banter, quick wittedness, touring with kindred spirits. If, in his cups, William were to muse on his earlier life there is a period from the summer of 1592 that would have been a recurring feature.

15. A Royal visit to Bisham and Cookham

O Mistris mine where are you roming?
O stay and heare, your true loues coming,
That can sing both high and low.
Trip no further prettie sweeting.
Iourneys end in louers meeting,
Euery wise mans sonne doth know.
Twelfth Night (3:3 715

For Emilia the three days she spent at Bisham Abbey and Cookham on the banks of the Thames from August 11 1592 was one *journey's end* because of her unplanned pregnancy, begun there, and was to be the harbinger of the end of her life at court as the mistress of the Lord Chamberlain.

In other respects this most memorable of occasions, at which Emilia sang *both high and low*, was a *lovers meeting* that was to mark the beginning of her relationship with Shakespeare and his obsession with her. A romance that was to inspire Shakespeare to write some of the greatest love speeches and poems - as well as quick-witted ripostes between man and woman - in the history of literature.

By 1592 the connection between the Queen and her namesake Elizabeth, Lady Russell went back decades. The 64 year old Lady Russell, who was five years older than the Queen, had much to be grateful to the monarch for. She was born at Gidea Hall in Essex the third of four daughters of the humanist scholar, Sir Anthony Cooke, tutor to Edward Vl. Unusually for the time, Cooke's daughters were educated as if they were sons, to a high academic level.

Elizabeth's sister, Anne Bacon, became a notable scholar and writer on religious subjects, the main literary discipline open to educated aristocratic women to write about at the time. Elizabeth herself was proficient in Latin and French and her extant letters show a poetic turn of phrase and sophisticated use of language.

40 Bisham Abbey

Elizabeth's first marriage was on 27 June 1558, to Thomas Hoby of Bisham Abbey close to Marlow in Berkshire. Four years before, during Mary's reign, Hoby had travelled overland to Italy, including a night at the Angel Inn in Bassano. Hoby and Elizabeth shared a love of languages. He was a diplomat and noted for his translation of Castiglione's *The Book of the Courtier* from Italian into English. This work quickly became essential reading for those in and around court.

In March 1566 the family moved to Paris following Thomas's appointment as ambassador to France when he was knighted. Sir Thomas died in France only four months later and his widow, just 30 years old, received a touching letter of condolence from the Queen. Elizabeth had given birth to four children by Sir Thomas, the eldest of whom, Edward, was educated at Eton and Oxford, and was in later life to enter into his father's profession as a diplomat.

He lived with his wife, Margaret, Lord Hunsdon's daughter, and his mother, at his birthplace, Bisham Abbey. Edward and Margaret also had a London residence in close proximity to Emilia and Alphonso in Westminster.

A few days before Christmas 1574, Elizabeth remarried John, Lord Russell's eldest son and heir to the earldom, at the Bisham Parish Church, All Saints. She had two daughters by this second marriage, Anne and Elizabeth. There was reportedly a son, William, who was apparently slow witted and the unjust recipient of beatings from his mother because of this learning difficulty. One morning Elizabeth thrashed William particularly badly because of his lack of progress - he might have been dyslectic - and locked him up in the tower until his work was completed. A little while later a message arrived commanding Elizabeth to go to court immediately, she left in a hurry forgetting to tell the servants where William was.

She did not return until two days later. When William failed to greet her on her arrival home, she raced up to the tower to find her son dead. Elizabeth never forgave herself and spent the remainder of her life in a state of deep contrition. Her guilt-ridden ghost is said to haunt Bisham Abbey.

In 1575 the Queen and her favourite, Robert Dudley, the Earl of Leicester stood as godparents to Elizabeth, Lady Russell's elder daughter, it is claimed that the Queen was also godmother to her second daughter, Anne. 1575 was the year that Robert Dudley who hosted the Queen at his spectacular *Entertainment* at Kenilworth, when, from the Dolphin speech in *a A Midsommer nights Dreame,* indicates the Shakespeares were present.

John Russell's death in 1584, predeceasing his father, an event which precluded Elizabeth becoming the Countess of Bedford. Following financially difficult times after the death of her second husband, the queen, recognising Lady Russell's predicament, granted her the custodianship of Donnington Castle near Windsor Forest, with all its attendant revenues, for life.

Lady Russell was a patron of the writer Sir John Harington, ingenious inventor of the flush toilet - who was also a school friend of her son Edward, from their Eton days - but more significantly she was patron of the composer and lutenist, John Dowland. Between 1588 and 1595 Mathew Holmes, Precentor and Singingman of Christ Church Oxford, copied four lute books. The second of these books contains Dowland's Lady Russell's Pavan, followed on the same page by a Galliard by Emilia's cousin, Lodovico Bassano.

Dowland's 1604 *Lachrimae* is a collection of seven pavans for a consort of viols and lute, each one based on the theme derived from the celebrated lute song *Flow my Tears.* Each dance has a dedication to a gentlemen. The first dedication is to the 3rd Earl of Essex (son of the disgraced and executed 2nd earl) another is entitled *M. Giles Hoby his Galiard,* Giles was a nephew of Thomas. I think it is most likely that before he moved to Denmark in 1598, if he didn't make his own instruments, Dowland's lutes were supplied to him by the Bassano family. By this time they had an extensive Europe-wide musical instrument dealership.

Examples of Elizabeth Russell's known writing are from a collection of letters - some held in the Cecil state papers - elegies, memorial inscriptions and other religious subjects. She translated the transubstantiation text

A way of reconciliation touching the true nature and substance of the body and blood of Christ in the sacrament

from Latin. Here are two disciplines; music and divinity which immediately give her strong connections to Emilia's known interests.

Lady Russell's London home was in the fashionable district of Blackfriars. In 1596, she was an active opponent of the reconstruction of the Blackfriar's Theatre, refering to the venture as a *Comon playhouse*. Her's was the first of thirty signaturies on a petition against it to the Privy Council, which ultimately failed. The second signature on the petition was *Hunsdon*, not Henry but his son, George, who that year had inherited, not only his father's title, but his company of actors too, *The Lord Chamberlain's Men.*

Lady Russell and her neighbours were concerned by the

great resort and gathering togeuther of all manner of vagrant and lewde persons

the *hoy polloi* groundlings - attending plays which they said would have a detrimental impact on the neighbourhood. Furthermore, as a Puritan, she was opposed to performances in the theatre *per se.* Curious then, that only four years before, Lady Russell organised and hosted a theatrical production at her country home, Bisham Abbey. Perhaps events that unfolded after the performance initiated Lady Russell's opposition to actors.

The entertainment was in the form of a short masque to welcome Lady Russell's old friend, the Queen. The performance would feature her daughters, the Queen's goddaughters, as prominent members of the cast. At the time of the Queen's visit the older girl, Elizabeth was eighteen and her sister Anne, a year or so younger.

Below is the complete script which includes brief stage directions for the three stations of the action as they are published in John Nichol's *Compendium of Royal Entertainments* printed by John Barnes in 1823.

At the top of the Hill going to Bissam, the Cornets [Cornetts] sounding in the Woods, a Wilde Man came forth and uttered this Speech:

I followed this sounde, as enchanted; neither knowing the reason why, nor how to be ridde of it; unusuall to these Woods, and (I feare) to our gods prodigious. Sylvanus, whom I honour, is runne into a Cave: Pan, whom I envye, courting of the shepheardesse: Envye I thee, Pan? No, pitty thee, an eie-sore to chast Nymphes, yet still importunate. Honour thee, Sylvanus? No, contemne thee: fearefull of Musicke in the Woods, yet counted the god of the Woods. I, it may bee, more stout than wise, asked, who passed that way? what he or she? None durst answere, or would vouchsafe, but passionate Eccho, who said Shee. And Shee it is, and you are Shee, whom in our dreames many yeares wee Satyres have scene, but waking could never find any such. Every one has tolde his dreame, and described your person; all agree in one, and set downe your vertues: in this onely did wee differ, that some saide your Portraiture might be drawen, others saide impossible: some thought your vertues might be numbered, most saide they were infinite: infinite and impossible, of that side was I: and first in humility to salute you most happy I: my untamed thoughts waxe gentle, and I feele in myselfe civility; a thing hated, because not knowen; and unknowen, because I knew you not. Thus Vertue tameth fiercenesse; Beauty, madnesse. You Majestie on my knees will I followe, bearing this Club, not as a Savage, but to beate down those that are.

At the middle of the Hill sate Pan, and two Virgins keeping sheepe, and sowing in their samplers, where here Majestie stayed and heard this:

Pan. Prety soules and bodies too, faire Shephardisse, or sweet Mistresse, you know my suite, Love; my vertue, Musicke, my power, a Godhead. I cannot tickle the sheepes gutts of a Lute, bydd, bydd, bydd, like the calling of Chickins; but for a Pipe that squeeketh like a Pigg, I am he. How doe you burne time, and drowne beauty, in pricking of clouts, when you should be penning of Sonnets? You are more simple that the sheep you keepe, but not so gentle. I love you both, I know not which best; and you both scorne me, I know not which most. Sure I am, that you are not so young as not to understand love, nor so wise as to withstand it, unlesse you think yourselves greater that gods, whereof I am one. How often have I brought you chestnuts for a love token, and desired but acceptance for a favour. Little did you know the misterye, that as the huske was thornye and tough, yet the meate sweete, so though my hyde were rough and hateful, yet my heart was smooth and loving: you are but the Farmer's daughters of the Dale, I the God of the flocks that feede upon the hils. Though I cannot force love, I may obedience, or else send your sheepe a wondering with my fancies. Coynesse must be revenged with curstnesse: but be not agaste, sweet mice: my Godhead cometh so fast upon me, that Majestye had almost overrun affection. Can you love? Will you?
Syb. Alas, poor Pan! Looke how he looketh, Sister, fitter to drawe in a harvest wayne, then talke of love to chaste Virgins. Would you have us both?

Pan. I, for oft I have hearde, that two Pigeons may bee caught with one beane.

Isab. And two Woodcocks with one sprindge.

Syb. And many Dotterels with one dance.

Isab. And all fooles with one faire worde
Nay, this is his meaning; as he hath two shapes, so hath he two harts; the one a man wherewith his tongue is tipped, dissembling; the other of a beast, wherewith his thoughts and poysoned lust. Men must have as manie , as they have hart-strings, and studie to make an Alphabet of Mistresses, from A to Y, which maketh them in the end crie Ay. Against this, experience hath provided us a remedy, to laugh at them when they know not what to saie; and when they speake, not to be-lieve them.

Pan. Not for want of matter. but to knowe the meaning, what is wrought in this sampler?

Syb. The follies of the Gods, who became beastes, for their affections.

Pan. What in this?

Isab. The honour of Virgins, who became Goddesses, for their chastity.

Pan. But what be these?

Syb. Men's tongues, wrought all with double stitch, but not one true.

Pan. What these?

Isab. Roses, egletine, harts-ease, wrought with Queenes stitch, and all right.

Pan. I never hard the odds between men's tongues and woemens's; therefore they may be both double, unlesses you tyell me how they differ.

Syb. Thus, woemen's tongues are made of the same flesh that their harts are, and speake as they thinke: men's harts of the flesh that their tongues, and both dissemble. But prythy, Pan, be packing; thy words are as odious as thy sight, and we attend a sight which is more glorious that the sunne rising.

Pan. What, does Jupiter come this waies?

Syb. No, but one that will make Jupiter blush, as guilty of his unchast jugglings; and Juno dismaise, as wounded at her Majesty. What our mother hath often told us, and fame the whole world, cannot be concealed from thee; if it be, we wil tell thee; which may hearafter make thee surcease thy suite, for feare of her displeasure; and honour virginitye, by wondering at her vertues.

Pan. Say on, sweere soule?

Syb. This way commeth the Queen of this Islande, the wonder of the world, and Nature's glory, leading affections in fetters, Virginitie's slaves: embracing mildnes with justice, Majesties's twinns. In whom Nature hath imprinted beauty, not art paynted it; in whome Wit hath bred leartning, but not without labour; Labour brought forth wisedom, but not without wonder. By her it is (Pan) that all our carttes that thou seest are laden with corne, when in other countries they are filled with harneys; that our horses are ledde with a whip, theirs with a launce; that our rivers flow with fish, theirs with blood; our cattel feede on pastures, they feed on pastures like cattel. One hande she stretcheth to Fraunce, to weaken Rebels; the other to Flaunders, to strengthen Religion; her heart to both Countries, her vertues to all. This is shee at whom Envie hath shot all her arrowes, and now for anger broke her bow; on whom God hath laide all his blessinges, and we for joy clappe our hands. Heedlesse Treason goeth hedlesse; and close Trechery restlesse: Daunger looketh pale, to beholde her Majesty; and Tyranny blusheth to heare of her mercy. Jupiter came into the house of poore Baucis, and she vouchsafeth to visit the bare farmes of her subjects. We, upon our knees, wil entreat her to come into the valley, that our houses blessed with her presence, whose hartes are filled with quietnes by her governement. To her wee wish as many years as our fields have ears of corne, both infinite: and to her enemies, as many troubles as the wood hath leaves, all intolerable. But whilst here she is, run downe, Pan, the hill in all hast; and though thou breake thy necke to give our mother warning, it is no matter.

Pan. No, give me leave to die with wondering, and trippe you to your mother. Here

I yeelde all the flockes of these fields to your Highnes: greene be the grasse where you treade: calme the water where you rowe: sweete the aire where you breathe: long the life that you live, happy the people that you love: this is all I can wish. During your abode, no theft shall be in the woods; in the fields no noise, in the vallies no spies: myselfe will keepe all safe. That is all I can offer. And heare I break my Pipe, which Apollo could never make me do; and follow the sounde which follows you.

At the bottome of the hill, entering into the house, Ceres with her Nymphes, in an harvest cart, meet her Majesty, having a crown of wheat-ears with a jewell; and after this Song, uttered the Speech following:

> *Swel Ceres now, for other Gods are schrinking,*
> *Pomona pineth,*
> *Fruitlesse her tree;*
> *Fair Phœbus shineth*
> *Only on mee.*
> *Conceite doth make me smile whilst I am thinking,*
> *How every one doth read my story,*
> *How every bough on Ceres lowreth,*
> *Cause heaven's plenty on me powereth,*
> *And they in leaves doe onely glory,*
> *All other Gods of power hereven,*
> *Ceres only Queen of Heaven.*
> *With robes and flowers let me be dressed,*
> *Cynthia than shineth*
> *Is not so cleare;*
> *Cynthia declineth*
> *When I appeere,*
> *Yet in this Ile shee raignes as blessed,*
> *And everyone at her doth wonder,*
> *And in my ears still fond Fame whispers,*
> *Cynthia shalbe Ceres Mistres,*
> *But first my carre shall rive asunder.*
> *Help, Phœbus, helpe; my fall is suddaine;*
> *Cynthia, Cynthia, must be Sovereigne.*

Greater than Ceres receives Ceres' Crowne, the ornament of my plenty, the honour of your peace. Here at your Highnes' feete, I lay down my feined deity, which Poets have honoured, Truth contemned. To your Majesty, whom the heavens have crowned with happines, the world with wonder, birth with dignitie, nature with perfection, we doe all homage, accounting nothing ours but what comes from you. And this much dare we promise for the Lady of the Farme, that you presence hath added many daies to her life, by the infinite joies shee conveys in her heart, who presents your Highnesse with this toye and this shorty praier, poured from her hart, that your daies may increase in happines, your happines have no end till there be no more daies.

At the top of this text in Nichol's book is the title

Speeches Delivered to her Majestie at the Last Progresse, At the Right Honorable the Lady Rvssels at Bissam, the Right Honorable the Lorde CHANDOS at Sudeley at the Right Honorable the Lord Norris at Ricorte.

John Barnes the printer notes:

I Gathered these copies in loose papers I know not how imperfect, therefore must I craue a double pardon; of him that penned them, and those that reade them. The matter of small moment, and therefore the offence of no danger

As you can see Barnes doesn't know who wrote the masque but assumes that it was a man, and yet the feminist text would suggest that it was written by a women.

Men's tongues, wrought all with double stitch, but not one true

as well as detailed knowledge of flowers and intricate embroidery stitches

Roses, egletine, harts-ease, (a tricolour Viola, also known as Johnny-Jump-up) *wrought with Queenes stitch* (An elaborate stitch forming a diamond shape)

The writer has a knowledge of mythology quoting a pantheon of gods - Jupiter, Juno, Apollo, Pomona Phœbus - apart from those who are in the cast but isn't above including some risqué dialogue.

Sybilla. then talke of love to chaste Virgins. Would you have us both? Pan. I, for oft I have hearde, that two Pigeons may bee caught with one beane.

Ceres, the goddess of agriculture, sings a song towards the end of the masque, the words of which have survived in another publication, *Englands Helicon* under the title *Cere's Song in Emulation of Cynthia*, but still with no attribution to authorship.

England's Helicon is a collection of verse from a variety of poets published in 1600 and includes a sonnet from *Loues Labour's lost* spoken by Dumaine. In the Helicaon it is given the title *The passionate Sheepheards Song,* since Dumaine was a lord at Navarre's court, this title is a misnomer.

The climax of the entertainment is the symbolic gesture of submission by the goddess, Ceres laying her crown of wheat ears at the feet of the Queen. In a *Lover's Complaint* the fickle maid wears on her head *a plattid hiue of straw* (ALC.8)

I have already mentioned the presence of a natural echo - rather than a synthetically produced one, common in early theatre - in *A Lovers Complaint,* there would appear to be an echo in the woods at Bisham too

None durst answere, or would vouchsafe, but passionate Eccho

Which is why I think that the venue for both the Bisham entertainment and *A Lover's Complaint* are one and the same.

There are sections of text which demonstrate were intentionally conceived as a hymn of praise to the cult of virginity of which the Queen was the figure head. There are five mentions mentions of virgin(s) or virginity but most significantly the line *The honour of Virgins, who became Goddesses, for their chastity* demonstrates the script's sycophantic approach to the Queen.

The preamble of the entertainment shows Rycote and Sudeley as two more houses to be visited on the progress, Oxford was unlisted but was visited in September. The venues make it clear that the Queen and her entourage travelled by land from Windsor, rather than by river. Bisham Abbey although a large building was insufficiently large to accommodate everyone in the Queen's entourage. The use of additional accommodation is referred to in Pan's speech

We, upon our knees, wil entreat her to come into the valley, that our houses blessed with her presence

and so servants, actors and musicians would have been housed in outlying buildings. The final six words would indicate that she may also visit other houses in and around the estate including Dyers at Cookham Dean, a 30 minute walk from the Abbey.

In Chapter 9 I proposed that it was Emilia who wrote the *Speeches to the Queen* and that she was influenced by seeing or reading Lyly's *Midas* a year or so earlier. I supported this suggestion by highlighting the concordance of words and characters between the *Speeches to the Queen* and *Midas*.

Another female candidate for authorship has been proposed by Alexandra Johnston from the University of Toronto who suggests that it was Lady Russell the *Lady of the Farme* herself who wrote the *Entertainment*. There is no doubt that Lady Russell, as hostess at Bisham was present on the occasion, no doubt either that she was highly literate, but there is nothing else in her known writing the comes remotely near the comic quips in the *Speeches to the Queen,* I think that Emilia is a much more likely candidate.

As you can see from the exchanges between Pan, Isabella and Sybilla - played by Lady Russell's teenage daughters, Elizabeth and Anne - there is a strong element of *feminism* that is typical of Emila's writing in *Salve Devs*. The very first line setting the scene *Cornets* [cornetts] *sounding in the Woods* cannot possibly have been envisaged as being easily achieved by Lady Russell. Emilia's Bassano and Lanier cousins, were the only cornett players in England at the time.

We know that Emilia was there and spoke with the Queen because she tells us so in *Salve Devs*.

FArewell (sweet Cooke-ham) where I first obtain'd
Grace from that Grace where perfit Grace remain'd;
And where the Muses gaue their full consent,
I should haue powre the virtuous to content:
Where princely Palace will'd me to indite,
The sacred Storie of the Soules delight. (*Selve Deus, The Description of Cooke-ham* 1-6)

Lines 5 and 6 tells us that the Queen spoke to her.

Forman reported *She hath been favoured much of her Majesty*. The Queen probably enjoyed the *Speeches to the Queen* but felt it lacked the seriousness Emilia was capable of. Commanding her to write on a deeper subject, a religious one, more suited to feminine literary ambitions. *Selve Deus* was Emilia's response.

The Queen would immediately have recognised Emilia as Hunsdon's mistress, but also the daughter of Baptista Bassano, her former lute tutor from her days as Princess Elizabeth incarcerated at Hatfield.

It is unlikely that *princely Palace* means what we would now understand by it. There was no palace near Cookham and a building could hardly will a poet to write anything. Given the propensity for phonetic spelling in Elizabethan times it should perhaps be read as *princely Pallas*. The Queen was often referred to by other names, Cynthia, as in the *Speeches to the Queen* and the opening lines of *Salve Devs* published eight years after the Queen death

Sith Cynthia is ascended to that rest Of endlesse joy and true Eternitie

Emilia liked to use the Queen's aliases. Another of the Queen's alternative names was Gloriana - as celebrated in Morley's 1601 madrigal collection, *The Triumphs of Gloriana* - but also as the Goddess Pallas Athena. Hence these lines show that whilst she was at Cookham the Queen (*princely Pallas*) willed Emilia to write about the story of Christ (*the soul's delight*). The Queen was moved to talk to Emilia about her writing because she knew she was capable of producing something more profound.

There is another reason indicating that Emilia was present at Bisham, that is Lord Hunsdon's notable absence, evidenced by his non-attendance at privy council meetings held in Bisham and at subsequent venues too. Even for a man as powerful as Hunsdon, to have his much younger mistress in a situation of high visibility - involving at least one day of rehearsal and probably more - in close proximity at his daughter's home, particularly, if his wife was present too, would be a tricky situation to handle comfortably. Better to absent himself. Hunsdon's absence from the very time that Emilia conceived shows that he cannot have been the father of Emilia's son, Henry.

Apart from the cornett players, concealed in the woods, and the silent roles of Nymphs, there are five speaking roles. The Wilde Man, Pan, the shepherdesses, Sybilla and Isabella, and Ceres the goddess of agriculture. It is almosty certain that Lady Russell's two daughters played the shepherdesses and Emilia herself played Ceres in her straw hat and sang Ceres's song accompanying herself on the lute - which Pan refers to in the script *I cannot tickle the sheepes gutts of a Lute* - and spoke the final encomium.

Who, though played the two male parts? Of course it could be any two actors belonging to an acting company with an aristocratic patron, particularly as the theatres had been closed since June. My belief is though because of his revelation that Emilia's child wasn't Hunsdon's in Sonnet 127 *Slandering creation with a false esteem* and the very hurried marriage with Alphonso only two months later that Shakespeare played one of them. He later borrowing three phrases from Emilia's brief entertainment.

Peter in *Romeo and Juliet* uses the phrase *heart's ease* addressed by him to the musicians. A second less oblivously appropriated phrase is *muske roses, and with Eglantine* from *A Midsommer nights Dreame* (2.2.613) where *Speeches to the Queen* was just *Roses, egletine.* The precise phrase *sheepes gutts* is given to Benedick in *Much adoe* in his comment regarding the lute's powerful capabilities, albeit developing it, with a bawdy *horne* pun.

Now diuine aire, now is his soule rauisht, is it not strange that sheepes guts should hale soules out of mens bodies? well, a horne for my money when all's done. (Much adoe 2.3.865)

Pan's role is a comic one - cosmetically attired in imitation of the hindquarters, legs, and horns of a goat and holding, and probably playing, a set of Pan pipes. I think it less likely that Shakespeare played Pan. He is much more likely to have taken the less verbose role of the Wilde Man with his speech of welcome to the Queen opening the play. The words of introduction are not so far removed from the chorus speeches that begin *Romeo and Juliet* and those that Professor Foster has suggested that Shakespeare played in the opening scenes of *Henry V* and *Pericles.*

If it was Emilia who was commissioned to write the entertainment how might this have come about? It is clear that the text of *Speeches to the Queen* has a very female slant to it, and was conceived partly as a vehicle for Lady Russell to present her daughters to the Queen as prospective *ladies in waiting.* A woman writer would warm to the overall female concept. It is possible that it wasn't Lady Russell but her son, Edward Hoby who commissioned *Speeches to the Queen*, which may have been intended as a surprise for his mother.

Because of their collaboration on *Songs of sundrie natures* four years earlier, William Byrd, who despite his catholicism was still the Queen's favourite composer, knew very well how good Emilia was at finding suitable words to set to music. It is possible that he made the suggestion.

By 1592 Lord Hunsdon's daughter, now Lady Margaret Hoby had been living at the Abbey with her husband, Edward since their marriage a decade earlier. Hunsdon was privy to his mistress's literary skills as well as her musical ones, but it seems unlikely that he would purposely suggest Emilia as an author for a masque at his daughter's home. He could though have made the suggestion unintentionally, in conversation with his daughter's family over the very few female writers existing in England at the time, not realising where this conversation might eventually lead.

Alternatively, maybe Emilia made the offer to write the masque herself, perhaps even writing the script in advance which could then have been presented to Lady Russell and her son for consideration for performance. Once Emilia had convinced them that she could write well and appropriately for the visit, and Lady Russell, or her son had accepted the script, or extended an invitation to write one - possibly through John Dowland - it would have been impossible for anyone to easily withdraw from the event, particularly if Lady Russell or her son had made the Queen aware of their intentions.

What happened after the performance of *Speeches to the Queen?* A banquet followed by a ball? After which the individual members of the entourage made their way to the accommodation provided. The Queen, her *ladies in waiting* and her favourite courtiers housed in rooms at the Abbey, the rest of the court to the outlying buildings, the lower in hierarchy the further the distance away from the Abbey.

I suppose I have taken part in literally hundreds of concerts away from home with orchestras, choirs and smaller ensembles. There is something about touring that encourages professional performers, some of them happily married, to behave in a less constrained, more liberal way, than they might if they were returning home after a performance. Social interaction away from home and family, meals and wine together, room parties where flirting fuelled by alcohol can lead to illicit sexual relations. This is what I suggest happened between William - unhappily married - and Emilia - as happy as one can be as an attractive young woman, shackled to a partner, four decades older - somewhere on the Bisham Estate, but probably Dyers.

Carousing late into the night, eating and drinking, with Emilia beguiling all with her singing and playing *HOw oft when thou, my musike musike playst* (128:1) and the other musicians performing for their fellow servants to dance. William and Emilia, having as performers, both a little earlier been elevated into the elite society of Queen and courtiers, mingling with all, they threw caution to the wind and ended up in bed together.

It isn't beyond the realms of possibility that the very first hand-fasting exchanges between *Romeo and Juliet* were a recollection of the words uttered by the eloquent couple whilst dancing. Just one occasion when, Shakespeare the borrower of ideas and phrases recycled his and Emilia's words. Neither of them had ever met anyone else like the other. They had fallen in love.

Romeo

If I prophane with my vnworthiest hand,
This holy shrine, the gentle sin is this,
My lips to blushing Pilgrims did ready stand,
To smooth that rough touch, with a tender kisse.

Juliet

Good Pilgrime,
You do wrong your hand too much.
Which mannerly deuotion shewes in this,
For Saints haue hands, that Pilgrims hands do tuch,
And palme to palme, is holy Palmers kisse. (1:5:654)

Emilia was probably a virgin when she took up with Lord Hunsdon at the age of eighteen or so in 1587. It is most unlikely that she had another lover between then and beginning her relationship with Shakespeare in August 1592. She was living with Hunsdon at Somerset House. Even if she wanted to try out the experience of a younger lover less than forty years her senior, with servants in the house, it was difficult to achieve.

Even when the opportunity arose, as it did at Bisham, why would she risk losing her life at court and everything that went with it - *maintained in great pride* Forman says - for a one-night stand with a married man? The end result might be even more serious for William, his freedom or his life even, if Hunsdon ever found out? Why did it happen? They simply couldn't help themselves.

One thing's for sure - even if the lack of an expected period remained unnoticed - within a month of pregnancy a man becomes aware of the physical changes in his bed-fellow.

The special licence to have Emilia and Alphonso married so quickly in less than ten weeks - 11 August impregnated, 18 October marriage - showed the urgency of it all from Hunsdon's point of view.

To be cuckolded was every Elizabethan man's nightmare, as Shakespeare, in this instance the cuckoo himself, was later to point out

The Cuckow then on euerie tree, Mockes married men, for thus sings he, Cuckow. Cuckow, Cuckow: O word of feare, Vnpleasing to a married eare

> *Loues Labour's lost* (5:2:2695)

As the initiator of many pregnancies, Hunsdon must have realised in early stages of Emilia's pregnancy that he probably wasn't the father and that copulation had occurred at Bisham. No matter how hurt Hunsdon must have felt, he would prefer the world at large to believe that he was the father. How could he best do that? By paying off Alphonso to take on the role of *father* with the promise of a job at court, and pensioning off Emilia with a generous £40 a year, allowing her to keep the jewellery and clothes he had given her, both displayed in the Hilliard miniature. A further stipulation, that if the child was a boy, that she named him Henry after himself.

The ploy worked and continued working, everyone from Forman onwards has assumed that Hunsdon was the father of Emilia's child. It maybe that Hunsdon didn't need to wait for physical changes in Emilia's body to realise he had been cuckolded. Had William and Emilia ended up in the same bed at Dyers, that would very probably have been spotted by other guests, even if not immediately, once they had spent the next couple of days together their romance would have been difficult to conceal.

What a juicy piece of gossip it would make. The Lord Chamberlain - after Burghley, the most powerful courtier in the country - cuckolded by a lowly actor. There is no doubt that the gossip did get out, because Robert Greene who died on the 2nd September only a couple of weeks later had time to write about it on his deathbed. In the introduction to *Groatsworth* Greene claims to be the recipient of special information

And how euer I haue beene censured for some of my former bookes, yet Gentlemen I protest, they were as I had speciall information

He would appear to have quickly received *special information* about the carryings on the riverside at Bisham

Mistris Lamilia like a cunning angler made readye her change of baytes that shee might effect Lucanios bane: and to begin she discouered from her window her beauteous enticing face, and taking a lute in her   hand that shee might the rather allure, shee sung this sonnet with a delicious voyce

Lamilias song.

> *Fie fie on blind fancie,*
> *It hinder youths ioy:*
> *Faire virgins learne by me,*
> *To count loue a toy.*

When Loue learned first the A B C of delight,
And knew no figures, nor conceited phrase:
He simplie gaue to due desert her right,
He led not louers in darke winding wayes:
He plainly wild to loue, or flatly answerd no,
But now who lists to proue, shall find it nothing so,
> *Fie fie then on fancie,*
> *it hinders youths ioy,*
> *Faire virgins learne by me,*
> *To count loue a toy.*

For since he learnd to vse the Poets pen,
He learnd likewise with smoothing words to faine,
Witching chast eares with trothles tungs of men,
And wronged faith with falshood and disdaine.
He giues a promise now, anon he sweareth no,
Who listeth for to proue shall find his changings so:
> *Fie fie then on fancie,*
> *It hinders youthes ioy,*
> *Faire virgins learne by me,*
> *To count loue a toy.*

The fifth line has a connection with the Bisham *Speeches to the Queen*, the line *Alphabet of Mistresses, from A to Y.* The second verse a reference to a newly sprung poet (Shakespeare) and has the feminist slant shown at Bisham too. Shakespeare later adopts Greene's angling metaphor

Why of eyes' falsehood hast thou forged hookes (137.7)

It has always been considered that it was Greene's reference to Shakespeare as a plagiarist *an upstart Crow, beautified with our feathers* that encouraged Nashe in *Pierce Penniless* to deny the rumour that had circulated that he'd written *Groatsworth of Wit.* However isn't the insult far more directed towards Emilia, than Shakespeare?

It intimates that she had already become the busy courtesan that Shakespeare accuses her of in Sonnet 137 *The baye where all men ride* and whore as Forman accuses in 1597. She had only ceased to be Lord Hunsdon's paramour a couple of months before *Groatsworth* was published. No wonder Nashe was worried about what might befall him if Hunsdon thought that he had written the scurrilous accusation. He strenuously protests

... a scald trivial lying pamphlet called Greene's Groatsworth of Wit is given out to be of my doing. God never have care of my soul, but utterly renounce me, if the least word or syllable in it proceeded from my pen, or if I were any way privy to the writing or printing of it. I am grown at length to see into the vanity of the world more than ever I did, and now I condemn myself for nothing so much as playing the dolt in print

Once the Queen had set off on the day's journey to Rycourt, Emilia and William would have returned to London, as yet unaware of the developing foetus in Emilia's womb, that was to turn their world upside down in a little over a month.

Hunsdon, for reasons unknown, stayed away from the travelling court of the Queen's progress until the Privy Council met at Newbury on 26 August, too soon for him to observe for himself that Emilia was pregnant.

The theatres which had been closed by order of the Privy Council because of the apprentice riots in June but hadn't reopened as anticipated because plague had broken out in August closing the theatres until mid-1594.

Did Hunsdon find out about Emilia & William's fling by means other than noticing his mistress's swelling breasts and stomach? Did she confess, or did he intuitively realise there was something different about her, or was he informed, before he knew about the pregnancy? Whatever and whenever Hunsdon found out about Emilia's breaking of her trust, preparations for as early a wedding as possible continued apace. Emilia and Alphonso coerced into marrying, John Jvoot entrusted with obtaining the special licence, and Emilia removed from Somerset House to Alphonso's relative's house in the Minories.

My assumption is that Alphonso was present at Bisham as one of a handful of cornett players in London at the time. So if he was Hunsdon's choice, it could be that Hunsdon knew he was homosexual and would never have expected him to be the father of Emilia's child. No one can have been very happy at Hunsdon's *force majeure*, except perhaps Alphonso offered a musician's job at court with unexpectedly better conditions than any other incumbent. William, not knowing quite what to do with himself, with no acting work because the theatres were closed, his new found love forcibly taken away from him, but with the memory of the Bisham affair fresh in his mind, he did what he had to do, he wrote.

A period of intense inspired writing. First with a public declaration of his love for Emilia in which specifically names her. He continued writing the on-going sonnets as a duty to Southampton, his patron and someone to whom he expressed his love, and began the twenty year task of *writing Emilia*, his new found love with her Venetian origins.

He began with a long poem which mirrored the identities of his two loves, an attractive young man, who resisted all attempts to be persuaded to enter sexual relations and dies in the process, and a stunningly beautiful young woman - in this case also a goddess - possessing the feminine guile of a Venetian courtesan.

Imaginatively alluring sexual techniques were a skill that Emilia very likely developed in order to keep Hunsdon happy for so long, and no doubt experienced by William, in bed.

The poem was called *Venvs and Adonis.*

16. The Shrew, Venus and Titus

Come faire Emelia, my louely loue,
Brighter than the burnisht pallace of the sunne,
The eie-sight of the glorious firmament,
In whose bright lookes sparkles the radiant fire,
Wilie Prometheus slilie stole from Ioue,
Infusing breath, life, motion, soule,
To euery object striken by thine eies
O faire Emelia, I pine for thee,
And either must enjoy thy loue, or die.

A Pleasant conceited Historie, called The Taming of a Shrew (2.1.56-64)

*T*he Taming of the Shrew comes in an early period of Shakespeare's writing, but it springs from an even earlier play, *The Taming of a Shrew.*

In the "A" play, first published in May1594, there are two characters - Emelia and Alfonso - the couple's uncommon names in the forefront of London theatre goers' minds because of their recent hasty marriage and Emilia's fall from the arm of the Lord Chamberlain. Given the timing of the writing of the "A" play, and the casting of Alfonso and Emelia in two important roles, this can't be a coincidence.

Since there can have been no liaison between the couple whilst the relationship between Emilia and Hunsdon existed, it is most unlikely to have begun being written before their marriage was organised, around the end of September 1592.

The fact that Alfonso is cast as Emelia's father, makes me think that Shakespeare thinks that Alphonso Lanier was old enough to be Emilia Bassano's father, and is bold enough to say so publicly.

I think that the profound terms of endearment that Shakespeare gives Polidor to speak Emelia are the affectionate words he wants to say to our Emilia himself, this unconditional declaration before his discovery of her sexual duplicity.

The second line *Brighter than the burnished palace of the sun* is reminiscent of Emilia's own *Of gold all burnisht, and brighter then sunne beames.* (*Songs of sundrie natures* XXXIV.1)

There are concordances in these brief nine lines with the *Dark Lady* Sonnets. Fourteen uses of the word *fair[est]* in the Sonnets, most significantly *For I haue sworne thee faire, and thought thee bright* (147:13) and again *For I haue sworne thee faire* (152.13).

Four uses of *thine eies. Thines eies* (132.1) *thine eyes* (140,14) *thine eyes* (142.10) *thine eyes* (149.12)

On the morning of the 14th August 1592 - some months before Shakespeare had written his public declaration of love to Emelia - the Queen and her entourage left Bisham and began their twenty mile journey towards Rycote in Oxfordshire. Those who weren't courtiers or members of the Queen's household returned home, in the case of Emilia and Shakespeare, that meant London.

In their brief time together at Bisham and Cookham and on their journey to London by horse, Emilia will have told Shakespeare many tales of Italy learnt from her family - Venice and the Veneto in particular - discussed their mutual literary tastes. Related her musical training, begun by her father when she was a young child, and continued by one of her professional musician cousins after her father's death. I'm certain that on this journey Emilia - who Forman reported *could hardly keep secret* - spoke of her affair with Hunsdon and how it all began.

It is hardly surprising that shortly after his return to London Shakespeare should choose a subject remembered from his school days from Book X of Ovid's *Metamorphosis* that contains philosophical thoughts on the nature of love - praying on his mind if he was bi-sexual - and whose title, *Venvs and Adonis,* starts with an alternative name for Venice.

In the Renaissance, it was the city state of Venice that had most in common with the mythological goddess, Venus. Not just the similarity in their names, but their relationship to the sea - Venus was born from the sea on the coast of Cyprus, a Venetian island, as Botticelli's famous painting shows - the story encouraged Venetians to identify with Venus as an iconic symbol for their city. Underlining this connection four great Renaissance painters all active in Venice; Bellini, Giorgione, Titian and most significantly Veronese, all made Venus, in various stages of dress and undress, the subject of their paintings

41 Botticelli: Birth of Venus

Malcolm Bull writes

Though they later spread throughout Europe, the reclining nude in a landscape, the Toilet of Venus, and the iconography of Venus and Adonis were all initially Venetian products....There are at least three interconnected factors in the Venetian production of Venusian imagery; the sea, prostitution and trade

Ovid's telling of the story of *Venus & Adonis* in sixty five lines is exponentially developed by Shakespeare into close on twelve hundred lines. Ovid precedes his version of the story with behaviour which may have been in William's mind; Orpheus's sexual migration after the loss of Eurydice:

Orpheus had refused to love a woman,
either because his love had ended badly
or because he'd made a promise not to.
But many women, passionate for him,
wished to wed the poet and were upset
when he declined. But Orpheus transferred
his love to tender boys and was the first
among the Thracian people to enjoy
their brief spring years and early flowering,
before they were young men.

translation by Ian Johnston

Wise men flattering may deceive you is a well known aria from Handel's *Judas Maccabeus..* Deception may not have been in Shakespeare's mind when he dedicated *Venvs and Adonis* to Southampton, but flattery certainly was, and not just on the dedication page.

Shakespeare casts Southampton in the role of Adonis, praising Southampton's looks and his renowned skill as a horseman. In a significant parallel sexual narrative Shakespeare introduces an important purpose for the horse, when Ovid doesn't mention the animal.

Shakespeare demonstrates he is still trying to finish the job he started in the first seventeen sonnets, persuading Southampton to marry and produce children.

Ovid's description of Venus differs from Shakespeare's. Ovid's Venus goes hunting with Adonis only to please him, but otherwise is uninterested in country sports or activities.

She wears her skirt tucked into her knickers, worries about her complexion, and hates wild animals. Shakespeare's Venus is a bit like a wild animal herself, she apparently goes naked, did Emilia do just this in private? She is not interested in hunting, but only in making love to Adonis, offering her body to him in explicit poetic language in the form of a blazon.

In the end, she insists that the boar's killing of Adonis happened accidentally as the animal, impressed by the young hunter's beauty, gored him while trying to kiss him. Venus's behaviour seems to reflect Shakespeare's own feelings of empathy towards animals which his touching lines over an injured stag from *As You Like It* show

The wretched annimall heau'd forth such groanes That their discharge did stretch his leatherne coat Almost to bursting, and the big round teares Cours'd one another downe his innocent nose In pitteous chase (2.1.623)

Venvs and Adonis devotes many lines to describe the feelings of the stallion in sexual pursuit and to the hare's despair as hounds run it down.

Southampton, like Adonis is a young man renowned for his incredible beauty and shares Adonis's view of women *but loue he laught to scorne* (V&Λ.4)

Since Adonis has not the slightest interest in the pursuit of love he prefers to go hunting. Venus by comparison falls in love with Adonis at first sight and descends to earth where she contrives to meet him as he is about to set off hunting. She wants him to dismount and speak to her but Adonis isn't interested in talking to women. A goddess isn't so easily dissuaded so she forces him to dismount and then she persuades him to lie down beside her, gazes at him, and talks of love.

She craves a kiss but he wants to leave and go hunting, he manages to get away and he goes to get his horse.At that moment, his horse becomes aroused by a mare in season, who at first resists his overtures, but soon the stallion breaks free and both animals gallop off together. Loss of his means of transport keeps Adonis captive to Venus, who persists in her aim of seduction, continuing to speak to him of love. He listens momentarily but then turns away scornfully, she is emotionally devastated and faints. Afraid he might have killed her, Adonis kneels beside her, strokes and kisses her. Venus recovers and requests one last kiss, which he reluctantly supplies.

42 Veronese: Venus and Adonis

Venus wants to see him again; Adonis tells her that he cannot tomorrow, because he is going to hunt wild boar. Venus has a vision, and warns him that if he does so, he will be killed by a boar. She then flings herself on him, tackling him to the ground. He prises himself loose, and lectures her on the topic of lust versus love. He leaves, she weeps.

The next morning Venus roams the woods searching for Adonis. She hears dogs and hunters in the distance. Recalling her vision that he will be killed by a wild boar, she is afraid, and hurries to catch up with the hunt. She comes across hunting dogs that are injured. Then she finds Adonis, killed by the boar, Venus is distraught.

Because this loss occurred to the goddess of love, she decrees that love will henceforth be mixed with suspicion, fear, and sadness. Adonis' body has grown cold and pale. His blood gives colour to the plants all around him. A flower grows from the soil beneath him. It is white and purple, like blood on Adonis' flesh. Venus, bereft, leaves the Earth to hide her sadness where the gods live.

Some verses give a hint that aspects of Venus's seductive techniques may have been experienced first hand by the poet in his physical relationship with Emilia.

Euen as an emptie Eagle sharpe by fast,
Tires with her beake on feathers, flesh and bone,
Shaking her wings, deuouring all in hast,
Till either gorge be stufft, or prey be gone:
  Euen so she kist his brow, his cheeke, his chin,
  And where she ends, she doth anew begin

(*Venvs and Adonis* 55-60)

Venus recounts her sexual encounter with Mars

I have been wooed as I entreat thee now,
Euen by the sterne, and direfull god of warre,
Whose sinowie necke in battle nere did bow,
Who conquers where he comes in euerie iarre,
  Yet hath he bene my captiue and my slaue,
  And begd for that which thou vnaskt shalt haue.

Over my Altars hath he hung his launce,
His batterd thield, his vncontrolled crest,
And for my sake hath learn'd to sport and daunce,
To toy, to wanton, dallie, smile and iest,
  Scorning his churlish drumme and ensigne red,
  Making my armes his field, his tent my bed.

(*Venvs and Adonis* 97-108)

There are indications that this early on in their relationship Shakespeare is referring to Emilia as dark complexioned *And, beautie dead, blacke Chaos comes againe* (1020) and using the moor/more pun in *More I could tell, but more I dare not say* (805)

Echoing Emilia's temperament in *Burneth more hotly, swelleth with more rage* (332) and, as in the *Merchant of Venice,* associating a moor (the Prince of Morocco) with gold *But gold that's put to vse more gold begets* (768).

With eight occurrences of *rose* and associated words are implied references to Southampton and his nickname. *Rose-cheekt Adonis hied him to the chace* (3) and with its underlying bawdy content *What though the rose haue prickles, yet tis pluckt* (574) Was *Venvs and Adonis* yet another attempt by Shakespeare to kindle a dormant ember of heterosexuality in his young Patron?

What about suggesting to Southampton that he try out his mistress, who knew a thing or two about seduction? Far fetched? It would seem so, but Sonnet 35 would indicate otherwise

All men make faults, and euen I in this, Authorizing thy trespas with compare, My selfe corrupting saluing thy amisse (35.5-7)

It isn't only this confession but his very next play, *The Two Gentlemen of Verona* has precisely this weird occurrence.

Venvs and Adonis was registered in the Stationer's Register on 18 April 1593 about a month before Emilia was due to give birth and six weeks before the death of Kit Marlowe. Pregnancy doesn't put emotional love on hold, in fact it can heighten it, and so it is highly likely that Shakespeare took every opportunity to see Emilia whilst Alphonso was away with the peregrinating court. Perhaps even indulging in what Forman was to do in Emilia's bed, four years later, when he *felt all parts of her body willingly and kissed her often*

It was in May, after Emilia had given birth and revealed she was going to call the boy Henry, that Shakespeare began writing the *Dark Lady* sequence of sonnets and possibly shared the first two poems with Emilia.

IN the ould age blacke was not counted faire,
Or if it weare it bore not beauties name:
But now is blacke beauties successiue heire,
And Beautie slanderd with a bastard shame (127.1-4)

It wasn't too long after Henry's birth that the intense physical relationship between William and Emilia resumed, and with it, some disquiet for Shakespeare's conscience.

Sonnet 129
Th' expense of Spirit in a waste of shame
Is lust in action, and till action, lust
Is periured, murdrous, blooddy full of blame,
Sauage, extreame, rude, cruell, not to trust,
Enioyed no sooner but despised straight,
Past reason hunted, and no sooner had
Past reason hated as a swallowed bayt,
  On purpose layd to make the taker mad.
  Made In pursut and in possession so,
  Had, hauing, and in quest, to haue extreame,
  A blisse in proofe and proved, a very wo,
  Before a ioy proposed behind a dreame,
    All this the world well knowes yet none knows well,
    To shun the heauen that leads men to this hell.

Three works that Shakespeare was to tackle in the next two years - *Two Gentlemen of Verona, Titus Andronicus* and *Lucrece* - were all to touch on the awful subject of rape and were all set in Italy.

William's comments in Sonnet 129 on the male state of pre- and post-coital condition and the guilt experienced by breaking a line of his marriage vow *forsaking all others, be faithful to her as long as you both shall live?* so carefully crafted by Archbishop Cranmer in the Book of Common Prayer, prayed on his mind.

Katherine Duncan-Jones in a footnote to her edition of the Sonnets comments on the last two words, *this hell.*

the hell of shame and hatred described in the preceding lines: the female sex organ: the identification of hell with the vagina is made in Boccaccio's Decameron

Here is the reference that Professor Duncan-Jones refers to

Charming ladies, maybe you have never heard tell how one putteth the devil in hell; wherefore, without much departing from the tenor of that whereof you have discoursed all this day"

She quotes two more instances of the word being used in the same vein by Shakespeare

But being both from me both to each friend, I gesse one angel in an others hel. (144.11-12)

and

Women all aboue: but to the Girdle do the Gods inherit, beneath is all the Fiends. There's hell, there's darkenes, there is the sulphurous pit

King Lear (4.6.127-30)

My shame and guilt confounds me (4.4.2150)

was a line that resonated with Shakespeare and which he gave to Proteus in *The Two Gentlemen of Verona.*

Sonnet 130 (*My Mistrcs eyes are nothing like the Sunne*) demonstrates that Emilia has shared her poetry (*Of guld all burnisht, and brighter then sunne beames*) with William, and for reasons best know to himself, he has chosen to parody it. Others will point to Shakespeare parodying other sonneteers too; Sidney, Spencer and Petrarch.

It is around this time that William suggests to Emilia that she tries to seduce Southampton in the hope that this will spark off in him the desire to procreate. When Emilia accepts the challenge and makes successful overtures to Southampton, Shakespeare doesn't like it.

Thou art as tiranous, so as thou art (131.1)

In nothing are thou blacke save in thy deeds (131.13)

My guess is that she successfully began a sexual relationship with Southampton in the autumn of 1593, when William was in Italy.

A Lover's Complaint which relates the *fickle-maid's* version of events retold at a riverside location, which I suggest is Bisham/Cookham, and takes place in the summer. The narrator tells us the maid was wearing a straw hat, as protection from the sun, so perhaps this is set in the spring or summer of 1594.

When in 1593 Shakespeare was completing *Titus Andronicus* he openly names his love, Emilia Bassano, in two of his characters, Æmilius and Bassianus. To have ones name paraded on stage, the most public arena of the age, was flattering. When Emilia published *Salve Devs* in 1611 she chose to spell her name Æmilia. In *Titus*, Bassianus is Caesar's son, but Caesar didn't have a son called Bassianus, as Shakespeare would know very well from his school days. Bassianus was the Roman name for the town of Bassano from which Emilia and her family took its surname.

In *Titus,* Shakespeare invents a character, Aaron, a moor. Aaron is involved in a sexual relationship with Tamora, Queen of the Goths, afterwards Empress of Rome, who gives birth to his child. Titus says *That comes in likenesse of a Cole-blacke Moore* (4.1.1453) is this the beginning of Shakespeare's thoughts on the nature of racism that were to dominate the themes of two later Venetian plays *The Merchant of Venice* and *Othello*?

Anselm Bassano has pointed out that the name Tamora is a version of *Ti amo mora,* Italian for *I love you Moor*. Did Emilia, an Italian speaker, suggest Tamora's name?

Despite more recent productions that have rescued *Titus Andronicus* from its poor reputation it is still regarded a problem play because of its unbridled brutality and violence - murder, rape, mutilation and cannibalism - all of which the modern mind believes beneath the consideration of a great renaissance writer.

Shakespeare was known to have his sights set on making money, and seeing the popularity of Thomas Kyd's revenge play, *Spanish Tragedy,* prompted him to write *Titus* which during Shakespeare's lifetime, was one of his most popular plays. *Titus* was Shakespeare's first printed play registered in February 1594, there were two subsequent editions before his death, in 1600 and 1602, and then another posthumous edition when it was included in the First Folio in 1623.

Does Shakespeare give any lines to either Æmelius or Bassianus that could have been uttered by Emilia in life, or actions that reflect her known conduct? No, I don't think he does, but *lovely* Tamora certainly has lines which could be assoicated with Emilia. Tamora's amorous approach is reminiscent of Venus' forward behaviour in a setting with an echo and a cave, like Bisham.

Tamora
My louely Aaron, Wherefore look'st thou sad,
When euery thing doth make a Gleefull boast?
The Birds chaunt melody on euery bush,
The Snake lies rolled in the chearefull Sunne,

The greene leaues quiuer, with the cooling winde,
And make a cheker'd shadow on the ground:
Vnder their sweete shade, Aaron let vs sit,
And whil'st the babling Eccho mock's the Hounds,
Replying shrilly to the well tun'd-Hornes,
As if a double hunt were heard at once,
Let vs sit downe, and marke their yelping noyse:
And after conflict, such as was suppos'd.
The wandring Prince and Dido once enioy'd,
When with a happy storme they were surpris'd,
And Curtain'd with a Counsaile-keeping Caue,
We may each wreathed in the others armes,
(Our pastimes done) possesse a Golden slumber,
Whiles Hounds and Hornes, and sweet Melodious Birds
Be vnto vs, as is a Nurses Song
Of Lullabie, to bring her Babe asleepe. (2.3.666-715)

Lute songs - which Shakespeare heard Emilia first perform at Bisham - as well as aids to love, are, in *Titus* cited as powerful antidotes to violence, by Marcus at the sight of the brutally ravaged Lavinia

Marcus
Oh had the monster seene those Lilly hands,
Tremble like Aspen leaues vpon a Lute,
And make the silken strings delight to kisse them,
He would not then haue toucht them for his life.
Or had he heard the heauenly Harmony,
Which that sweet tongue hath made:
He would haue dropt his knife and fell asleepe (2.31054-62)

Was Emilia so nervous that when she played in public her hands shook? As in Sonnet 128 Shakespeare refers to parts of an instrument *kissing fingers.* *Since saucie Iacks so happy are in this, Giue them their fingers, me thy lips to kisse.* (128.13/14)

Only three months after *Titus* was registered, the anonymous, *The Taming of a Shrew* was published. Authorship of the "A" play is contested but I would hope that the inclusion of the characters of Emelia and Alfonso make it clear that Shakespeare had a hand in writing it.

The setting is Greece where Kate, a recalcitrant student, is taking lessons on the lute from Valeria.

Enter Valeria with a Lute and Kate with him
Valeria
The fencelesse trees by musick haue bin mou'd,
And at the sound of pleasant tuned strings,
Haue sauage beasts hung down their listning heads,

As though they had beene cast into a trance.
Then it may be that she whom nought can please,
With musickes sound in time may be supprisde,
Come louely mistresse wil you take your lute,
And play the lesson that I taught you last?
Kate
It is no matter whether I do or no,
For trust me I take no great delight in it.
Valeria
I would sweet mistresse that it lay in me,
To helpe you to that thing thats your delight.
Kate
In you with a pestlence, are you so kind?
Then make a night cap of your fiddles case,
To warme your head and hide your filthy face.
Valeria
If that sweet mistres were your hearts content,
You should command a greater thing then that,
Although it were ten times to my disgrace.
Kate
Your so kinde twere pitty you should be hang'd,
And yet methinks the foole doth looke asquint.
Valeria
Why mistresse do you mocke me?
Kate
No, but I meane to move thee.
Valeria
Wel, wil you play a little?
Kate
I, give me the lute

She plaies

Valeria
That stop was false, play it againe.
Kate
Then mend it thou, thou filthy asse
Valeria
What do you bid me kisse your arse?

(*The Taming of a Shrew* 2.1.1-27 The Shakespeare Library edition)

It seems as if the author here is referring to an actual event - no doubt celebrated in the Bassano family - involving three of Emilia's cousins who, as servants of the crown, had immunity from arrest. On 22 September 1584, John Spencer, a former Sheriff of London, after complaints had been made against him, was asked to account for himself when he unlawfully arrested and briefly imprisoned Arthur, Edward and Jeronimo Bassano for loitering near Christ Church.

They had been watching some workmen labouring when Spencer ordered them to move on but they obstinately refused - being the Queen's servants, unbeknown to the Sheriff - saying *This is the Queen's ground and we will stand here.* When told if they would not depart *by fair means* they would be sent to ward. Spencer recounted that *one of them - a little black man who was booted - answered*

"Send us to ward? Thou wert as good as kiss our arses"

Was this little Chaucerian anecdote one retold to Shakespeare by Emilia? When Elizabethans used the word *Black* to describe someone they meant hair, rather than skin colouring.

The dialogue between Kate and Valeria continues

Kate
How now iackfause, your iolly mate,
Your best be still least I crosse your pate,
And make your musicke flie about your eares,
Ile make it and your follish coxcombe meet.

She offers to strike him with the lute

Valeria
Hold mistresse, souns wil you break my lute?
Kate
I on thy head, if thou speake to me

The earliest known performance of *The Taming of the Shrew* is recorded in Philip Henslowe's diary on 11 June 1594.

In the "The" play, the lute lesson remains but characters Emelia and Alfonso disappear, was this at Emilia's request because she hated her name associated with a husband she despised? Shakespeare also transported the setting from Greece, to the one we know today, Italy.

17. Shakespeare in Italy

Venice, Who does not see you cannot praise you
I may speake of thee as the traueiler doth of Venice, vem chie, vencha, que non te
vnde, que non te perreche

(*Loues Labour's lost* 4.2.1170)

Did Shakespeare see Venice? Did he hear the old Mantuan dialect spoken that he puts in the mouth of Sir Nathaniel whilst he was in Mantua?

Emilia's talk of Italy, had already preoccupied him with the country, choosing the Roman settings of *Lucrece* and *Titus* as his 1592 subjects. From the beginning of 1594 he became even more concerned with Italy in his writing, particularly the northern towns and cities. In *The Taming of the Shrew* Vincentio: says *Thy father: oh villaine, he is a Saile-maker in Bergamo* but Bergamo is an inland town. C20 critics have thought this comment shows Shakespeare's ignorance of North Italian geography, but the reality is that because of the C16 waterway systems of North Italy Bergamo very likely did have a sail maker.

An opportunity for Shakespeare to visit came in the autumn of 1593, he mentions another sail, retrospectively, in Sonnet 117. *All the winds* would suggest a sea journey longer than just a channel crossing.

I have hoysted saile to al the windes Which should transport me farthest from your sight. (117.7-8)

There is compelling evidence that on that trip, as a professional adviser to three of Emilia's cousins, Shakespeare visited the town of Bassano and passed through other towns in the North of Italy on the way to Venice that would later appear as settings for plays that were fermenting in his mind.

There is general agreement that Shakespeare may have joined Lord Strange's Men by 1592, and that the first of Shakespeare's plays to be performed in Kent was probably *Henry VI* Part 1. *Lord Strange's Men* had played at the Rose Theatre between February and June 1592 until the outbreak of plague closed the theatres and forced the actors to tour the provinces. I think that Shakespeare preferred to accept a more interesting and lucrative offer to tour abroad.

Three Bassano brothers found themselves in a profitable trade dealing in a commodity of which they had no experience, but one in which Shakespeare was steeped because of his childhood, as the son of a glove maker, leather. Servants of the crown, which as court musicians, the Bassanos were, often used their connections to obtain licences to import and export all kinds of goods that eventually proved to be far more remunerative than their modest court wages.

This was Alphonso Lanier's experience, with his weighing of hay grant in London, but happened very early on shortly after the Bassanos arrival from Venice when Anthony and Jacomo were granted a licence to import three hundred tuns of Gascon wine, previously held by Mark Raphael. Importing though is a much easier commercial enterprise for a merchant than exporting.

On August 27 1593 Arthur, Andrea and Jeronimo Bassano were licensed to export six thousand dickers of calfskins. Very likely this licence had been promised for some time before the official date of the grant, so they would have been preparing for the new venture. The archaic term *dicker*, which unlike the word *dozen*, has disappeared from modern usage, means a quantity of ten. It was used specifically for calfskins.

Sixty thousand calfskins is a lot to export, it needs colossal man-power to herd the cattle together for slaughter, remove skin from flesh which then needs tanning - the sexton in Hamlet has something to say about the preservative quality to the skin of its practitioners *A Tanner will last you nine yeare* (*Hamlet* 5.1.3250) - but more than anything else, for the licence holder, it needs a sales market.

By 1593 the Bassanos had a long established Europe wide market for musical instruments on the various overland routes from London to Venice. It would have been a question of using their local connections to help expand the market for the inclusion of leather.

Bassano instruments still exist in private collections and museums in Brussels, Augsburg, Munich, Linz, Vienna and Venice as well as London and Oxford their current location often reflecting the general locality of their last home. One early Bassano instrument, a boxwood pipe, was recovered from the *Mary Rose* the Tudor war ship was sunk in 1545 and reclaimed in 1982 when the ship resurfaced and the wreck preserved.

The manufacture of brass instruments, particularly sackbuts was centred in and around Nuremberg, and so it is highly likely that a bartering system was in place whereby the wind instruments manufactured by the Bassanos, were exchanged for sackbuts and possibly trumpets, from the Nuremberg makers like Neuschel and Schnitzer.

By 1571, the Bavarian court in Munich owned a chest of Bassano instruments, six unidentified wind instruments of different sizes. Records show that the Bassanos distributed the instruments that they built in London, throughout the Hapsburg Empire, as far south as Toledo in Spain. As instrument makers the Bassano's use of leather was restricted to strips of the material covering the wooden cornetti and shaped hide in the manufacture of instrument cases, lute and viol cases, for example. Shakespeare shows his knowledge of the subject in the *Comedy of Errors*

Dromio of Syracuse.
No? why 'tis a plaine case: he that went like a BaseViole in a case of leather (4.1.1118)

Shakespeare possessed the experience in dealing with the production of leather that the Bassano family lacked. The closure of the London theatres was a good time to seek his assistance in a mercantile trip to Venice.

The early Shakespeare biographer, John Aubrey claimed that as a boy, Shakespeare would kill calves *in a high style and make a speech.* Katherine Duncan-Jones has published research exploring the links between the Shakespeares and leather-dressers and butchers, with particular reference to the various forms of dramatic entertainment that the young William may have encountered and learned to devise, such as dramas concerning the *Prodigal Son and the fatted calf,* or *Guy of Warwick,* legendary slayer of the Dun Cow of Dunsmore Heath. Professor Duncan-Jones paper makes connections between such entertainments and images of butchery and calf-killing throughout Shakespeare's writings, the most frequent and elaborate instances being found in early plays such as *King John* and the *Henry VI.*

The details of what I am about to suggest were first extensively written about, by Roger Prior, in 2008 in a rather obscure academic journal.

More than a hint of the veracity of a connection between the poet and the Bassano brothers is found in Thomas Nashe's *Strange News* of 1593, the same time as the Bassano brothers calf skin grant. It indicates that Shakespeare's reputation as a *kill-cow* followed him to London, and his experience as a bovine slaughterer, spoken of with Emilia.

Nashe writes

From the admonition of these uncourteous misconstruers, I come to The kill-cow champion of the three brethren

Although in this specific instance Nashe may have had Spencer, as well as Shakespeare, the *kill-cow champion* in mind. Arthur, Andrea and Jeronimo were *three brethren*, three of the five sons of Anthony Bassano.

The benefit of an export licence was that it effectively exempted the licence holder from the trade laws which banned certain types of export. It was often granted with certain stipulations, in this case, the complete 60,000 skins had to be exported within seven years, with a steep five shillings per dicker paid in customs duty - the usual rate was only one shilling - and they were forbidden to use the ports of Bristol, Chester or Liverpool during the continuous grants made to others relating to these ports.

Because as musicians they were generally required to be in attendance at Court, none of the brothers could have devoted their time exclusively to the new lucrative business, but developing local sales outlets with their established connections *en route* to Venice, seems what was initially in the three brother's minds before handing over the business to an administrator.

All three brothers, were members of the Court Recorder Consort along with Alphonso Lanier. The last received payment by the Court to them was made in June 1593, the next, not recorded until 1598. This doesn't necessarily mean they were paid nothing in those intervening five ycars, the records may just be missing, but what it may also indicate is that the lucrative licence may have been made in lieu of payments, in which case the brothers will have been more easily able to negotiated three months away from Court employment in order to establish their leather sales market.

In addition to his knowledge of the product, Shakespeare, because of his farming contacts in and around Stratford had access to good pedigree cattle. No wonder that as soon as he had the cash available, he chose to buy farm land - 107 acres of grazing - close to his family home, capitalising on the profitable opportunity offered to him by the Bassano brothers. This was not only over the seven year term of the original licence but, as it happened, continuing until the end of Shakespeare's life and after, up until 1621. This was because the licence was renewed three times, on each occasion adding younger members of the Bassano family.

I have been unable to trace passports for any of the three brothers, or Shakespeare, but it's hardly surprising that any papers relating to this - with an intervening civil war - are missing. Gentlemen, which the armigerous Bassano brothers were, were granted travel documents which allowed them to takc horses and be accompanied by servants. I imagine that Shakespcare, would bc categorised as a servant, so no travel document needed in his name.

The most direct overland route to Venice from London is some nine hundred miles including crossing the English Channel. At a modest thirty miles a day by horse the one way journey would take a month, the least mountainous route via Switzerland into Italy finally takes the traveller through Italian towns familiar to Shakespeare audiences because they are mentioned in several of the plays. Milan, *The Two Gentlemen of Verona* and *The Tempest*, Bergamo, *The Taming of the Shrew*, Verona, *Romeo and Juliet*, *The Two Gentlemen of Verona*, and Padua, *The Taming of the Shrew, The Two Gentlemen of Verona, The Merchant of Venice* and *Much adoe about Nothing*. Padua lies some twenty five miles inland from Venice, the city state is mentioned in *The Taming of the Shrew, The Two Gentlemen of Verona, Othello, The Merchant of Venice, Loues Labour's Lost, Richard ll* and *Much adoe about Nothing*.

Perhaps the return journey was made via Mantua (*Love's Labours lost*) where the Bassanos may have been strongly motivated to seek out the twenty eight year old composer, Claudio Monteverdi, employed at the Gonzaga court. In 1593 Monteverdi had just published his third book of madrigals, it was to be a few more years before he developed into the magnificent opera and liturgical composer he was to become.

From what follows, it is clear that Bassano (del Grappa) was visited. It lies on an easterly mountainous journey from England to Venice. It was the route taken by Thomas Hoby on his well documented journey to Italy in May 1554 and Shakespeare and the Bassano Brothers could have followed in his footsteps but that would have meant by-passing the towns that |I have mentioned.

The town of Bassano doesn't lie on the route from Milan to Venice and at fifty miles, was a long day's journey from Venice and so at least one overnight stay was required.

Bassano was founded as an agricultural estate in the 2nd century BC by a Roman whose name was Bassianus, identical to the character in *Titus Andronicus*. It's most prominent architectural feature is the cpvered bridge spanning the River Brenta built in 1569 to a design by Palladio.The town lies in the shadow of the 1,775 metre high Monte Grappa. For a traveller leaving England for the first time in his life to cross the Alps, mountains make a strong initial impression. The silence, pure air and views from on high are literally awe inspiring. When Shakespeare visited Bassano, he can hardly fail to have noticed that Monte Grappa is a beautiful mountain, he will have heard someone utter the Italian words *bella montana*. He shortened this phrase into the name of Portia's home, Belmont.

I have one significant hurdle to overcome with my suggestion of the timing of Shakespeares visit. If the rival poet is indeed Christopher Marlowe, Sonnet 86 dates from shortly after his death in May 1593, if all of the sonnets before the start of the *Dark Lady* sequence (126) were chronological, then Sonnet 86 clearly comes a long way after Sonnet 40 which is the betrayal of the *Dark Lady* with the *Fair Friend*.

Since Emilia was giving birth around the time of Marlowe's death, if there is indeed a chronological sequence between sonnets 40 and 86 she can only have been sharing her bed with Shakespeare and Southampton when heavily pregnant, or there has to be some other explanation.

We have already seen that Sonnets 40 and 133 are contemporaneous with one another indicating that there are two sonnet sequences overlapping. If the visit to Italy in the autumn of 1593 is correct, this means there is a third sequence numbers 78-86 dealing with the *Rival Poet*; so three overlapping sequences, with No 86 shortly after the death of Marlowe on 30 May 1593.

If it is his stabbing that is referred to in

the coward conquest of a wretches knife (74.11)

shows that Sonnet 74 was written after 30 May 1593, it could be contemporaneous, which doesn't help me very much, but it is even more damaging to the concept that Thorpe's numbered sequence was chronological, coming twelve sonnets before Marlowe's death.

Sonnet 74 could have been written months, or even a year later, than the writing of Sonnet 86. If Sonnet 74 relates to Marlowe but it is a distant memory of both the method of his death and the character of his killer, this makes my timing for Emilia's affair with Southampton perfectly feasible. We have much to be grateful to Thomas Thorpe for publishing the sonnets without authorisation, but with his numbering, he is also the source of much confusion.

In 2008 I sent Roger Prior a photograph I had taken of a fresco displayed in the civic museum of Bassano. It had originally been painted on an external wall of a house in the centre of the old town, the wall on which it was painted had been carefully preserved and transported to the museum.

43 Dal Corno fresco

The photograph showed a faded painting which included naked and semi-clad figures, cherubs and musical instruments, but most significantly, goats and monkies.

When he saw it, Roger recalled Iago's enigmatic lines, having planted the seeds of doubt in Othello's mind over his wife's fidelity, and inferring that he will never see Desdemona and Cassio making love with his own eyes.

It is impossible you should see this, Were they as prime as Goates, as hot as Monkeyes, As salt as Wolues in pride (capital letters G, M and W as in the First Folio 3.3.405-7)

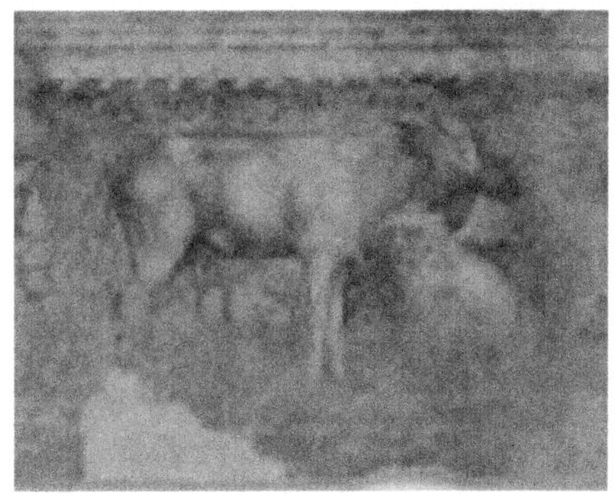

44 Dal Corno fresco detail

After studying the photograph and undertaking extensive further research, Prior concluded that Shakespeare must not only have seen the fresco with his own eyes, but drawn a sketch of it too. Further enquiry showed other connections between Othello and the town of Bassano. Why should Shakespeare have been so drawn to this fresco?

I think it was the naked women. Although exposed breasts in unmarried ladies were allowed in England, the completely naked female figure in Tudor portraiture hardly existed and then only in private collections. The medieval nudes, murals of Adam and Eve on church walls for example, were whitewashed from public view at the Reformation, certainly nothing so publicly displayed in England. It was a new and thrilling experience for him arousing the enthusiastic heterosexual side of his nature.

Shakespeare's knowledge of the Veneto and the Po valley is strikingly accurate. He knows that nearly all the chief cities, such as Padua, Verona, Bergamo, Mantua and Milan are accessible by water, and are commonly reached in this way by ship. The thirty principal tributaries of the Po were all navigable, and were then linked by an extensive system of canals. It is possible that the Bassano brothers and Shakespeare when they arrived in Milan continued their journey to Venice by water.

In *The Tempest* Prospero and Miranda are sent from Milan to the sea by an inland waterway, and then transferred to an unrigged *butt* when they reach the coast, a journey that was perfectly achievable in the way Shakespeare suggests. In the *Two Gentlemen of Verona* Shakespeare implies that a river (the Adige) which can carry ships flows through Verona.

Panthino
Launce, away, away: a Boord: thy Master is
ship'd, and thou art to post after with oares; what's the
matter? why weep'st thou man? away asse, you'l loose
the Tide, if you tarry any longer.

Launce
"It is no matter if the tide were lost, for it is the
vnkindest Tied, that euer any man tied." (2.2.610-5)

The phenomenon of a tide in a river has been questioned - it could, of course, just be the playwright unable to resist punning - but contemporary travellers testified to the fact that fast flowing rivers in the region could be reduced in strength and volume by the diversion of water through irrigation channels.

By this method their water levels could be made to rise and fall, just like a *tide* or *flood*, as Panthino later calls it.

Between 1592 and 1594 Shakespeare studied the works of several Italian poets in the original, and used them freely as sources for his plays. He borrowed much from Tasso's *Aminta,* and influenced by Boiardo's *Orlando Innamorato* and Ariosto's *Orlando Furioso* as he wrote *Loues Labour's lost.* Perhaps these works were owned by the Italian speaking Bassanos.

The town of Bassano, stands in the foothills of the Trentine Alps on the river Brenta. In the 1590s it was a prosperous market town, a centre for the manufacture of leather and silk and the cultivation of silkworms and former home to a substantial Jewish population, expelled by the time of Shakespeare's visit. As well as the former residence of the Bassano musicians, it was the home of the well known dal Ponte family of painters, almost always referred to these days as Bassano. The *pater familias*, until his death in 1592, was Jacopo dal Ponte.

Whilst they were resident in Bassano the family of musicians were known by the name Piva, renaming themselves Bassano, when they moved to Venice. The English Bassanos retained ownership of a house in the town until 1571 when ownership was transferred to the Venetian branch of the family, but in his will, Jeronimo Bassano mentions another property still in his ownership as late as 1623.

Nearly all of the Jews in the Shakespeare plays, are like the Bassanos, Venetian, although Tuball may have been named after a contemporary London resident. Shylock's dislike of music may be deliberately designed to contrast him with the Jewish, but highly musical Bassanos.

By the time he came to write *The Merchant* Shakespeare had acquired an extensive knowledge of the town of Bassano. There is much detailed knowledge of both Bassano and Venice, in *The Merchant* and *Othello*, that would have been difficult to assimilate from books or informants.Shakespeare names two of his protagonists, Bassanio and Othello, after families who were well known in the town. The Italian form of the name Othello, Otello, has so far only been found in the town, where it was common, and nowhere else.

There were ten men with the name spanning three generations from 1430-1597 all of whom at some stage in their lives lived in Bassano. Several of them were related and it is likely that they were all members of the same extended family. Among their number were two teachers of grammar, notaries and three priests including one who was a Jesuit and interestingly, one very prosperous leather handler. Even today leather remains an important industry in the town, showing that business, as well as family sentiment, was a motivation to visit.

Two Otello brothers, both notaries, commissioned paintings from Jacopo Dal

Ponte. There were Otellos living in the town when Shakespeare visited. His choice of the name Othello for his play, and its leading actor, shows he will either have heard of the family or met one of them whilst he was in Bassano.

One of the additions to his main source, Cinthio's story of *The Moor*, is the association he makes between Othello and drugs. Desdemona's father Brabantio is convinced that Othello must have won the love of his daughter by employing drugs.

Abus'd her delicate Youth, with Drugs or Minerals, (1.2284)

corrupted her *By Spels, and Medicines, bought of Mountebanks* (*Othello* 1.2.384).

The link between Othello and drugs may have been suggested to Shakespeare by the fact that Giovanni Otello had been part owner of an apothecary's shop in Bassano. Besides Giovanni Otello, drugs and medicines in Bassano were associated with a Moor. A popular apothecary in the same piazza as Giovanni Otello was known as *the Moor* because of the sign of a Moor's head which hung outside his shop. Spretti's *Famiglia Stemma* depicts a Neapolitan family bearing the name Bassano, featuring a moor with a turban and crescent moon, in the crest of their Italian grant of arms.

Bassano was known for for the cultivation of silk worms, the Bassano family coat-of-arms displays three silk worm moths and a mulberry tree. Shakespeare took a particular interest in this subject in the early months of 1594, since he then read - in manuscript - Thomas Moffet's treatise *The Silkwormes and their Flies.* He used it as a major source for two plays, *Romeo and Juliet* and *A Midsommer nights Dreame,* as well as Sonnets 54, 94, 98 and 128 which seem to be influenced by Moffet's writing. He also refers directly to silkworms when Othello links Desdemona's lost silk handkerchief to the silk-worms and magic drugs.

The Wormes were hallowed, that did breede the Silke, And it was dyde in Mummey, which the Skilfull Conseru'd of Maidens hearts (3.4.2171-4)

When the Bassano family of musicians lived in Crespano del Grappa and later Bassano del Grappa they went under the name Piva, meaning bagpipe, as well as the insulting anti-semitic colloquial terms, common at the time, of *big-nose* and *penis.*

From 1510 the town council of Bassano regularly voted to expel its Jewish residents, and succeeded in doing so by 1524. The history surrounding the Bassano family and the town of Bassano seems to have been in Shakespeare's mind when he was writing both Venetian plays. He spent the best part of two months traveling with the three Bassano brothers so he will have learnt a great deal about the family's story, their home town, and Venice from them. He associates bagpipes, nose and penis with the Venetian Jew, Shylock, when he gives him the following line

And others, when the <u>bag-pipe</u> sings i'th <u>nose</u>, Cannot containe their <u>Vrine</u> for affection (Merchant 4.1.1885-6 my underlining)

In *Othello* the musicians are told

Then put vp your <u>Pipes</u> in your <u>bagge</u> (3.1.1499)

Enter Cassio, Musitians, and Clowne
Cassio
Masters, play heere, I wil content your paines,
Something that's briefe: and bid, goodmorrow General.
Clown
Why Masters, haue your Instruments bin in Na
ples, that they speake i'th'Nose thus?
Musician
How Sir? how?
Clown
Are these I pray you, winde Instruments?
Musician
I marry are they sir.
Clown
Oh, thereby hangs a tale.
Musician
Whereby hangs a tale, sir?
Clown
Marry sir, by many a winde Instrument that I
know. But Masters, heere's money for you: and the Ge
nerall so likes your Musick, that he desires you for loues
sake to make no more noise with it. (Merchant 3.1.1494)

The Clown asks the musicians if thcir instruments - from which hangs a tail (or penis) - have been in Naples, that is caught a venereal disease. Untreated syphilis causes the nose to disintegrate so that the sufferer speaks with a nasal twang.

When Shakespeare visited Bassano there was one sight he could not fail to have seen. The large and remarkable fresco painted on the wall adjacent to the street from the first floor upwards of a private house in the centre of the town.It was pained by Jacopo dal Ponte, who had died in Bassano in 1592. It is highly likely that whilst they were resident in Bassano, the Pivas and dal Pontes, knew one another.

The dal Ponte family were musical enough to perform together. Leandro dal Ponte's Concert is a portrait of his own family singing a madrigal together accompanied by lute and keyboard. The evidence that this is the dal Pontes is given by the appearance of Leandro's father Jacopo - recognised from his self portrait - as a member of the musical ensemble.

The fresco that Shakespeare refers to was painted in 1539 and so the colours would be far more vivid and detail much more focussed in 1593 than the wall appears now. The fresco is preserved in the Bassano del Grappa Museum.

It was commissioned by the Dal Corno family, who owned the house. Zuanne Dal Corno, a nobleman from Treviso, appears to have paid for the painting and either he, or his son-in-law, Lazzaro, had an important influence on what symbolism should be included and the overall design of the fresco. Lazzaro had taken his wife's aristocratic maiden name as his own. The Dal Corno coat-of-arms was featured as a wooden carving on the fresco. Shakespeare shows a detailed knowledge of the fresco which would indicate he has seen it himself.

The fresco is divided into four horizontal bands, the highest of which is a *Trompe-l'œil* frieze showing eleven cherubs either side of three window apertures which would have given light to the third floor of the building. The second band shows a man's head, five goats, two monkeys and what could be a swan with its wings expanded - a common heraldic symbol - as well as the bird with which Shakespeare was identified by Ben Jonson's *Sweet swan of Avon.*

As well as the animals there are musical instruments, unfortunately the faded painting makes it difficult to identify with absolute certainty what the instruments are. There are definitely cornetts. the inclusion of cornetts is emblematic of the family name, Dal Corno. What appears to be a brass instrument, a trumpet or a sackbut - cornetts and sackbuts went together as the conventional wind ensemble in the Veneto. so it is most likely a sackbut. By the time of Shakespeare's visit to Bassano, Giovanni Gabrieli's compositional techniques for separated choir music - *cori spezatti* - was in the ascendent. Finally two different size viols, most likely a tenor and bass.

Two juxtaposed animals seem to have caught Shakespeare's eye, a goat which stands over a seated monkey. This pair stand out partly because the goat is large - the same size in fact as some of the human figures on the band beneath - and partly because the monkey is differentiated from the other animals. It is the only figure to be seated, and the only one which faces from right to left.

Shakespeare seems to have associated the Dal Corno fresco with sexual desire. He may have been influenced by both the family name, Corno, translating as horn, and the family trade as salt merchants. The Dal Cornos were the official sellers of salt in Bassano, and their house was located in the Piazzotto del Sale - the little square of salt. Shakespeare regularly uses salt as an adjective to mean *lustful*, and in *Othello* he links it to the goat and monkey in the fresco. In *Othello,* and no other work, Shakespeare brings together goats and monkeys as twin examples of lechery. In Iago's words he also associated them with the act of seeing.

It is impossible you should see this, Were they as prime as Goates, as hot as Mon-

keyes, As salt as Wolues in pride, (3.3.2004)

In Act 4 Scene 1 Desdemona has referred to *the love I bear to Cassio* (*Othello* 4.1.2560) and Othello takes this as a sexual boast. In their subsequent exchanges he strikes her, insults her and orders her to leave. *Cassio shall have my place* (4.1.2598), he says to Lodovico, with a sexual double meaning on the word *place*, and immediately exits crying *Goates, and Monkeyes* (4.1.2601)

Besides the word *salt* other clues suggest that in both scenes Shakespeare had in mind the goat and monkey of the Dal Corno fresco. for example the phrase *well-painted passion* six lines before Othello's exit recalls the painted fresco. In the earlier scene the goats and monkeys of Iago's speech are immediately followed by other visual features of the fresco.

Were they as prime as Goates, as hot as Monkeyes, As salt as Wolues in pride, and Fooles as grosse As Ignorance, made drunke. But yet, I say, If imputation, and strong circumstances, Which leade directly to the doore of Truth (4.1.2008)

The last two phrases both describe scenes from the fresco. On its lowest band are depicted four scenes of debauchery from the Old Testament, each in a separate oval frame. Looking from left to right, the third of these which is vertically below the goat and monkey depicts the drunkenness of Noah. Here is Shakespeare's *Ignorance, made drunke.* Since the drunken Noah is shown naked lying on his back with his legs apart, he might well be called a

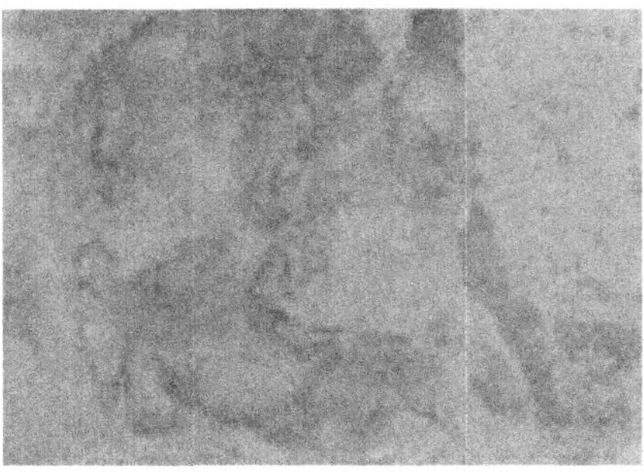

45 Dal Corno fresco Noah

Foole as grosse As Ignorance, made drunke, where *gross* has its common Shakespearean meaning of *sexually shameless.* Shakespeare may have had in mind the description of Noah in the Geneva bible *And he drunk of the wine, and was drunken; and was uncovered in the midst of his tent.* In Iago's lines Shakespeare's eye traveled vertically down and to the right in the fresco from the goat and monkey to the drunken Noah. On this trajectory his eyes would take in another figure in the third band, one which is even larger than Noah beneath it.

This is the figure of a woman, entirely naked, who stands by herself, flanked by two tall arched windows of the *piano nobile.* She has her right arm raised and in that hand she holds what appears to be a torch. She is one of three large female figures who stand between the windows and who were traditionally identified as *Prudence, Rhetoric and Industry* This identification was recorded a century after the paining was done so may not be correct, in fact the Rubinesque nude is unlikely to be associated with any of these three virtues. The central women is more likely to be *truth* who when used symbolically often appears as a naked woman holding a flaming torch above her head. It is hardly

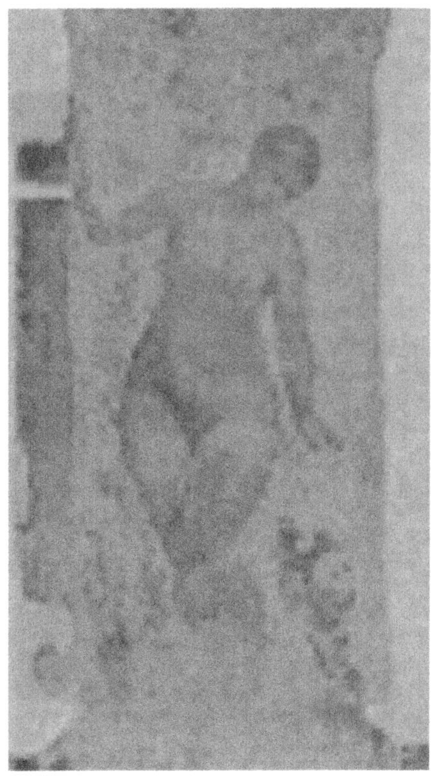

46 Dal Corno fresco
Naked Truth

surprising if Shakespeare identified the nakedwoman as *truth*. He used the phrase *the naked truth* in *Loues Labour's lost*. (5.2.2497)

In the fresco the images of the goat, monkey and Noah could be said to *lead directly* to the naked figure as Truth which physically unites them. But why does Shakespeare refer to *the doore of Truth* (capital letter T as in First Folio). The naked figure had doors on either side of her, vertical wooden shutters would enclose the figure of *Truth*. When opened outwards during the day these shutters would cover the nude figure, hiding her nakedness, as Shem and Japheth had hidden their father Noah's nakedness.

We know from Jacopo dal Ponte's notebook that the shutters on the Dal Corno house were called *gelosie* literally *jealousies*. A wooden *gelosia* has downward facing slats from which an observer can see but not be seen. The Dal Corno *gelosie* have an obvious relevance in *Othello*, and Shakespeare seems to have been well aware of their double meaning.

In the long Scene 3 of Act 3 Shakespeare uses images that appear to owe their inspiration from the Dal Corno fresco. Iago and Othello have a lengthy emotional exchange on the subject of jealousy, and the reasons for suspecting Desdemona's honesty. The words *jealousy* and *jealous* occur seven times within fifty lines (*Othello* 3.3.1714-1764) and are associated with cuckoldry (3.3.1737) and goats (3.3.1751).

The owner of these *gelosie* was a Dal Corno, whose name in itself made him what Othello calls *A Horned man* (capital letter H as in First Folio) or cuckold. With so many references to *gelosia* in his mind Shakespeare seems to recall the closed wooden *gelosie*. Iago points out that

She [Desdemona] *did deceiue her Father, marrying you* (3.3.1778) To do this, she was able

To seele her Fathers eyes vp, close as Oake, He thought 'twas Witchcraft (3.3.1786)

The enigmatic phrase *close as oak* is easier to understand if Shakespeare is comparing her father's eyes to closed wooden shutters, traditionally made of oak. Later he was to associate the oak tree *Herne's oak* with Falstaff's horned cuckold guise in the Forrest in *The Merry Wiues of Windsor.*

The fresco's second scene from the Old Testament to the left of Noah is of *Lot and his Daughters,* and it too seems to have been based on Genisis. In chapter 19 Lot's two daughters gave their father wine and *lay with* [their] *father* whilst he was asleep, both became pregnant by him. In the lines which follow *the door of truth,* Iago describes how he *lay with Cassio lately* (3.3.2013) According to Iago's retelling of the story, the sleeping Cassio makes sexual advances to him, dreaming that he is making love to Desdemona.

Both Lot, and Cassio in Iago's invention, make love whilst they are asleep, and neither is aware of what he is doing. The parallels between the two tales go even further than this. Cassio's sexual approaches to Iago even in sleep are symbolic acts of sodomy. Lot and his daughters were originally citizens of Sodom.

Shortly after Desdemona has taken her dying breath, Æmilia talks to her dead mistress. She recalls the song that Desdemona has sung to her that she had first heard from her mother's maid Barbarie which she had sung as she died. Singing is of course something that Emilia did in life recalling the swan of the fresco

I will play the Swan, And dye in Musicke: Willough, Willough, Willough (5.3.3458).

Perhaps within the lines of *Salve Devs* Emilia was making a cryptic reference to both Shakepeare and Southampton when she refers to the symbolic colours, white and red, mentioning a swan and a rose.

No Dove, no Swan, no Iv'rie could compare
With this faire corps, when 'twas by death imbrac'd;
No rose, nor no vermillion halfe so faire
As was that pretious blood that interlac'd
His body, which bright Angels did attend
(*Salve Devs,* to the Ladie Katherine Countesse of Suffolke 79-83)

Lodovico Bassano, was a cousin of Emilia and the three brothers, he died in July 1593 at the age of 40, just before the brothers began their journey, so it is possible that Shakespeare names one of his characters, Lodovico *in memoriam.*

References to the Dal Corno Bassano town fresco appear in the earlier play, *The Merchant of Venice* as well as in *Othello.* Through the name Bassanio, both the Bassano family and the town of Bassano are constant presences throughout the play. Antonio is the Venetian name of Anthony Bassano the father of the three Bassano brothers that accompanied Shakespeare to Italy.

The cornett, an instrument associated with the Dal Corno fresco and the Bassano family is specified in the script to be sounded on five occasions, more than any other of the four Shakespeare plays in which the instrument appears. By the time Shakespeare was writing *The Merchant,* the Venetian musician, Giovani Bassano, Emilia's cousin once removed, had established himself as Europe's foremost virtuoso on the instrument.

Commenting on Antonio's changeable mood, Solanio mentions the Roman god, Janus *Now by two-headed Ianus* (*The Merchant* 1.1.51) There is a two headed figure on the Dal Corno fresco, where the central of the three women has two heads facing in opposite directions.

In *The Merchant* Shakespeare shows a particular interest in the two men that commissioned the fresco, the jurist Lazzaro dal Corno and his father-in-law Zanetto, both of whom lived in the house. In 1532 Lazzaro recited a Latin eulogy in the presence of the Emperor Charles V on his visit to Bassano, in return the Emperor confirmed upon Lazzaro the title *Conte Palatino.* This title *the Countie Palentine* occurs twice in *The Merchant* (1.2.231,244) where it belongs to one of Portia's suiters.

The Count is the only suitor whose place of origin isn't identified, perhaps a sign of his Venetian provenance that is well known to Portia and Nerissa. Portia judges him to be so gloomy that

I feare hee will proue the weeping Phylosopher when he growes old (1.3.234)

The real-life Conte Lazzaro has also been described as a philosopher, and he wrote at least one gloomy or *weeping* sonnet which Shakespeare may have seen in print in Lorenzo Maruchini's *Il Bassano* published in Venice in 1577. Perhaps it was Maruchini's Christian name that influenced Shakespeare to call Antonio's friend Lorenzo.

In 1648 an observer noted that one of the Dal Corno fresco cherubs was accompanied by death's-heads *fra teschi di cadaeveri* now no longer visable. Two crossed bones with the motto *Mors omnia aequat* can still be seen. Shakespeare noticed them, since Portia comments on her two Italian suitors

I had rather to be married to a deaths head with a bone in his mouth, then to either of these: God defend me from these two (1.3.236)

Another resident in the Dal Corno house was Lazzaro's father-in-law, Zanetto dal Corno. He was the authorised seller of salt in Bassano. Amongst the inhabitants of Bassano he was known as *Ser Zanetto Salarol, Zanetto the salt merchant.* Some of the payments for the fresco were in salt and Jacopo's account book describes him as *S alarolo in Bassano.*

The archaic Italian word *salaro,* of which *salaròl* and *salàrio* are alternative forms, means both a shop which trades in salt and a table salt cellar. Zanetto probably sold salt from the frescoed house in which he lived. Both Zanetto's name *Corno*, (horn) and *salt*, his trade commodity had sexual connotations for Shakespeare. The word *salt* occurs four times in *Othello.*

As well as bringing the Conte Palatino into the *Merchant* Shakespeare also alludes to his father-in-law.

Three Venetian men in the play owe their names to Zanetto's trading title of *Salaròl.* They are Salarino, Salanio and Salerio.

In *The Merchant* 2.6 as in *Othello* 3.3 Shakespeare may again be thinking of the images in the Dal Corno fresco - *the torch of Truth* and the the obscuring effect of the *gelosia* - when Jesica, like Emilia Bassano, the daughter of a Jew - is planning to elope with Lorenzo.

Lorenzo
Descend, for you must be my torch-bearer.
Iesica
What, must I hold a Candle to my shames?
They in themselues goodsooth are too too light.
Why, 'tis an office of discouery Loue,
And I should be obscur'd. (Merchant 2.7.909)

Jessica fears that her torch will reveal her *shames* and that she is *too too light* or immodest. Her position on the first floor of her father's house, equates with the elevated position of the naked figure of *Truth* on the *piano nobile* of the fresco. Moreover she herself appeals directly to the truth, with the rhyme *goodsooth.* Lorenzo later reinforces her identification with *Truth.*

Lorenzo
And true she is, as she hath prou'd her selfe:
And therefore like her selfe, wise, faire, and true (2.7.920)

Shylock's house has windows that can be closed with shutters, since he has told Jessica *But stop my houses eares, I meane my casements* (2.7.840) and to *Doe as I bid you, shut dores after you* (2.7.859)

Shakespeare may be alluding to Venetian shutters when Jessica, standing in the window, says *And I should be obscur'd* (2.7.909). It seems unlikely that Shakespeare would have placed any particular significance on a fresco in Bassano and include details of it when he was writing a play set in Venice, unless it had very personal meanings for him.

The innovation of the Venetian *piano nobile* may have been fermenting in Shakespeare's mind as the pioneering additional acting space, that it became on the London stage, to be used to such beguiling effect in the balcony scene of *Romeo and Juliet.*

If Shakespeare hadn't seen the fresco himself, then he can only have got the information about it second hand from an Italian living in London at the time, Emilia or her cousins being the most likely. In 1593 all of the first generation Bassano family were dead, including Emilia's father, who was born in Venice, not in Bassano del Grappa, anyway. The second generation, even though they continued to speak Italian, were all born in London, it is unlikely that anyone would have known the kind of detailed knowledge of the fresco that the playwright shows in both his Venetian plays.

It isn't though just in the fresco of Bassano that Shakespeare demonstrates such a wealth of knowledge, he knows a great deal of detail about Venice too. He knows that there is a synagogue in Venice since Shylock uses it as a *rendezvous* for as meeting with his fellow worshiper Tubal

goe Tuball, and meete me at our Sinagogue, goe good Tuball, at our Sinagogue Tuball. (Merchant 3.2.1287)

His knowledge that the Rialto was the centre of commerce was at precisely the time when every Venetian had the Rialto at the forefront of his mind. The iconic stone-bridge so familiar to us today, which replaced a wooden one, was completed in 1591 to a design by Antonio da Ponte, creatng a new architectural marvel of the city.

Shakespeare knows that there is a church called San Giobbe - the patron saint of silk merchants - in Cannaregio the same sestiere as the synagogue. He has found out that two of the Christian guards who were chosen to man the bridge securing entrances to the Ghetto were named Gobbo and is so influenced to call the clown in *The Merchant*, Gobbo.

It has been suggested that Cinzio's *Moor* from the *Gli Hecatommithi* was based on a real life Venetian, Christoforo Moro, *Moro* is the Italian word for Moor, even though, despite his name, Christoforo Moro wasn't a Moor. Cinzio doesn't give his Moor a name but he does his wife, Desdemona, which Shakespeare adopts. Christophoro Moro became Doge in 1462 at a time of war with the Turks. His tomb is in in San Giobbe, it is decorated with the same feature as the Bassano coat-of-arms. mulberry leaves, the food for silk worms.

If the connection with Otello, the apothecary in Bassano, and his Moor's head trade sign had Shakespeare thinking about Moors, when he arrived in Venice there were plenty of other Moorish icons to further consolidate his interest. In St Mark's Square alone there are four types of Moor, the most obvious the great bronze statues that strike the hour at the top of the clock tower, built by Mauro Codussi at the end of the C15. These impressive male figures are clad in animal skins. The Venetian name for the clock tower is *Torre dei Mori*, Tower of the Moors.

Two levels down from the bells, under the winged lion of St Mark are two doors, on specified occasions, from the right hand side emerge an angel and the three Magi in circular procession recessing through the left hand door. One of the Magi, the dark skinned Balthazar may have influenced

Shakeapeare to write *The fixed Figure for the time of Scorne, To point his slow, and mouing finger at* (4.2.2685) that Othello fears he will become.

On the corner of the basilica and the Doge's Palace are the group of figures known as the *Tetrarchs.* These are four warriors embracing each other, created in Egypt from a single block of porphyry in the C4. They are said to depict the Emperor Diocletian and other members of the tetrarchy. Venetians though prefer to believe that they are sculptures of the four Moors who were turned to stone as they tried to steal the Treasure of St Mark's.

The fourth Moorish image can be found on the C14 *capital of the Peoples of the Earth,* the third from the left on the water side façade. He is turbaned with the thick lips Roderigo refers to *What a fall Fortune do's the Thicks-lips owe If he can carry't thus?* (1.1.69)

47 Torre dei mori

If the suggestions over the timing of Shakespeare's visit to Italy are correct he would have been in Venice either for the feast of St Jerome on 30 September or, more likely, the feast of All Souls on 1 November 1593.

The three Bassano brothers would have met up with their cousin Giovanni Bassano, composer as well as cornett virtuoso and inventor of a new wind instrument, the bassanello. No original examples of this intriguing instrument have survived, only an illustration in Michael Praetorius's *Syntagma Musicum.*

The annual celebrations of St Jerome and All Souls were important ones in the Venetian liturgical calendar and Giovanni had composed motets, voices combined with instruments - *O doctor optime* and *Salvator mundi* - especially for the Vesper services in St Marks for these feast days. Although less renowned than Andrea and Giovanni Gabrieli and Claudio Monteverdi - his musical colleagues at St Marks - at the time of Shakespeare's visitGiovanni Bassano was as celebrated as the Gabrielis. In 1581 Francesco Sansovino published *Venetia città nobilissima et singolare,* his book in praise of Venice. Of the services in the basilica he wrote *rare music, more singular than any part of the world for voice and instruments all because of the most excellent masters, the three Giovannis; Croce, Gabrieli and Bassano*

Although if Shakespeare had played the Wild Man in Emilia's *Speeches to the Queen* he will have heard cornett playing in the woods at Bisham, he would though have heard nothing of the order of Giovanni Bassano's outstanding virtuosity, it would have stuck in his mind.

The cornett is specified to play four times in the *Merchant* stage directions, the most often that he ever specifies the instrument to sound in any of the plays. In London, the Cornett was exclusively associated with the Bassanos and the Laniers, its foremost Venetian exponent bore the name of Antonio's friend, Bassan(i)o. The Cornett is only specified in four other plays; *Coriolanus, All's that Ends Well, Henry Vl Part 1* and *Henry Vlll.*

The trumpet, by comparison is called for in twenty seven plays. As William Lyons has pointed out, in martial scenes trumpets sound various calls: *parley, tucket, sennet, alarum, flourish.* They are often sounded 'afar' to denote distance, action occurring elsewhere, or the imminent arrival of royalty or opposing armies. It is possible that professional trum-

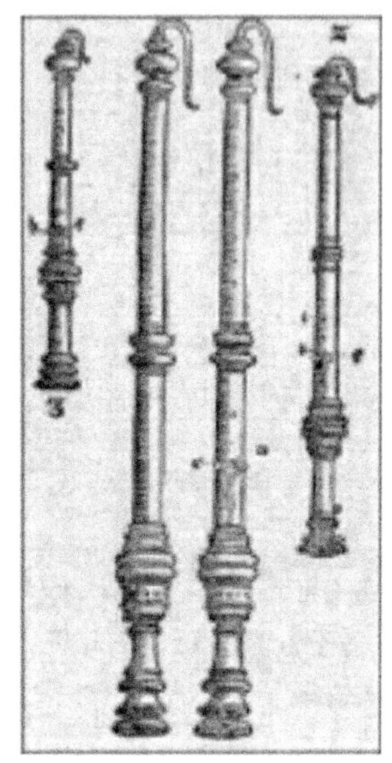

48 Praetorius: Bassanelli

peters were hired to play, not only the realistic martial calls, but also to sound the advent of the play, by playing the same short fanfare three times, before the players entered. In *A Midsommer nights Dreame* the mechanicals enter to perform their play preceded by a professional trumpet player, named in the text, William Tawyer.

If Shakespeare had been so inclined and could afford to, he might have paid a visit to one of the two hundred prostitutes listed in a *Catalogue of all the principal and most famous Courtesans in Venice,* a directory which listed names, addresses and fees, and showed that many of the practioners were married woman. By 1593 the catalogue was a couple of decades out-of-date so many of those listed, if still active, would probably have been forced to drop their prices. Perhaps Shakespeare did visit a brothel and confessed to his friend Ben Jonson who was mischievously inclined to write the following in Old Knoell's speech

Well, I thank heaven, I never yet was he That travell'd with my son, before sixteen, To shew him the Venetian courtezans.

Shakespeare seems to be well aware of the Venetian sex trade because early on in *Othello* he writes a part for one of the practitioners of the world's oldest profession, Bianca, a courtesan is enamoured of Cassio, who leads her on

Iago
Now will I question Cassio of Bianca,
A Huswife that by selling her desires

Buyes her selfe Bread, and Cloath. It is a Creature
That dotes on Cassio, (as 'tis the Strumpets plague
To be-guile many, and be be-guil'd by one)
(*Othello* 4.1.2423)

Like the two shepherdesses in Emilia's *Speeches to the Queen* Bianca is skilled in needlework and agrees to copy the strawberry motive on the handkerchief that Cassio gives her. Later she throws it back at him, in high dedgeon, jealously believing it is the token of his new love.

Anyone with an interest in the symbolism of Venice will be struck by just how much knowledge Shakespeare displays on this esoteric subject. In 1177, Pope Alexander III, in gratitude to the Venetians for their protection of him from Frederick Barbarossa, granted Venice six symbolic gifts, or *Trionfi* which over the centuries became inextricably wound up with the civic and religious ritual so beloved of the Venetian state.

They were

The right to carry a white candle in processions, as a sign of noble honour.

The exclusive right to use a lead seal, a papal prerogative.

A sword, symbol of justice and assurance of salvation to all who touched it.

A gold ring and the right to marry the sea as a token of the doge's lordship of the sea.

A golden umbrella

Eight banners and eight long silver trumpets

There are a number of allusions to five of these *Trionfi* in *The Merchant;* the gold, silver and lead of Portia's caskets for a start.

On the symbolism of the candle:-

Portia
Thus hath the candle sing'd the moath (2.9.1149) there are three moths in the Bassano coat-of-arms, and *How farre that little candell throwes his beames, So shines a good deed in a naughty world* (5.1.2424)

Jessica
What, must I hold a Candle to my shames (2.6.906)

Bassanio
And by these lessed Candles of the night (5.1.2559)

The Prince of Morocco gives his views on his understanding of lead, the second of the *Trionfi*

What saies this leaden casket?

Who chooseth me, must giue and hazard all he hath.
Must giue, for what? for lead, hazard for lead?
This casket threatens men that hazard all
Doe it in hope of faire aduantages:
A golden minde stoopes not to showes of drosse,
Ile then nor giue nor hazard ought for lead. (2.7.955)

The Prince of Arragon isn't much taken with the quality of lead either *And so haue I addrest me, fortune now To my hearts hope: gold, siluer, and base lead* (2.9.1088)

Like a true Venetian who understands the imprtant significance of lead, Bassanio chooses the apparently least attractive casket, and in so doing wins Portia's hand.

but thou, thou meager lead
Which rather threatnest then dost promise ought,
Thy palenesse moues me more then eloquence,
And here choose I, ioy be the consequence. (3.2.1398)

On the third of the *Trioni*, the sword of justice bringing with it the assurance of salvation, there a number of allusions. Shakespeare uses the word *sword* thirteen times in *Othello*. There is Othello's monosyllabic *Keep up your bright swords, for the dew (Jew?) will rust them.* (1.3.268) Is Shakespeare referring to Shylock, his usury rusting the brightness?

Othello muses on his resolve to kill the sleeping Desdemona *Oh Balmy breath, that dost almost perswade Iustice to breake her Sword.* (5.2.3173)

Roderigo

Let loose on me the Iustice of the State (1.2149) The word *sword* doesn't feature in *The Merchant* but there are sixteen appearances of the word *justice*.

Portia's speech on the quality of mercy highlights the specific qualities of the *Trionfi* sword; justice and salvation

And earthly power doth then shew likest Gods
When mercie seasons Iustice. Therefore Iew,
Though Iustice be thy plea, consider this,
That in the course of Iustice, none of vs
Should see saluation (4.1.2034-7)

and Salerio's association of justice with the upholding of Venetian liberty *And doth impeach the freedome of the state If they deny him iustice* (3.2.1577)

The huge symbolic importance that Shakespeare places on rings in *The Merchant* and the persistence with which he uses the word, thirty nine times, and curiously, not at all in *Othello*. When Portia gives away her possessions she says *giue them with this ring, Which when you part from, loose, or giue away, Let it presage the ruine of your loue (3.2.1466)*

In *Othello* Shakespeare uses Monkeys as a symbol of lechery. The exchange between Tuball and Shylock on the ring given to him by his wife Leah and exchanged by Jessica for a monkey seems to hark back to the Dal Corno fresco.

Tuball
One of them shewed me a ring that hee had of your daughter for a Monkie (3.2.1279).

Shylock
Out vpon her, thou torturest me Tuball, it was my Turkies, I had it of Leah when I was a Batcheler: I would not haue giuen it for a wildernesse of Monkies (3.2.1282)

The ritual importance placed on the marriage of the sea ceremony where the Doge accompanied by Venetian hierarchy casts a ring into the lagoon. The ceremony is enacted with a huge flotilla of boats with great pomp annually on Ascension Day is mirrored in *Like Signiors and rich Burgers on the flood, Or as it were the Pagants of the sea* (1.1.10)

The eight silver trumpets - so long they needed a small boy to support the bell end - were spectacularly sounded around St Mark's Square on every important feast day heralding the arrival of the doge or the elevation of the host in St Mark's. There are sixteen uses of the word *trumpet* in *Othello* - both in the script and as stage directions - often strongly associating it with Venice or Venetians, but *trumpet* only appears twice in *The Merchant* - although as an important symbol - as in the remark of Lorenzo to Portia after her marriage to Bassanio the Venetian.

A Tucket sounds.

Lorenzo
Your husband is at hand, I heare his Trumpet (5.1.2459)

and then on its sound's arresting qualities on a restless herd of colts *If they but heare perchance a trumpet sound, Or any ayre of musicke touch their eares, You shall perceiue them make a mutuall stand, Their sauage eyes turn'd to a modest gaze,* (5.1.2408)

The Merchant is Shakespeare's most musical play, the theme of music is apparent throughout. Moreover in Lorenzo's serenade the poet equates malevolence with the hatred of music *The man that hath no musicke in himselfe, Nor is not moued with concord of sweet sounds, Is fit for treasons, stratagems, and spoyles* (5.1.2418)

While Bassanio makes his choice of casket Portia - with another reference to the fresco swan - commands *Let musicke sound while he doth make his choise,*

Then if he loose he makes a Swan-like end, Fading in musique (3.2.1337)

and later

Here Musicke. A Song the whilst Bassanio comments on the Caskets to himselfe.

Tell me where is fancie bred,
Or in the heart, or in the head:
How begot, how nourished.
Replie, replie.
It is engendred in the eyes,
With gazing fed, and Fancie dies ,
In the cradle where it lies:
Let vs all ring Fancies knell.
Ile begin it.
Ding dong, bell.
All.
Ding, dong, bell. (3.2.1363)

Bassanio, a name identified with musicians, is the only one of Portia's suiters to have his own song whilst he considers which casket to choose. The rhyming *nourishéd* at the end of the first three lines pointing him towards *lead* accompanied by the base metal bells of the famous *campanile*.

In the uses of the word *trumpet* in *Othello* along with its symbolic association with authority, particularly Venetian authority is made clear. Iago's line shortly before the entry of Othello with attendants *The Moore I know his Trumpet* (2.1.930)

Hearke how these Instruments summon to supper:The Messengers of Venice staies the meate, (4.2.2817)

There exist several allegorical paintings depicting the presentation of the *Trionfi*, by Il Vicentino, Girolamo Gambarato, Leandro and Francesco dal Ponte - sons of Jacopo the Dal Corno fresco painter - and others.

A line from Ben Jonson's *Valpone*, which is set in Venice reads *I had read Contarine, took me a house* indicates that he, at least was aware of Gasparo Contarini's *De magistratibus et republica venetorum*. However, neither Cardinal Contarini, nor Sansovino mention the *Trionfi*.

Where did Shakespeare hear about the symbolic importance to the Venetians of the *Trionfi*? Where did he learn about the Bassano fresco to retell its features in such detail?

There can only be one convincing answer. When he was there.

18. London again

Full often hath she gossipt by my side,
And sat with me on Neptunes yellow sands,
Marking th'emburked traders on the flood,
When we haue laught to see the sailes conceiue,
And grow big bellied with the wanton winde:
Which she with pretty and with swimming gate,
Following (her wombe then rich with my yong squire)
Would imitate, and saile vpon the Land,
To fetch me trifles, and returne againe,
As from a voyage, rich with merchandize.

A Midsommer nights dreame (2.1.485)

In order for Shakespeare to be back at court acting over Christmas he will need to have left Venice by mid-November. A journey across the Alps by land in winter would be hazardous, it would be more practical if the return jouney was made by sea. *I have hoysted saile to al the windes Which should transport me farthest from your sight.* (117.7-8) *All the winds* would indicate an extensive voyage, not just an English Channel crossing.

The Port of London records show frequent visits from Venetian and Genoese ships. A voyage from Venice would entail a long route from the Adriatic around the south of Italy. A sailing from Genoa would have been much quicker and would have involved the Bassano brothers and Shakespeare travelling there via Milan.

Although *Othello* seems to have been written some years after Shakespeare's visit to Venice and probably after the end of his affair with Emilia, she was still in the forefront of his mind because in the character of Æmilia, he puts Emilia Bassano on stage with lines that find feminist echoes in *Salve Devs*, *Speeches to the Queen* and *A Louer's Complainte*. On men, Æmilia comments:- *Tis not a yeare or two shewes vs a man: They are all but Stomackes, and we all but Food, They eate vs hungerly, and when they are full They belch vs* (*Othello* 3.4.2204)

But Iealious soules will not be answer'd so; They are not euer iealious for the cause, But iealious, for they're iealious. It is a Monster Begot vpon it selfe, borne on it selfe. (3.4.2264)

He call'd her whore: a Begger in his drinke: Could not haue laid such termes vpon his Callet (4.2.2761)

Unafraid to speak her mind to the master who had just murdered her mistress, Desdemona

Othello
She's like a Liar gone to burning hell, 'Twas I that kill'd her.
Æmilia
Oh the more Angell she, and you the blacker Diuell.
Othello
She turn'd to folly: and she was a whore.
Æmilia
Thou do'st bely her, and thou art a diuell.
Othello
She was false as water.
Æmilia
Thou art rash as fire, to say That she was false. Oh she was heauenly true (5.2.3312)

Damning her husband and insulting her master on news that it was her husband, Iago, who falsely told Othello of Desdemona's betrayal *If he say so, may his pernicious Soule Rot halfe a graine a day: he lyes to'th'heart, She was too fond of her most filthy Bargaine (5.2.3344)*

Confronting Iago with his slander

Æmilia
But did you euer tell him, She was false?
Iago
I did.
Æmilia
You told a Lye an odious damned Lye: Vpon my Soule, a Lye; a wicked Lye. Shee false with Cassio? Did you say with Cassio?
Iago
With Cassio, Mistris? Go too, charme your tongue.
Æmilia
I will not charme my Tongue; I am bound to speake, My Mistris heere lyes murthered in her bed (5.2.3369)

Shakespeare adopts Emilia's anaphoric hallmark

Æmilia
Villany, villany, villany: I thinke vpon't, I thinke: I smel't: O Villany:I thought so then: Ile kill my selfe for greefe
(5.2.3387)

I would like to leave Æmilia, Desdemona's maid, with the last word. She reflects in drama the feminism that Emilia Bassano espoused in life, she was indeed Shakespeare's *Dark Musical Lady* his great love but a love that drove him *frantick madde with euer-more vnrest* (147.10).

In the last lines of A.L.Rowse's letter to me dated 3rd September 1994 he wrote *The proper method was to collect all the facts - and they point overwhelmingly to Emilia Bassano. She was the woman. "This is She" wrote Professor Nevill Coghill. He was no ordinary human fool* There was a P.S. *If down this way don't bring wives and babies!*

When Emilia died in 1645, she had lost both of her children, Odillia as an infant in 1599, and the forty year old Henry in 1633, his wife had died the following year. This left the widowed Emilia, at the age of sixty four, to bring up two grandchildren, Mary aged six and Henry, aged four. Henry began his training as a flute player with his uncle, Andrea Lanier, in the expectation that he would follow his father's profession, that of a royal musician.

It is said that Andrea was imprisoned during the Commonwealth, his alleged crime is unknown. Those royal musicians who had lost their employment during the Civil War, believed that the end of court employment was permanent, once the regicide had occured.

Although a very few musicians were re-employed by Cromwell most had lost their only form of income. Their economic situation had seriously deteriorated, their difficulties highlighted in a petition to parliament dated 1655 from some fifty former servants to the crown which stated that they had *tried all other means in vain for them to get bread for themselves and their families, hoping to arouse pity for their plight. They only decided to take this last step after a number of their kin had died of starvation.*

Two years later, John Lanier (1631 Greenwich - 1683 Virginia), Clement's son and Alphonso's nephew, and his wife Lucrece decided to emigrate to Virginia. 1657 was the year in which Oliver Cromwell was offered the crown - which he declined - and in the same year that he lifted the legal exclusion of Jews in England. It is a minor irony that John Lanier who had inherited Jewish blood through his grand-mother Lucrece Bassano, should leave England just at the moment when Jews were permitted to stay. Howell Pryce was given a patent to transport forty seven persons to Virginia in exchange for a 2350 acres of land there. Two of his passengers were John and Lucrece Lanier, but might another have been Emilia's grandson Henry Lanier 2, who happened to be Shakespeare's grandson too?

In 1657 Henry Lanier 2 was twenty seven years old, trained as a flute player by his uncle. He now had no close living relatives, no work as a musician, because of the abolition of the monarchy and an anti music puritan parliament. Both sides of his family had, almost exclusively, been royal musicians, this career path at the time seemed to have been permanently closed, so a new life in America could be attractive. I can find no record for Henry Lanier 2's death, which makes me think he went to America. If so his literary and musical genes were transported with him.

An American with a given middle name associated with Shakespeare's Stratford, is Sidney Clopton Lanier (1842-81), a soldier on the confederate side in the American Civil War, a renowned professional flute player, a founder member of the Peabody Orchestra and a poet and essayist.

Late in his short life, he became first a student, then a lecturer and finally, a faculty member at the John Hopkins University English Department where he specialized in the works of the Shakespeare, other Elizabethan sonneteers, Chaucer and other old English poets. His reputation in America was sufficiently high for him to have a school and a bridge named after him.

Only thirty years after the death of Sidney Lanier a distant relative of his, Thomas Lanier Williams III was born in 1911, in Columbus, Mississippi. Thomas was born into something of a dysfunctional family from English, Welsh, and Hugenot ancestry.

49 Sidney Clopton Lanier

His father was a traveling shoe salesman, an alcoholic, who was frequently away from home. His mother, Edwina, was the daughter of Rose Dakin, a music teacher, and the Reverend Walter Dakin, an Episcopal priest from Illinois who was assigned to a parish in Clarksdale Mississippi, shortly after Thomas' birth.

Thomas' parents separated due to his father's intemperance and his sister Rose was diagnosed with schizophrenia. He lived in his grandparent's parsonage with his remaining family for much of his early childhood and his relationship with his grandparents was a close one.

There were no notable literary figures in Thomas' immediate family but he had read Homer's *Illiad* by the time he was eight and wrote his first play when he was a student. Thomas went on to become one of the most successful Amercian writers of the C20. He is better known to us as Tennessee Williams.

There is a physical resemblance between them. Might Tennessee Williams have inherited Shakespeare's literary genes?

50 William Shakespeare - Tenessee Lanier Williams

Postlude - Venice Preserved

As I was writing this book I became increasingly aware of extraordinary coincidences linking me with my Venetian musical ancestors of more than four centuries ago.

Early in my career as a performer I had been privileged to take part in concerts and recordings of Gabrieli and Monteverdi with Andrew Parrott, John Eliot Gardiner, Denis Arnold, Roger Norrington, Seiji Ozawa and Michael Tilson Thomas.

Awareness of a Venetian connection began in late 1989, but the coincidences that I refer to go back much further. It was as a trombone and sackbut player, rather than a conductor, that over years, I became very familiar with the music of the North Italian masters. One pivotal performing experience in the 1980s was playing all of the instrumental pieces of Gabrieli's 1597 *Sinfonae Sacrae* collection with the *Equale Brass Ensemble* in historic buildings in Rimini and Citta di Castello, under the inspired direction of Roger Norrington.

I was apponted a professor of trombone at the Royal College of Music in London in 1978. In 2003 I became Head of Brass, a position I held for eleven years. A year or so before my appointment as Head of Faculty, I conducted a student concert for voices and wind instruments, *Christmas at San Marco.* The repertoire consisted entirely of works by Giovanni Gabrieli and Claudio Monteverdi, composers with whom I feel a particularly strong empathy.

I was then very much a performer, rather than an academic, but I was obliged to write programme notes for the RCM concert. It was while I was researching I chanced upon the name Bassano.

Venice has a very special magic - it takes an unusually hard heart not to succumb to her charm. It isn't uncommon for a musician exposed to the genius of her composers to become passionate about their music. However, a number of curious events have led me to believe that there is more than meets the eye with my love affair with 'La Serenissima' Any musician with an interest in music of this period will be familiar with the name of Giovanni Bassano employed at St Mark's from 1576 until his death, dates which coincide with the whole 22 years of Giovanni Gabrieli's tenure as organist and choirmaster and the first five years of his successor, Monteverdi. Giovanni would also have become familiar with Gabrieli's student the young Heinrich Schütz during his prolonged his period of study in Venice. As well as playing the cornett, Giovanni Bassano's duties at St Mark's included directing the wind instrumentalists at services. Canzonas and sonatas were an important element of the Venetian liturgy.

I was less familiar with the other Bassanos listed with Giovanni in Grove's *Dictionary of Music and Musicians:* five brothers, Alvise, Anthony, Jasper, Baptist and John, sons of the Venetian sackbut player, Jeronimo di Bassano. Jeronimo was employed from 1506 to 1512 by the *Scuola di Santa Maria dei Mercanti,* one of the religious confraternities in Venice. As you will know from Chapter Two the five brothers had been recruited in Venice by Henry VIII's agent there, Harvel, to settle in London and join the *King's Musik.*

It had, of course occurred to me when I first heard of the Tudor Bassano musicians in the early 1970s that I ought to invtigate my ancestry. However, I believed that any connection with the musicians was most unlikely, and this, coupled with lack of time, postponed indefinitely any research. The reminder of the name while browsing through Grove gave me renewed interest.

In the days before quick referencing genealogical search engines, a labouriously slow visit to the Registry for Births, Deaths and Marriages was my only option. St Katharine's House wasn't the most hospitable of government buildings: overheated and generally over-crowded with members of the public vying for space on the reading desks to rest heavy indices of births, deaths and marriages. I entered this unwelcoming edifice believing that my search would probably reveal mid-Victorian ancestors arriving in London to escape the poverty of the Neapolitan slums, but after only an hour or so, the rarity of Bassano entries made me realise that everyone bearing the name in England were all related.

Working from birth certificates and one marriage certificate I managed to draw a family tree going back to Philip Bassano who was born in Derby in 1789. Then I had a stroke of luck which must be the envy of anyone involved in genealogy, a footnote in David Lasocki's paper *Professional Recorder Playing in England, 1500 - 1740* told me that there was a Bassano family tree in Glover's *History and Gazeteer of the County of Derby,* published in 1835. A visit to the British Library showed that the family tree in Glover and the one I had drawn up overlapped by a generation. In less than a month I had got back to 1539.

I shared my discovery with the conductor, academic and director of the Tavener Consort and Players, Andrew Parrott, who when I mentioned my grandmother's name Emily, immediately said, *ah that name. A.L.Rowse nominated Emilia as his candidate for Shakespeare's Dark Lady.* This was the first occasion on which I heard mention of the *Dark Lady.* Glover's book showed that my pedigree came through Anthony Bassano, instrument maker, recorder and sackbut player. The sackbut/trombone was the instrument that at that time I had been earning my living by playing for some twenty five years. It raised questions in my mind; why music, why the trombone?

The inspiration for me to play a brass instrument came when I was eleven years old. At my local cinema in Southend-on-Sea, I saw William Fairchild's *John and Julie*, a film about two young children who ran away to London, to witness, first hand the coronation of Elizabeth II. Philip Green's score of the 1955 film featured the searing trumpet playing of Eddie Calvert - popularly known as the *Man With The Golden Trumpet*. I was impressed with the music and become a big fan of Calvert's playing.

From the first exposure to Calvert's playing I pestered my parents - who were of modest means - to buy me a trumpet for Christmas so that I could teach myself to play *Oh Mein Papa* and *Stranger in Paradise,* two of Calvert's most popular hits.

When I unwrapped my long-anticipated present, what I got was a pastic toy trumpet with four valves, the only brass components, harmonica reeds used to produce unattractive adenoidal sounds, not at all reminiscent of the trumpet. Needless to say I was less than happy with my gift - albeit kindly meant - and so I continued to whinge.

The small RAF estate home of my aunt and uncle and their three children in Bourton-on-the-Water, the picturesque Cotswold village and at a time long before it became the international tourist attraction that it is today, was a regular venue for me and my family to spend Christmas. It was usual for my parents to return home at the end of the festivities leaving me in Bourton to see out the rest of the school holidays. My father, without prior reference to me, took it upon himself to enrol me into the Young People's Band of the local Southend Salvation Army Corps. He wrote to me in Gloucestershire to tell me what he'd done.

Although I welcomed the opportunity to learn to play a real brass instrument, I was less than happy about the religious implications of this *conversion* by post, to say nothing of the fact that my perception then, was that most members of the Salvation Army were all a bit deranged. Open-air meetings featuring *personal testimonies* from strangely attired tambourine twirling ladies in bonnets with ribbons and black silk seam stockings, were frequently encouraged by other comrades with cries of *Praise the Lord* or *Hallelujah.* It was all a bit too much of an alien world for a shy, only child.

I dutifully arrived on Sunday morning and was introduced to Ray Gilson, the Young Peoples' Bandmaster, his occupation was as skipper of a coastal trawler and member of the Life Boat crew, who presented me with an old, but ornately engraved Bb cornet (a close relation to the trumpet) and mouthpiece complete with battered, but sturdy, velvet lined case. There was no fingering chart, no printed tutor and the only technical advice to produce a sound I was given, was *imagine you're spitting a bit of tobacco off your tongue.* I subsequently discovered this rather unhygienic method of initiating children into playing a brass instrument was common in the 1950s.

I took this advice seriously because at my first attempt at blowing the cornet - which was taken *al fresco* when I had nearly arrived home on my two mile bike journey - I placed my tongue between my teeth and lips and blew a raspberry into the mouthpiece. I was to continue using this unorthodox method of note-production for the next eight years, not without some degree of success.From the beginning I practised daily. *Men of Harlech* could be heard in the neighbourhood emanating from the outside toilet - but my ambition to tackle triple and double tonguing, so much a feature of brass band cornet solos, knew no bounds, with the necessary *tu, tu, ku* tonguing practised on every cycle journey but, despite which, was never properly achieved.

A few months into my short cornet playing career I was seduced by the trombone; not by its sound quality, but by its attractive serpentine shape and the even more by the William Morris style floral decoration on bell and slide which I had ample time to admire during tedious sermons and embarrassingly emotionally prayer-meetings. I swapped my cornet for an ancient SA Bb tenor small bore trombone, but since the arrival of the large-bore instruments, now affectionately known as a *peashooter,* closer to a sackbut than the modern trombone, which I transported without a case from home to the SA Hall by bike; both cargo and carrier uninsured.

A family move to Hackney in the East End of London when I was 1fifteen, a job with Morton Brothers a family firm of stock brokers and a transfer to Cambridge Heath SA Band - which posessed a number of ex-army bandsmen - plus regular attendance at concerts at the Royal Festival Hall, meant I was introduced to a more sophisticated environment than my earlier Southend schoolboy days. A much keener selection of brass players in my new band quickly spotted my technical eccentricities and suggested that lessons might be a good idea.

Denis Wick, the virtuoso principal trombone of the London Symphony Orchestra was destined to become one of the most successful teachers of trombone technique ever. It was with a great deal of trepidation I arrived at Denis's house in Kenton for my first lesson. I can recall the walk from the station, the truly wintery weather, the words used and the amazing playing of Denis at close quarters during this lesson, precisely, as if it was yesterday. The date, Friday 22nd November 1963, which is also the most effective of *aides mémoire.* Everyone old enough to remember, never forgets what he was doing on the day President John F. Kennedy was assassinated in Dallas. It never entered my head that within a decade I would be walking through New York's poignantly named JFK Airport on the start of an American tour as a guest trombonist in Denis's LSO section.

Less than two years after my first lesson with Denis Wick his influence had ameliorated my trombone playing to the point that in September 1965 I entered the Royal College of Music in London. At the RCM I studied with Morris Smith, a former trombonist, whose surviving reputation as a player was less than glowing and whose main job had emerged as orchestral manager at the Royal Opera House, Covent Garden. Morris was well connected and generous, he brought into the RCM, the great Wagnerian bass, David Ward to sing through Sarastro's aria from *Zauberflaute,* (accompanied by a section of trombones) and also gave free tickets to his trombone students to attend dress-rehearsals at the ROH.

With this benevolence, between 1965-67, I and my fellow students were fortunate enough to hear some of the world's best singers - Hotter, Fischer-Dieskau, Resnik, McCraken, Sutherland, Caballé - conductors Solti, Davis, Giulini, Pritchard - and to see iconic dancers, including Fonteyn and Nureyev and witness outstanding productions: Wagner's complete Ring cycle, as well as *Fliegende Hollander,* and *Parsifal, Benevenuto Cellini, Die Frau ohne Schatten, Falstaff, Il Trovatore, Ondine, Romeo and Juliet,* and *Zauberflaute.*

When I left the RCM my trombone playing career was launched at a thriving and exciting time in the cultural life of London. Kenneth Clark's *Civilisation* and later Jacob Bronovski's *Ascent of Man* were to become two corner stones in my journey of self-education.

The capital had four full-time symphony orchestras, plus two BBC orchestras and the BBC Big Band, two opera-house orchestras, numerous smaller modern music ensembles, many west-end theatres were employing large orchestras on a regular basis, and there were many opportunities for freelance musicians to work with rock-groups. Touring with the *Bee Gees* and *Pink Floyd* and recording with *The Who* and *The Beatles.* As well as *Much Ado* for the National Theatre I also took part in Charles Wood's *H, Being Monologues at Front of Burning Cities* a play about General Havelock and the Indian Mutiny, Chekov's *Three Sisters* and a run of Stravinsky's *Soldier's Tale* at the Young Vic.

I left the RCM with no interest in composers earlier than Bach and the strong perception that *Early Music* was dull and boring and that the practitioners of Early Music on *authentic* instruments were poor players with little technical ability, appalling intonation, and a painfully slow rehearsal expectations which meant that knocking a performance into shape took inordinately longer than *professionals* would. In 1970 I joined *Sinfoniae Sacrae* a brass ensemble (which took its name from the two great collections of instrumental and vocal music by Giovanni Gabrieli) with not a clue that my cousin twelve times removed, Giovanni Bassano had worked with Gabrieli at St Marks.

Sinfoniae Sacrae was managed by the energetic, witty, eccentric bass trombonist, Martin Nicholls, known as *Nutty Nicholls,* who had the ability to sing a three octave range. The players in *Sinfoniae Sacrae* were, like me, all conservatoire trained on modern orchestral instruments. As freelance players we were aware that there was an opportunity to diversify into *authentic* Early Music performance by procuring historic instruments, cornetts and sackbuts. Cornetts were not such a great financial outlay since instrument makers like Christopher Monk reconstructed cornetti and produced them quite cheaply. Trumpet players found that once they had mastered cornetto fingering, a compromise mouthpiece, more resembling trumpet contours than an original acorn-style cornett mouthpieces, worked well for them.

51 Sinfonae Sacrae

Sackbuts, then were a different matter; German brass manufactures were making copies of original Nuremberg instruments preserved in museums but they were exorbitantly expensive; some four or five times the cost of the modern American instruments played by professional orchestral players.

Most of the freelance trombone players of the 1970s seeking to acquire a small-bore instrument resembling a Renaissance sackbut embarked on an act of vandalism. They bought a modern second-hand small or medium bore trombone - freely available and inexpensive - and had the bell flare literally sawn off to reduce its size from some 7" to 4". These adapted instruments became known as *sawn-off shotguns*.

Like the 1960s cornett players, trombonists didn't, at that stage use copies of mouthpieces of original historic instruments but played on modern versions with slightly smaller rims and shallower cups than they would use with their everyday orchestral instruments. The most notable exception to this adaptation of the cheap *sawn-off shotgun* was Alan Lumsden, who acquired, at great expense, a Meinl and Lauber copy of an instrument by Hans Neuschel. Holding the instrument was a painful exercise, which could only be achieved without bloodletting by shielding the hand from a plethora of sharp contoured stays and ornate hinges with a piece of chamois leather. Alan became the butt of several jokes about this but he finally had the last laugh when within a few years, all professional sackbut players had felt obliged to buy historic replicas.

It was because *Sinfoniae Sacrae* had already established some personal connections with David Munrow that when he needed to expand his core-ensemble into something closer to a Renaissance Dance Band that our divergent musical paths first crossed. The first concert in which I took part with the Early Music Consort of London was on the 28th January 1971 at the Queen Elizabeth Hall in London in a programme called *Dance Music of Four Centuries*. This programme was a sequence of twelve groups of pieces presented almost chronologically; anonymous Basse Dances and Ducta, Trouvere Songs,

52 David Munrow

Italian Carnival music from the time of the Medicis, a suite of Anthony Holborne's beguiling dances and what was destined to become the mainstay of one of Munrow's best selling recordings, Tielman Susato's Twelve Dances from *The Danserie*.

The title and choice of repertoire was typical of David's innate ability to construct clever, diverse and appealing programmes that made the resurrection of so much music unearthed, after centuries of neglect, thrilling, for both performers and audience. When David died in 1976 at the age of just thirty three, it was a terrible shock, the cause of profound grief to me personally, and the musical world at large Two years before my first sackbut performance with David Munrow, I was engaged by Philip Jones to play the modern trombone for a Promenade Concert on 11 September 1969. This was to be some music by Monteverdi never before played at the Proms, motets from the 1640 *Selve Morale* collection and the Prologue and Acts 1 and 2 of *L'Orfeo*.

This concert was conducted by John Eliot Gardiner, the first time I had worked with the conductor and was to be the start of a professional relationship that was to last for twenty seven years and was to be hugely influential over my musical development. Gardiner is a supurb vocal trainer and his choir, the *Monteverdi Choir*, was second to none. In addition he takes great care with choosing soloists, finding the perfect voices to fit the dramatic various roles, operatic and liturgical.

This was the first time I had ever heard any Monteverdi performed in this startling way, the musical encounter was like an electric shock going through me, emotionally draining. Again I had no idea that Giovanni Bassano at the end of his life worked with Monteverdi and very likely played the cornett in a number of the works that I took part in that evening.

Taking music back to its source was something that Gardiner regarded as important if a musician really wanted to fully understand a composer's intentions. in recent years this included performing the Bach Cantatas in their rightful place in the liturgical calendar in venues associated with the composer. Other examples are Berlioz in the old Paris Conservatoire, Handel in Halle, Rameau in Versailles and Bruckner motets in St Florian's, the Augustinian Priory at which the composer was organist.

It was my priviege to perform and record Monteverdi's *1610 Vespers* in St Mark's Venice having previously performed the work in two other cities associated with Monteverdi; Cremona, his birthplace and Mantua, where he wrote the Vespers. By this time I was aware that my early Bassano ancestors worked in the basilica on a daily basis.

My work with Paul McCreesh's *Gabrieli Consort and Players* took me back to Venice again, this time to another building associated with the Bassano family, the *Scuola de San Rocco*, for a concert and video recording of a reconstruction of a concert of music by Gabrieli.

I was for ten years a member of *His Majesties Sagbutts and Cornetts*, a group who take their name from a renonwned work for these instruments by Matthew Locke King Charles ll's *Master of the King's Musick*. With HMSC I found myself retracing the steps of my Tudor ancestors playing similar, if not the same music that they played in venues like Westminster Abbey, Hampton Court, Windsor Castle and St George's Windsor.

Like my English ancestors I found myself in close proximity to members of the royal family. As a student I played a fanfare for HM the Queen when she visited St Martin-in-the-Fields. When Queen Elizabeth I died in 1604 her funeral was accompanied by much pomp and ceremony - there were four musicians bearing the name Bassano attended to provide appropriate music.

Such great state occasions are rare, but in 1981 when Lady Diana Spencer - the 12 times great-grand-daughter of Henry Writhiosley - married the Prince of Wales at St Pauls, I was there, as a member of the Philharmonia brass section performing the same function as my Tudor ancestors.

As Head of Brass at the Royal College of Music it was my responsibility to rehearse the fanfares for the annual graduation ceremony attended by Primce Charles. When the ceremony was over it was my delightful duty to introduce the student players to the Prince. It was in the same role that I was asked to organise and conduct the music for an Investiture Ceremony at Buckingham Palace when Prince Charles deputised for his mother. I included instrumental works by Augustine and Jerome Bassano.

With the death of Henry Bassano in 1665 full time professional music making at court had come to an end for the family. Music continued as an important interest in the family's life. Christopher (1679-1745) was a Vicar Choral of Lichfield Cathedral, a collection of his compositions - six anthems - was published some years after his death.

Mary (1759-1833) was painted by Joseph Wright of Derby; she appears as model for '*Maria and her dog Silvio*'. Maria is a melancholy young widow from Laurence Sterne's '*Sentimental Journey*' - in her hand she holds a descant recorder, an instrument played and made by the Tudor Bassanos.

In the early 1900s George Henry Bassano owned a small factory in Derby that made wind-up horn gramophones called '*Bassanophones*'. What would the Tudor Bassanos making instruments in their workshops at the Charterhouse have made of that coincidence?

In more recent years my father sang as a soloist and in choirs, he played the piano without ever having had any formal tuition. Shortly after I was born he began what was to be a long career conducting a local amateur choir. I have learnt that most of the surviving Bassanos have an appreciation of music, and in some instances play instruments, too. Four of my children were awarded Music Scholarships at their well known schools.

When I began researching into my family history, it felt as if I was being taken by the scruff of the neck to all of the right places, as if there was a guiding hand directing me. If anyone from beyond the grave had the determination to get their story told, it was Emilia.

Buccleuch and Queensbury

6 Never resting time - Dating the Sonnets

17 Esalas van Hulsen: Lopez conspiring to poison the queen Wellcome Trust ICV No 29206
18 Anonymous: Ferdinando Stanley 5th Earl of Derby Public Domain 2118
19 Anonymous: thought to be Christopher Marlowe. Corpus Christi College, Cambridge

7 The Elusive Mr Shakespeare

20 Shakespeare Droeshout engraving First Folio, © British Library C.39.k.15.
21 Shakespeare (Overbury) Shakespeare Birthplace Trtust
22 Sit Thomas Overbury © Bodleian Library, University of Oxford
23 Janssen: Shakespeare Holy Trinity Bust © Sicinius, CC BY-SA 4.0
24 Dugdale The Antiquities of Warwickshire illustrated Engraving made by Wenzel Hollar
25 John Hall's painting of the bust Earl of Warwick Collections loaned to the Shakespeare Birthplace Trust

8 Did Shakespeare authorise publication of the Sonnets?

26 Sonnets Dedication page British Library
27 Venus Dedication page © Bodleian Library, University of Oxford
28 Rape of Lucrece dedication page

9 A Louers Complaint - the Dark Lady's voice

29 A Louer's Complaint title page British Library
30 Salve Devs title page

10 Emilia and Hunsdon

31 Byrd dedication page
32 Gheerarts: Hunsdon Berkeley Castle
33 Lady in Black Gheerarts © The Bowes Museum, Barnard Castle, Co. Durham)
34 Emilia and Alphonso St Botolph-without-Aldgate Parish register

11 Life After Marriage

35 Jan van Belcamp the Great Picture Abbot Hall Art Gallery Kendal

12 William Shakespeare and appraisal of the Evidence

Peter Bassano

A descendant of Anthony Bassano (born Italy c. 1500 died London 1574) the eldest of six musical brothers brought to England by Henry VIII. He studied trombone and singing at the Royal College of Music, London (1965-68) becoming a professor at his amla mater in 1978. A worked as a free-lance trombone player in London 1968-1973, before joining the Philharmonia Orchestra where he remained until  2000. After extensive periods of study, in the last two decade he has worked as a conductor. Shakespeare and Emilia is his first book.

Praise For Author

"absolutely riveting" Crispian Steele-Perkins

"Fascinating material, lucidly presented. Peter Bassano brings a scholarly attention to detail and a musician's insight to Shakespeare's intimate life, and to the identification of his Dark Lady." Cynthia Harrod-Eagles

"I was spellbound. Of course, a lot I already knew but how much I didn't: the music, musical life and musical detail, the Italian history of your family and the wholly convincing Venetian journey with WS and the possible illegitimate child. The concordances between Emilia's and WS's life and the plays are startling." Charles Duff

"Peter Bassano has put together a fascinating study of the Shakespeare circle as it impinges remarkably on his own ancestors. An intriguing read, impeccably researched" Sir Roger Norrington

Printed in Great Britain
by Amazon

76104627R00169